CRIMINAL SLANG

The Vernacular of the

UNDERWORLD

LINGO

BY

CAPTAIN VINCENT J. MONTELEONE

New Introduction by
Bryan A. Garner
President, LawProse, Inc.

THE LAWBOOK EXCHANGE, LTD.
Clark, New Jersey

ISBN 978-1-58477-300-9

Lawbook Exchange edition 2004, 2015

The quality of this reprint is equivalent to the quality of the original work.

THE LAWBOOK EXCHANGE, LTD.
33 Terminal Avenue
Clark, New Jersey 07066-1321

*Please see our website for a selection of our other publications
and fine facsimile reprints of classic works of legal history:*
www.lawbookexchange.com

Library of Congress Cataloging-in-Publication Data

Monteleone, Vincent Joseph.
    Criminal slang : the vernacular of the underground lingo / by Vincent
J. Monteleone.
        p. cm.
    Originally published: Rev. ed. Boston: Christopher Pub. House, c1949.
    ISBN 1-58477-300-6 (cloth: alk paper)
    1. Cant—Dictionaries. 2. English language—Slang—Dictionaries. I.
Title.

PE3721.M6 2003
427'.973—dc21   2002043283

Printed in the United States of America on acid-free paper

Criminal Slang:
An Introduction

Bryan A. Garner

This relatively obscure glossary first appeared in 1949, the same year as Eric Partridge's far more ambitious *Dictionary of the Underworld: British and American*. The material for Captain Monteleone's work appears to have been gathered firsthand exclusively from his years in law enforcement. Partridge, on the other hand, was working primarily with literary sources. A mere glance at the two books reveals Partridge as a thoroughgoing lexicographer at the height of his career, and Monteleone as an amateur who wasn't as interested in lexicography per se as he was in recording the idioms he heard at work.

Oddly, Captain Monteleone's compilation isn't mentioned in the Select Annotated Bibliography that J.E. Lighter included in his magisterial book on slang, *The Random House Dictionary of American Slang* (1994). Even more surprisingly, it doesn't appear to have been cited anywhere in the three-volume (and counting) text.

One wonders about the purpose of the book and its intended audience. The appendix in back — titled "Whether You Believe It or Not" — does have a Ripley-style feel to it, as Monteleone lists some interesting factoids about legal history, especially crimes. Then there are the "secret signs" of hobo life, a symbolic language for which Monteleone has given the key.

This is a book that fell out of date more quickly than most: slang, and especially criminal slang, evolves more rapidly than probably any other type. But undoubtedly researchers will find it useful to know the state of criminal slang in the 1940s.

If you're looking at a mid-20th-century transcript and read that the prisoner "complained about the Hixer Hiney frigging the frog legs in the next cell when the Hiney's side dish got thrown in the slammer and announced that the Hiney was upholstered," you might be at a loss to know what's going on. This book will help you sort it out as few books can.

For the work of a lexicographic amateur, it's admirably thorough.

Dallas, Texas
October 2003

CRIMINAL SLANG

The Vernacular of the

UNDERWORLD

LINGO

BY

CAPTAIN VINCENT J. MONTELEONE

THE CHRISTOPHER PUBLISHING HOUSE
BOSTON, U. S. A.

FOREWORD

During my thirty-two years of law enforcement, as United States Custom Inspector Mexican Border, Deputy United States Marshal and Deputy Sheriff, I have gathered slang words and their meanings used by criminals of the underworld, tramps, hobos, etc. These words I have compiled into book form.

We all know that every business and game has its own peculiar characteristic of language. None is more colorful and sometimes more comical and incongruous, than the slang of the gangster, tramp or hobo. It is not strange that it creeps into the vocabulary of policemen and others. Frequently one word expresses an entire chapter, while at other times an entire phrase in slang is needed where one good English word would suffice.

Any gangster with a proper respect for his calling would deeply resent being called a murderer, but if referred to as a "torpedo," or a "dropper," his chest would swell.

In this glossary many words will be found that have been used in wholesale murder undertakings and by underworld gangsters for generations, while some are comparatively new, but all of them are universally used and understood in the big family of gangsters, racketeers, tramps and hobos.

It is almost a hopeless undertaking to attempt tracing the origin of many of the slang words that have been in constant use for decades.

In this glossary I omit much of the slang that is common to all America, and confine myself to words and phrases used only by the new race of racketeers, gangsters, tramps and hobos. Some of their terms are merely adaptations of older terms; others are quite new.

5

In my first book, on grounds of decorum, I omitted the very pungent ones, however, in this revised volume I have not.

It gives me great pleasure to take this opportunity of expressing my appreciation for the valuable assistance given me by Ruth L. Busbey of the U. S. Department of Agricultural Research Center, Beltsville, Maryland, in reading all of the manuscript and making many helpful suggestions.

I wish also to express my gratitude to my fellow officers for their help and hope it will prove of valuable assistance to them.

Vincent J. Monteleone

Los Angeles
California

RESPECTFULLY DEDICATED TO
MY CO-WORKERS AND ALL LAW
ENFORCEMENT OFFICERS.

CRITICAL SLANG

A

A CONNIVING RAT (N) A law enforcement officer who secretly betrays fellow officer under his command, by false pretences; one who feigns to be other than he is; a false pretender.

AB (N) Abscess; a collection.

ABE (N) A Jew.

ACADEMY (N) A jail.

ACE (N-V) A one dollar bill; a good fellow; a clever crook; a one year prison sentence; to endure or bear up under a third degree without talking.

ACE IN THE HOLE (N) An asset held in reserve for use in time of need; an emergency fund; surprise evidence.

ACE OF SPADES (N) A widow.

ACROSS THE RIVER (N) Dead.

ACT (N) The cross examination of a prisoner.

ACT ONE'S AGE (V) To behave sensibly and with propriety.

ACTIVE CITIZENS (N) Fleas; mites; lice.

ADAM (N) A bailiff; a jailor; a prison guard.

ADAM AND EVE (N) Two eggs.

ADAM AND EVE ON A RAFT (N) Two eggs served with toast.

ADAM'S AND EVE'S TOG (N) The bare skin without any clothing.

ADENOID (N) A radio tenor who sings in a forced, strained voice.

ADMIRAL'S WATCH (N) A good sleep.

ADVENTURE BUNDLE FROM HEAVEN (N) A new born baby.

AFRICAN DOMINOES (N) Dice.

9

AFRICAN GOLF   (N)   Dice shooting.
AFTER THE BEEF   (Adv)   After a complaint has been made to the police.
AHEAD OF THE BEEF   (Adv)   Before a complaint is made to the police.
AIR-CONDITIONED   (Adj)   Full of holes.
AIREDALE   (N)   A guard or watchman; a petty vice runner; an employee of bootlegger and drug peddler; a special guard; one who is employed on the water front by bootleggers.
ALARM CLOCK   (N)   A chaperone; a baby.
ALBERT   (N)   A watch chain.
ALIAS   (N)   A false name.
ALIBI   (N-V)   An excuse; a burglar's mask; to present an excuse.
ALLIGATOR BAIT   (N)   Liver; a negro child; poor food.
ALIVE   (Adj)   Having plenty of money.
ALKALI   (N)   Coffee.
ALKI   (N)   Alcohol; alcohol diluted with water.
ALKI COOKER   (N)   One who distills alcohol.
ALKY   (N)   Alcohol.
ALKY KING   (N)   A liquor gang leader.
ALL BONES   (N)   A skinny person.
ALL IN   (N-Adj)   An introduction which places one in a position to secure favor or bribe; tired out; exhausted.
ALL RIGHT GUY   (N)   One who can be trusted.
ALL SET   (Adj)   Ready for action.
ALL SHOT   (Adj)   Tired; fatigued; exhausted.
ALL TO THE GOOD   (Adj)   All right.
ALL WET   (N)   Wrong; mistaken; without value.
ALL WORKED UP   (Adj)   Eager to possess; feeling a strong emotion of sexual desire.
ALLEY APPLES   (N)   Stones or other missiles used in street fights.
ALLEY CAT   (N)   A private watchman; a prostitute; a night prowler.
ALLEY RAT   (N)   A night prowler; a thief who looks for his victims in alleys, or takes them there to be robbed.

ALMA MATER (N) A prison in which a convict has served time.

ALTER (N) A toilet seat.

ALTER ROOM (N) A toilet; a privy; a rest room.

AMBULANCE CHASER (N) A lawyer who specializes in damage suits for automobile accident victims.

AMBULANCE LAWYER (N) A lawyer who specializes in automobile accident cases.

AMBULANTER (N) One who travels in a cheap automobile with a family.

AMDRAY (N) A dram of narcotics.

A MISFORTUNE (N) A new born baby.

AMMO (N) Bullets.

AMMUNITION (N) Toilet paper; beans; bullets.

ANCHOR (N) A reprieve or stay of execution of sentence; a temporary suspension of a criminal sentence; a safety catch on a stick pin; a wife.

ANCHORED (Adj) Married.

ANCHOR ON PROP (N) A stick pin having a safety catch.

AN END (N) A share.

ANGEL (N) A person or backer of a show or actress; a person easily victimized; a sucker; a sap; an easy mark; one who gives a beggar more than he anticipated; one who has a fair face; a female; a woman; an effeminate man who has womanish traits or qualities; a male homosexual.

ANGEL-FACE (N) A male who has the traits and qualities of a woman; an effeminate man.

ANGEL FOOD (N) Preaching religion.

ANGEL FOOD CAKE (N) Bread.

ANGEL FOOD CAKE AND WINE (N) Prison fare of bread and water.

ANGEL-PUSS (N) One with an angel face; a slightly ironic term of endearment.

ANGELINA (N) A boy tramp who travels with an older tramp; a male homosexual.

ANGLE (N-V) An idea; a trick; a mode of procedure; a plan; a lead; a scheme; to select a victim; to steal through windows with a stick and hook.

ANGLER   (N)   A confidence man.

ANGLER-FISHER   (N)   One who steals through windows by means of a stick with a hook.

ANIMAL   (N)   A woman of easy morals; a prostitute.

ANKLE   (N-V)   A female; a woman; the mother of an illegitimate child; to walk.

ANNEX   (V)   To steal.

ANNIE OAKLEY   (N)   A pass; a free or complimentary ticket; a meal ticket; a pardon or discharge certificate given a convict.

ANOINT   (V)   To flog.

ANTIQUE   (N)   An old man or woman.

ANTS IN THE PANTS   (N)   Displeasure or irritation.

A ONE   (N)   A clever crook; in good condition. (Used by tramps in place of the personal pronoun I, in descriptive objects.)

APACHE   (N)   A thief; one who steals.

APARTMENT   (N)   The cell of a jail.

APE   (N)   An adolescent child; a child with ugly features.

A PINCH   (N)   A steal.

APPARATUS   (N)   The external organs of generation; the male sexual organs.

APPLE   (N)   A baseball.

APPLE KNOCKER   (N)   A yokel; a blunderer; a farmer; an apple harvester.

APPLES   (N)   The female breasts.

APPLES AND PEARS   (N)   Stairs.

ARM   (V)   To rob a victim by the application of the strangle hold.

ARMFUL   (N)   A baby; a beautiful female.

ARM OF THE LAW   (N)   A policeman; a law enforcement worker.

AROUND THE HORN   (Adj)   Detained on a minor charge.

AROUND THE TURN   (V)   To be through the severest part of the withdrawal distress after the last dose of narcotic by an addict.

ARTILLERY   (N)   Firearms; baked beans; any food

causing stomach gas; biscuits and doughnuts; the hypodermic needle or syringe used by a dope addict.

A SHOT IN THE ARM (N) An injection of narcotic.

ASK FOR IT (V) To put oneself knowingly in a precarious or dangerous position; to lay oneself open to blame or censure.

ASS (N) A pimp; pertaining to copulation.

ASS PEDDLER (N) A prostitute; a whore.

AT THE SPRING (Adj) Laced up in a strait jacket.

ATTABOY (Excl.) Bravo; that's fine; you are doing well.

ATTABOY LINGO (N) Slangy, sturdy and forceful speech.

AUNT (N) An old prostitute; a brothel hostess.

AUNTIE (N) The keeper of a house where young girls, who live with their parents, are hired to ruin; a brothel hostess; a prostitute; an old man who takes the part of a catamite.

AUTO COP (N) A policeman patroling in an automobile.

AUTO HOBO (N) A tramp who travels from place to place in a cheap automobile and works only when in need of money.

AUTO TRAMP (N) One who travels, with a family, in a cheap automobile.

A VISITOR (N) A female menstruating period.

AWAY FROM ONE'S HABIT (V) To quit using narcotics.

AXE (N) A knife.

AXLE GREASE (N) Butter.

AXMAN (N) A barber.

B

BABBLING BROOK (N) A crook.

BABY (N) A pretty girl; any girl or woman; a female; a newly painted stolen car; a male homosexual.

BABY ACT (N) An excuse; inexperience; defence of oneself on the ground of legal infancy.

BABY BOUND (N) Pregnant.

BABY BUGGY (N) A wheelbarrow.

BABY-BUNTING (N) A baby.

BABY DOLL (N) A pretty young woman; a pretty female.

BABY FACE (N) One with an angel face; one with an innocent looking face; an effeminate man.

BABY KISSER (N) A politician.

BACHELOR BAIT (N) An unmarried girl; a female; a woman.

BACHELOR'S BABY (N) An illegitimate child.

BACHELOR'S WIFE (N) A mistress; a prostitute.

BACK DOOR (N) Death in prison.

BACK DOOR TROT (N) Exit from a gang gathering by the back door.

BACK FISCH (N) An adolescent girl.

BACK FRIEND (N) Fleas; mites; lice.

BACK GATE PAROLE (N) The death of a convict, in prison while serving time.

BACK NUMBER (N) A person who is old-fashioned in appearance, ideas or habits.

BACK PAY (N) Alimony.

BACK TALK (N) Rude replies; lack of respect for others.

BACK UP (N) An addict causing the veins to stand out by tying up the arm or leg between the place where he desires to make an injection.

BACK WAY (N) The buttocks or rectum.

BACON (N) A large plunder.

BAD ACTOR (N) A tramp who lives on money sent him by his family to keep him from returning home.

BAD BABY (N) A woman of easy morals; a desperado or thug.

BAD DOG (N) A dishonest person; a vicious person; a no good person.

BAD DOUGH (N) Counterfeit money.

BAD FALL (N) Arrested.

BAD LANDS (N) The underworld outside of prison.

BAD NEWS (N) A restaurant check; a bill; trouble; a pistol or revolver; shooting; in trouble with the law.

BAD NUMBER (N) An exconvict; any dangerous criminal.

BAD PAPER (N) Forged securities; a bad check.

BAD SHAPE (N) Pregnant.

BADGER (N) A blackmailer who plays the badger game; a licensed huckster; a petty trickster.

BADGER GAME (N) Shakedown; grafting; the enticing or decoying of a man by an immoral woman to a place where a male confederate is concealed, who demands money of the victim under threat of exposure or bodily injury, alleging himself to be the husband of the woman; blackmailing of a man by a woman placing him in a compromising position.

BADGER WORK (N) Blackmailing of a man by a woman by placing him in a compromising position where a male confederate demands money, alleging himself to be her husband.

BADGER WORKER (N) A blackmailer who plays the badger game.

BAG (N) The female genitals; the pouch which contains the testicles; the scrotum; a woman of easy morals; steal.

BAG GUY (N) A vendor of toy balloons.

BAG OF BONES (N) An excessively thin person; a skinny person.

BAG OF WATER (N) The fluid of the rudimentary embryo-sac; the amnion.

BAG OPENER (N) Female dip who operates in stores, making her touch by opening bags, carried by woman shoppers.

BAGGAGE-SMASHER (N) A porter who handles baggage for railroad, steamship, etc.

BAGGED (N) Pregnant.

BAIL JUMPER (N) One who flees while on bond.

BAIL OUT (V) To pay bail charges for another to be released from custody.

BAIT CAN (N) A dinner pail.

BAKEHEAD (Adj) Insane; crazy.

BALDHEAD (N) An old man.

BALDY (N) An old man.

BALE OF HAY (N) Salad of greens; blonde woman.

BALK (N) A victim of a hold up, resisting same.

BALKER (N) One who resists a holdup man.

BALL (N) A tear gas bomb; a jail sentence; a prison allowance.

BALL AND CHAIN (N) A boy tramp, usually a catamite, who travels with an older tramp; a wife; marriage.

BALL AND CHAIN DRAGGING (N) Condition where the husband or wife is causing, one or the other, considerable trouble.

BALL GRUNT (N) A cook's helper; a woman of easy morals.

BALL THE JACK (V) Go fast; in a hurry.

BALL TOSSER (N) A bomb thrower.

BALL UP (V) To spoil; to confuse.

BALLOON (N) A hobo's bed roll.

BALLS (N) The testicles.

BALLS AND BAT (N) The testicles and penis.

BALM (N) Breach of promise; damage.

BALONEY (N) An automobile tire; woman of easy morals; the male organ of copulation.

BAMBOO (N) An opium addict; an opium pipe.

BAMBOO PUFFER (N) An opium addict; an opium smoker.

BAMBOOZLE (V) To deceive by hoax; to cheat by hoax; to practice fraud and trickery.

BANANA OIL (N) Nonsense; bunkum; insincere praise.

BAND (N) A woman of easy morals.

BAND BOX (N) The work house; a jail; a house of prostitution.

BAND HOUSE (N) A jail; a house of prostitution.

BANDOG (N) A policeman.

BANG (N) A tip off; information; a narcotic injection.

BANG TO RIGHTS (Adj) Caught with the stolen property; caught in a criminal act.

BANG UP (N) The apprehension of a pickpocket operator.

BANJO (N) A short-handled shovel.

BANNER (N) A report for the violation of prison rules.

BANNER CARRIER (N) A tramp who walks the street all night.

BANTY (N) A small person.

BAPTIZED BOOZE (N) Cut liquor.

BAR FLY (N) Habitual drinker of alcoholic beverages.

BARBER (N) One who slashes the cheek of a stool-pigeon for a price.

BARGAIN (N) A reduction of sentence upon plea of guilty; a reduction of an original charge or sentence.

BARGE AROUND (V) To walk about; to stroll.

BARGE IN (V) To enter; to intrude; to meddle.

BARK UP THE WRONG TREE (V) To pursue an incorrect or useless course.

BARKER (N) An auctioneer; a street or sidewalk solicitor; a bally-hoo man; a person who solicits attention in a loud voice; a pistol or revolver.

BARKING (N) A gunfire; discharging a gun.

BARKING IRON (N) A pistol or revolver; firearms.

BARNACLES (N) A gang of criminals who persistently stick to another, whether a hindrance or disadvantage.

BARNEY (V) To travel in style.

BARNEY MACGUIRE (N) A fire.

BARON (N) A lodging house beat; a hotel beat; a swindler who defrauds hotels or firms, who sends goods to his hotel to be checked to his account.

BARREL DOSSER (N) A tramp who frequents barrel houses.

BARREL FEVER (N) Delirium tremens.

BARREL HOUSE (N) A cheap saloon.

BARREL-HOUSE BUM (N) A tramp who frequents barrel houses.

BARREL STIFF (N) A low-class tramp who frequents barrel houses.

BASE METAL MAN (N) Metal counterfeiter; one who makes coins out of lead or some base metal.

BASH (V) To assault; to break.

BASKET (N) The female external genitals; testicles.

BASTILE (N) A jail; a prison.

BAT (N) A woman of the street; a woman of easy

morals; a prostitute; the male pudendum; a dollar; a noisy celebration.

BAT CARRIER   (N)   A stool pigeon; an informer.

BAT HOUSE   (Adj-N)   Insane; crazy; a hospital for the criminally insane.

BATCH KICK   (N)   A hip pocket.   (A pickpocket slang.)

BATS   (Adj)   Crazy; insane; delirium tremens.

BATS IN THE BELFRY   (Adj)   Crazy in the head; insane.

BATTER   (V)   To beg.

BATTER THE DRAG   (V)   To beg on the street.

BATTLE   (N)   Imprison; placed in prison.

BATTLE-AXE   (N)   A woman of domineering disposition; a woman who causes her husband considerable trouble; an old woman; an ugly woman.

BATTLE WAGON   (N)   A police patrol car.

BATTY   (Adj)   Foolish; eccentric; insane; crazy; delirious.

BAWL OUT   (V)   To scold; to reprimand severely.

BAY STATE   (N)   A hypodermic syringe.

BAY WINDOW   (N)   A protuberant abdomen; a bulging abdomen.

BAZOO   (N)   The mouth; loud bragging; boasting.

BE ACES   (V)   To be able to bear up under the third degree.

BE SOLID   (V)   To bear up under the third degree.

BEACH COMBER   (N)   One who loafs along the water front and gathers articles carried by the waves on the beach.

BEAGLE   (N)   A sausage; a plain cloth officer; a detective; a town constable.

BEAK   (N)   A nose; a judge; a magistrate.

BEAK HUNTER   (N)   A church thief.

BEAK HUNTING   (N)   Chicken stealing.

BEAN   (N-V)   The head; a dollar; a Mexican peon; to beat on the head.

BEAN POLE   (N)   A tall lean lanky person.

BEAN SHEET   (N)   A meal ticket.

BEAN SHOOTER (N) A shot gun.

BEANSTOCK (N) A tall lanky person.

BEANERY (N) A restaurant.

BEANERY QUEEN (N) A waitress.

BEARD JAMMIER (N) A whore monger; a dealer or trader in prostitution.

BEAT (N-V) A large plunder; flee; escape; indicating that the pickpocket has taken the victim's purse; to defraud; to swindle.

BEAT A DUMP (N) A convict sentenced for committing burglary.

BEAT A MARK (V) To follow and pick the pockets of a victim. (Term used by pickpockets.)

BEAT CLEAN (Adj) Term used by pickpocket indicating that the victim's purse was taken cleanly.

BEAT IT (V) To go away; to leave hastily; to warn that a policeman is coming.

BEAT MOLL (N) A prostitute who walks the streets for trade of her profession.

BEAT POUNDER (N) A uniform policeman.

BEAT THE GONG (V) To smoke opium.

BEAT THE RAP (V) To evade legal punishment for a criminal offense; to evade or escape punishment.

BEAT THE STIR (V) To escape prison sentence.

BEAT UP (V) To assault.

BEAR (N) A Russian.

BEARCAT (N) A good prize fighter; one with plenty of gumption.

BEAUTY DOCTOR (N) A club with a piece of metal on the end, used by criminal in massaging a victim's face.

BEAUTY PARLOR (N) A brothel; a whore house.

BED OF ROSES (N) A place in which one may lead an easy life.

BED-PAN ALLEY (N) A hospital.

BEE AND HONEY (N) Plenty of money.

BEEF (N-V) Gossip; a fight; to complain; to inform the police; to turn states evidence.

BEEF-STEW SINGER (N) A very bad soloist.

BEEFER (N) One who talks too much; one who be-

trays confidence; a talkative person; one who squeals or
gives away a criminal; a District Attorney; a stool
pigeon; an informer; a fault finder.

BEEFY (Adj)   Stout; large and heavy.

BEETLE (N)   A woman of easy morals; a loose girl or
woman.

BEEZER (N)   The nose; the face; sometimes the head.

BEFORE THE BEEF (Adv)   Before a complaint is
made to the police.

BELCH (V)   To complain; to talk; to turn states evidence or informer.

BELCH-SONG (N)   A confession.

BELCHER (N)   A stool pigeon; an informer.

BELL JOINT (N)   A bank.

BELLOWS (N)   The lungs.

BELLY (N)   The under bracing of a freight car.

BELLYACHE (V)   To complain; to whine; to express discontent.

BELLY-BOUND (N)   Constipated; a morbid inactivity
of the bowels.

BELLY-GUN (N)   A short barrel pistol or revolver.

BELLY-UP (Adj)   Pregnant.

BELLY WRINKLES (N)   Hunger.

BELOW-DECK (Adj)   Stupid but pretty.

BELT (N)   Narcotic exhilaration; the effect of narcotic
on a user, producing an increase of vital energy and
cheer.

BEN (N)   A coat; a vest.

BENCH NIBS (N)   A judge.

BENCH RIBS (N)   A judge.

BENCH WARMER (N)   A park loafer.

BEND (V)   To steal.

BENDER (N)   A thief; a cheater; a petty thief; the
back; a marihuana smoker; a stolen automobile.

BENDIN (N)   An addict full of narcotic.

BENJAMIN (N)   An overcoat.

BENNY (N)   An overcoat; a vest; sometimes a hat.

BENNY WORKER (N)   A pickpocket who operates
under the protection of an overcoat; shoplifting under
the protection of an overcoat.

BENSER (N) A noisy drinking feast; a boisterous gathering of drunks.

BENT (N) A stolen automobile; stolen.

BENT GOODS (N) A large plunder; stolen goods; stolen property.

BENT HARDWARE (N) Stolen jewelry.

BENT SPARK (N) A stolen diamond stick-pin or ring.

BERG (N) A small town.

BERNIES (N) Cocaine contained in a remedy put out by a doctor of that name.

BERRIES (N) Dollars; crystallized cocaine.

BERRY (N) A dollar.

BETTER HALF (N) One's wife.

BETTY (N) A burglar's jimmy.

BIBLE (N-V) Referring to the taking of an oath; to take the oath.

BIBLE-BACK (N) A religious hypocrite.

BIBLE BELT (N) A district in which religious hypocrisy flourishes.

BIDDY (N) An Irish woman; a servant girl.

BIFF (N-V) A blow; to strike; to hit.

BIG-BLOKE (N) Cocaine.

BIG BOY (N) A high court judge; judge of the Supreme court; a term of address implying recognition.

BIG BRAINS (N) A gang-leader.

BIG BROWN EYES (N) The breasts of a female; the mama.

BIG BUG (N) A wealthy person; an important person.

BIG BULL (N) A foreman; the principal keeper of a jail; the warden of a penitentiary; a Chief of Police.

BIG CORNER (N) The larger share.

BIG CUTOR (N) District Attorney.

BIG DAY (N) The visiting day in prison.

BIG DICK (N) Ten on a pair of dice; a large penis.

BIG DITCH (N) An Ocean. (Mostly used as to the Atlantic Ocean.)

BIG DOUGH (N) A great deal of money.

BIG END (N) The larger share.

BIG EYES (N) A detective; a plain cloth officer.

BIG GUN (N) An important person; a wealthy person; a gang leader.

BIG GUY (N) A gang leader.

BIG HAND (N) Loud applause.

BIG HEAD (N) Over-estimate of one's own abilities; vanity; principal keeper of a jail; warden of a penitentiary.

BIG HOLE (N) A sudden stop.

BIG HOUSE (N) A penitentiary.

BIG JOLT (N) A long sentence.

BIG MAN (N) A Pinkerton detective; a distributor who handles large amounts of narcotics.

BIG MITT MAN (N) A confidence man.

BIG MOUTH (N) A noisy person.

BIG ROD (N) A machine gun.

BIG SHOT (N) The leader of a band of criminals; head of a gang; a person of power; a person of importance; a pretentious criminal of no importance.

BIG-SHOT CONNECTION (N) One who peddles large amounts of narcotics.

BIG SMOKE (N) A city.

BIG STICK (N) A machine gun.

BIG STICK WIELDER (N) A machine gunner.

BIG STORE (N) A wealthy gambling house or dive; the headquarters of confidence men.

BIG TAKE BUNDLE (N) A large plunder.

BIG-TIME (N) Major criminal activities.

BIG TOP (N) A prison; the cell house; a bank.

BIG TOWN (N) A city.

BIGGER CORNER (N) Larger share of the spoils.

BILE HOUSE (N) The gall bladder.

BILGE (N) Soup.

BILLPOSTER (N) A forger; a passer of counterfeit money; a passer of bad checks.

BILLPOSTING (N) Passing counterfeit money or checks.

BILLY (V) To club.

BILLY CAN (N) A small cooking vessel.

BILLY COCK (N) A hat.

BIMBO (N) A girl or woman; a girl or woman of loose morals.

BINDLE (N) Package of narcotics, usually small, folded in a special way; a bundle or roll of blankets, carried by hobos; a small account.

BINDLE STIFF (N) A hobo; a tramp; a hobo who carrys a roll of blankets; a drug addict; a narcotic smuggler.

BING (N) A narcotic injection.

BING ROOM (N) An opium den.

BINGE (N) A drunken celebration; a drunken spree.

BINGO (N) A narcotic injection.

BINGO-BOY (N) A drunk.

BINNY (N) An overcoat.

BIRD (N) A twenty-five cent piece; a popular person; a person; a police criminal record; an informer; a stool pigeon.

BIRD BRAIN (N) An individual with little intelligence.

BIRD CAGE (N) A jail; a brothel house; a whore house.

BIRD-CAGE HYPS (N) The poorer class of drug addicts.

BIRD CLUB (N) Prison stool pigeons; an inmate; an informer.

BIRD DOG (N) A reconnoiterer of thieves; a locater of thieves.

BIRD HOUSE (N) A jail.

BIRD HOUSE STIFF (N) A prisoner; an exconvict.

BIRD MINDED (Adj) Foolish; flighty; irresponsible.

BIRD OF PASSAGE (N) An established tramp; a tramp who does not voluntarily work.

BIRD OF THE NIGHT (N) Night pleasure seeker.

BIRD TAKER (N) A sodomite.

BIRDIE (N) Male homosexual; the attraction of persons of the same sex.

BIRDIE POWER (N) Morphine; cocaine; heroin.

BIRDSEYE (N) A small amount of narcotic; a weak injection of narcotic.

BIRDS-EYE MAPLE (N) An octoroon; the offspring of a quadroon and a white person.

BIRD'S NEST (N) A cup made of putty into which nitroglycerine is kept.

BISCUIT (N) A pistol; a revolver.

BISCUIT SHOOTER (N) A waitress; a cook.

BIT (N) Twelve and one half cents; a prison sentence; a share; a gag.

BITCH (N) An improvised lamp made by placing a wick in a can of grease; an untidy or negligent woman; a catamite.

BITE ONE'S EAR (V) To beg in the street.

BITTER ALMOND (N) Cyanide of potassium.

BIZ (N) The hypodermic syringe used by a drug addict.

BLAB (V) To talk too much; to talk or reveal without caution or correct judgement.

BLABO (N) One who talks too much.

BLACK (N) Opium.

BLACKBIRD (N) A negro.

BLACK BOTTLE (N) Poison; chloral hydrate; opiate; knockout drops.

BLACK BOX (N A criminal lawyer; a coffin.

BLACK CAT (N) A preacher.

BLACK DIAMOND (N) A negro of good traits.

BLACK DOLL (N) A negress.

BLACK GOLD (N) A cheap watch.

BLACK GOLD SOAPER (N) A cheap watch.

BLACK HAND (N) A gang of criminals, consisting mostly of Italians.

BLACK HANDER (N) Extortionist; one who obtains by threats, violence or injustice.

BLACK HEAD (N) A negro.

BLACK JACK (N) A billy; a loaded club; strong black coffee.

BLACKLEG (N) An unscrupulous criminal lawyer; a dishonest gambler.

BLACK MARIA (N) A police patrol wagon; a vehicle in which prisoners are transported.

BLACK MEAT (N) A negro female.

BLACK MIKE (N) Stew.

BLACK OINTMENT (N) Raw meat.

BLACK OUT (V) To assassinate; to kill; to murder.

BLACKSMITH (N) One who does the actual work of opening a safe.

BLACK SPOT (N) An opium den.

BLACKSTONE (N) A judge.

BLACK STRAP (N) Strong black coffee.

BLACK STUFF (N) Opium.

BLACKED EBONY (N) A mulatto.

BLACKY (N) A negro.

BLADE (N) A knife.

BLAH (N) Nonsense; foolish talk.

BLANKET (N) A top coat; an overcoat.

BLANKET MORTGAGE (N) A conveyance to defraud creditors.

BLANKET STIFF (N) A tramp who generally carries a blanket roll with him on his back. (Western Slang.)

BLANKETS (N) Pan cakes; cigarette paper.

BLAST (N-V) The blowing of a safe; an explosive; a charge of explosive used in safe blowing; to shoot; to turn on the heat.

BLAST OUT (V) To shoot to death.

BLASTER (N) A safe cracker; one who kills.

BLASTING OIL (N) Nitroglycerine.

BLAZER (N) A large diamond.

BLEAK (N) Attractive; having good qualities.

BLEATER (N) An informer; a stool pigeon.

BLEED (V) To extort money.

BLEEDER (N) An extortionist; an officer who by color of his office, claims and takes money that is not due, or more than is due.

BLESSED EVENT (N) A new born baby.

BLIMP (N) A girl of questionable character; a prostitute; a very large girl.

BLIND (Adj-N) The front end of a baggage car; unlawful; a bet made before a player has seen his cards.

BLIND BAGGAGE (N) The front end of a baggage car having no door.

BLIND FENCE (N) Innocent purchaser of stolen property or goods.

BLIND JAM (N) An arrest without specific charge.

BLIND MAN (N) One who operates a legitimate business as a screen for criminal activity; a tramp who rides the blind baggage.

BLIND PIG (N-V) A place in which liquor is sold illegally; a speakeasy; to run an illicit liquor establishment.

BLIND TIGER (N) A place in which liquor is sold illegally.

BLINK (N) A hiding place.

BLINKY (N) A blind or one-eye person.

BLISTER (N) A woman of the street; a prostitute; a slut.

BLOAK (N) A man.

BLOCK (N) A solid gold watch; the head; a bindle of morphine; a cubic pack of morphine; a fire-proof vault.

BLOCK AND SLAG (N) A watch and chain.

BLOCK AND SLANG (N) A watch and chain.

BLOCK AND TACKLE (N) A shackle; a watch and chain.

BLOCKHEAD (N) A stupid fellow; a dolt; a person deficient in understanding; want of natural cleverness.

BLOCK JACK (N) A laxative food.

BLOCK SCRAPINGS (N) Scrap meat begged from a butcher.

BLOKE (N) A fellow; stiff; being tired.

BLOOD (N) Catsup.

BLOOD DISEASE (N) Syphilis.

BLOODHOUND (N) A detective; a plain cloth officer.

BLOOD SUCKER (N) One who gives the Wassermann test; an extortionist.

BLOODTHIRSTY HACK (N) A rigid prison guard.

BLOODUCKER (N) A doctor or physician who gives the Wassermann test.

BLOOMER (N) An empty safe; an empty purse; a mistake.

BLOSSOM (N) A female no longer a bud or virgin; a fulminate cap.

BLOTTER (N) The book upon which an officer makes a record of the arrest of the offender; a police record; a weapon.

BLOTTO (N) No good; scornful.

BLOW (N-V) A pistol or revolver; to brag or boast; to go away; to escape; to run away; to spend money; to inhale cocaine; to betray.

BLOW A SHOT (V) To waste an injection of narcotic; to miss the vein in an injection of narcotic.

BLOW DOWN (V) To modify; to soften; to squash.

BLOW GUN (N) A short barreled shot gun; a pistol with a large barrel.

BLOW-IN (N) The new arrival of a prisoner.

BLOW OFF (N) The end; death; a climax; the attainment of the highest point.

BLOW ONE'S BRAINS OFF (V) To shoot one through the head.

BLOW ONE'S TOP (N) To commit suicide; to lose control of one's self.

BLOW ONE UP (V) To blow a safe. (A term used by safecrackers.)

BLOW RAG (N) A handkerchief.

BLOW THE COKE (V) To inhale cocaine.

BLOW THE GAFF (V) To confess.

BLOW THE MEET (V) To fail in keeping an appointment with a narcotic peddler.

BLOWTORCH (N) The penis.

BLOW TOWN (V) To flee from a town.

BLOW UP (N) Nervousness; losing one's confidence; a rumor; confidential information.

BLOW WISE (V) To grasp the meaning of a sudden calamity of infiction of evil.

BLOWED IN THE GLASS STIFF (N) An established tramp who does not voluntarily work; an experienced tramp or crook; a professional crook; a trustworthy pal.

BLOWER (N) A marihuana smoker; an informer; a stool pigeon; a handkerchief.

BLOWING (N) Treating; boasting; taking narcotic via the nostrils.

BLOWING A PETER (N) Blowing open a safe; forcing a safe with the aid of explosive.

BLOWING COKE (N) Sniffing cocaine into the nostrils.

BLOWN SAFE (N) A female no longer a bud or virgin.

BLUBBERS (N) The female's breasts; the mamma.

BLUDGEONER (N) The man who pretends to be the outraged husband in a badger game.

BLUDGET (N) A woman blackmailer; a woman who plays the badger game; a female thief; one engaged in extortion or prostitute.

BLUEBALL (N) Venereal disease.

BLUEBELLY (N) A policeman.

BLUE BOAR (N) Venereal disease.

BLUE BOY (N) A policeman.

BLUE CAT (N) A tenderfoot tramp.

BLUE COAT (N) A policeman.

BLUE DEVIL (N) Delirium tremens.

BLUE GOOSE (N) The principal or main compartment in a jail; a convict cage at a prison work camp.

BLUE LIZ (N) A police patrol car.

BLUE MURDER (N) Killing; murdering.

BLUE NOSE (N) A Canadian.

BLUE ONE (N) A poor place for committing a crime; an unsuccessful crime.

BLUE SKY (N) Forged securities.

BLUE TICKET (N) A pistol or revolver.

BLUFF (V) To promise but fail to fulfill; to deceive by speech or manner, so as to accomplish some hidden purpose or ward off some change or false impression.

BLUNDERBUSS (N) A shot gun with the barrel sawed off.

BO (N) A tramp; vagrant; a hobo.

BO-BO-BUSH (N) Marihuana.

BO CAMP (N) A hobo camp.

BO CAVE (N) A shelter where hoboes congregate.

BO PARK (N) A hobo camp; a railroad yard frequented by tramps and hoboes.

BOAR (N) A man; a he man.

BOARD (N) A restaurant check.

BOARD STIFF (N) A walking advertisement; one who carries a board with advertisement, on his back; a sandwich-man.

BOARDING-HOUSE MAN (N) A prison cook; a kitchen worker.

BOARD'S NEST (N) A hobo camp.

BOB (N) A shoplifter.

BOBE (N) The nose.

BOBBER (N) A woman barber.

BOBBERY (N) Shoplifting.

BOBBY (N) A cop. (English slang.)

BOCHE (N) A German.

BODY BY FISHER (N) An attractive young woman; a young girl with a perfect physique.

BODY CLAIMING (N) Kidnapping.

BODY LIFTER (N) An undertaker.

BODY SNATCH (N) A kidnapper.

BODY SNATCHER (N) A kidnapper; an undertaker; a foreman who entices workers away from other work.

BODY WAX (N) Dung; sediment; a worthless matter.

BOETTLE (N) A female tramp.

BOGEY (N) A detective; a plain cloth officer.

BOGUS (N) A counterfeiting machine.

BOGUS MONEY (N) Counterfeit coins.

BOHUNK (N) A European; one from the central or northern part of Europe.

BOIL (V) To brew or distill liquor.

BOIL-OUT (N) Taking the narcotic cure; abstaining from the use of narcotic.

BOIL UP (N-V) A cleaning of the person; a tramp boiling his clothes to get rid of body-lice; to get rid of body-lice.

BOILED DINNER (N) An Irishman.

BOILER (N) A moonshine still; an automobile thief; a stolen automobile; a camp cook.

BOILER-MAKER (N) A ladies man; a lover.

BOLONEY (N) An automobile tire; loose talk.

BOLT   (N-V)   A bank-roll; to flee; to leave in haste; to allow a prospective victim to go unmolested.

BOLTS AND NUTS   (Adj)   Insane; crazy.

BOMB   (N)   An egg; a boiled egg.

BONE   (V)   To steal.

BONE BENDER   (N)   A wrestler.

BONE BOX   (N)   A coffin.

BONE CRUSHER   (N)   A wrestler.

BONEHEAD   (N)   A prisoner; a fool; an exconvict.

BONE-HOUSE   (N)   A hospital.

BONE-ON   (N)   Passion; lust; being passionate.

BONE ORCHARD   (N)   A cemetery; a graveyard.

BONEYARD   (N)   A hearse; a cemetery; a hospital where students practice on cadavers; a departed hobo.

BONES   (N)   Dice.

BONNET   (N)   Cap used for exploding dynamite.

BON-TON   (N)   A prisoner who has an easy job; a rich or wealthy person.

BOOB   (N)   The lockup; a station house; a City prison; a victim; a dupe.

BOOBY HATCH   (N)   A jail; an insane asylum; the hospital for the criminally insane; a police station.

BOOBY HUTCH   (N)   The hospital for the criminally insane.

BOODLE   (N)   A roll of paper or stage money supposed to represent a large roll of money; loot; money; a large plunder; a petty prison official who practices graft on prisoners.

BOODLE BAG   (N)   A hobo's bed roll.

BOODLE CARRIER   (N)   One who carries a large quantity of counterfeit coin which he passes to a second party, so that the latter may cash it.

BOOGIE   (N)   A negro; a negro informer.

BOOGIE HOUSE   (N)   A prison hospital.

BOOGIE MAN   (N)   A turnkey in a jail or prison.

BOOK   (N)   Everything; a pocketbook; a life sentence.

BOOK MAKER   (N)   One who makes a business of accepting bets on horse races.

BOOKMAN   (N)   A purse snatcher; one serving a life sentence.

BOOKED (Adj) Registered at a jail.

BOOMER (N) A transient worker; a high-class traveling criminal.

BOOZER (N) A drunk; one who consumes much liquor.

BOOST (N-V) A shoplifting job; to flatter; to assist; to shoplift; to rob at the point of a gun; to crack a safe.

BOOSTER (N) A woman shoplifter; a shoplifter; one who operates under the protection of an overcoat.

BOOSTER BLOOMERS (N) Bloomers worn by female shoplifters to conceal stolen goods.

BOOSTING (N) Shoplifting.

BOOT-AND-SHOE FIENDS (N) The poorer class of narcotic addicts.

BOOTLEG (N-V) Contraband whiskey; prison coffee; inferior coffee; illicit goods; to sell illicit whiskey; to smuggle.

BOOTS (N) The poorer class of narcotic addicts.

BOOTY (N) A large plunder.

BOOZE (U) Intoxicating liquor.

BOOZE BARON (N) A liquor gang leader.

BOOZE-HISTER (N) A drunkard.

BOOZE-HOUND (N) A drunkard.

BOOZE MOB (N) A liquor gang.

BOOZE STIFF (N) A tramp who is a drunkard.

BORMET (N) A cap used for exploding dynamite.

BORNIE (N) A knife.

BORROWED (N) Stolen.

BOSOM CHUMS (N) Fleas; mites; lice.

BOSS'S EYE (N) A detective or spy hired to watch workers.

BOSTON BUM (N) A highbrow tramp.

BOTTLE (V) To make one stop talking.

BOTTLE WASHER (N) A cook's helper; a wife.

BOTTLES AND STOPPERS (N) Containers of drugs or liquors.

BOTTLES AND BOOZE (N) Shoes.

BOUNCE BACK (N) The return of a bad check.

BOUNCER (N) A worthless check; a slugger for a dive

or saloon; a strong-arm man; a keeper of order in a low
resort.

BOUNCING PAPER (N)   Bad checks.

BOUQUET (N)   A bundle of wheat.

BOW AND ARROW (N)   A male Indian.

BOW-SOW (N)   Narcotics.

BOWIN (N)   A drug addict full of narcotics.

BOX (N)   A safe; a cell; a safe within a safe; a steel
compartment in a safe; a female pudendum.

BOX-CAR ARTIST (N)   A tramp who steals train
rides.

BOX-CARS (N)   Twelve on a pair of dice.

BOX MAN (N)   A safe blower or cracker; an expression used to apply to any safe burglar.

BOXED IN (Adj)   Surrounded by officers of the law
and unable to make an escape.

BOY SCOUT (N)   An effeminate man.

BOX SCREW (N)   A bank guard.

BOX UP THE DOUGH (V)   To bake.

BOX WORKER (N)   A safe cracker.

BOXER (N)   A box car.

BOZO (N)   A fellow; a man.

B.R. (N)   Bank roll.

BRACE (V)   To speak to a person; to beg; to ask.

BRACE GAME (N)   A swindling activity or trick; a
confidential game.

BRACELETS (N)   Handcuffs.

BRACES (N)   Handcuffs; the legs.

BRAG (V)   To talk boastfully; to boast.

BRAIN (N)   The combination of a safe or vault.

BRAIN BOX (N)   The combination of a safe or vault.

BRAKEY (N)   A brakeman.

BRAND BLOCKER (N)   A cattle thief.

BRASS (N)   Cheap or imitation jewelry.

BRASS BUTTONS (N)   A policeman.

BRASS GUTS (N)   A brave person; a plucky person.

BRASS MAN (N)   A huckster on the public highway,
going in and out of small towns and informing safe
burglars of good locations to blow safes.

BRASS NUTS (N) The principal keeper of a jail; the warden of a penitentiary.

BRASS PUNDER (N) A telegraph operator.

BRASS PEDDLER (N) A peddler of cheap jewelry.

BRASS UP (V) To divide stolen goods or spoils; to split; to divvy.

BRASSES (N) Brass knuckles.

BRASSIERE (N) A strait jacket.

BRASSIES (N) Brass knuckles.

BRAT (N) A child; an adolescent child.

BREAD AND BUTTER JOHN (N) A tramp who begs from house to house.

BREAD BOX (N) A safe easy to open.

BREADLINE (N) One satisfied with a hand to mouth existence.

BREAK (V) To conquer; to give way; to confess; to give in; to quit using narcotics.

BREAK A BOX (V) To crack a safe.

BREAK A LEG (V) To get married; to be seduced; to make a woman.

BREAK A PETER (V) To crack a safe.

BREAK A PRISONER (V) To conquer his unruly spirit for a time; to make him confess.

BREAK AWAY (V) To separate.

BREAK UP (V) To separate a pickpocket from his victim.

BREAKER (N) A burglar.

BREAST KICK (N) The inside pocket of a vest or coat.

BREED OF PUPS (N) An association of criminals.

BREEZE (V) To depart; to flee; to escape; to leave.

BRIAR (N) The sudden making without preparation of a key; a hacksaw blade.

BRICK (N) Gum opium.

BRICK GUN (N) Gum opium.

BRIDE AND GROOM ON A RAFT (N) Two fried eggs.

BRIDEWELL (N) The workhouse; a jail; a place of detention.

BRIDGE (N) A pickpocket picking a pocket by reaching around the victim.

BRIDGE MONKEY (N) A bridge builder or carpenter.

BRIDGE STIFF (N) A bridge builder or carpenter.

BRIDLE (N) A gag.

BRIEF (N) A ticket.

BRIGHT (N) A pocket.

BRIGHT EYES (N) A female criminal lookout.

BRIGHT LIGHTS (N) Night life.

BRIGHT MULATTO (N) An Octoroon.

BRIGHT SKIN (N) A white person.

BRING UP (V) To cause the veins to stand out by tying up the arm or leg between the place where the addict desires to make the injection.

BROAD (N) A gangster's moll; a girl; a prostitute; a woman of easy morals.

BROAD JUMPER (N) A gangster who deserts his sweetheart; one who rapes women.

BROADWAY BROAD (N) A prostitute.

BRODIE (N) A leap; a failure.

BRODY (V) To fling spasm by a narcotic addict.

BROKE (V) To be without funds or means; to escape.

BROKEN LEG (N) The mother of an illegitimate child.

BROKEN PITCHER (N) A corpse.

BROKEN RIB (N) A divorced woman.

BRONCO (N) A boy kept for unnatural purpose.

BROOM (V) To flee; to escape.

BROTHER-IN-LAW (N) A man who has two women of the street working for him; a procurer for two prostitutes of the street.

BROWN BUCKET (N) The hinder part; the rectum.

BROWN POLISH (N) A Mulatto.

BROWN SUGAR (N) A negress.

BROWN-SKIN BABY (N) A young negress.

BROWNEY (N) A boy; a young tramp.

BROWNIE (N) A freight car burglary.

BROWNIE BUSTER (N) A burglary of freight cars.

BRUM (N) A woman of the street; a negligent, careless or untidy woman.

BRUNSER (N) A boy kept for unnatural purpose; a young boy who keeps company with an older tramp.

BRUSH (N) Whiskers.

BRUSH OFF (V) To kill; to murder.

BUBBIES (N) The female breasts.

BUBBLES (N) Champagne.

BUBBLY (N) Champagne.

BUCK (N-V) A dollar; a catholic priest; a male negro; a male Indian; to oppose.

BUCK NIGGER (N) A male negro.

BUCKET BRIGADE (N) Prisoners emptying their chamber pots.

BUCKET BROAD (N) A prostitute who practices a type of sexual variant; a prostitute whose sexual style is variable.

BUCKET OF BLOOD (N) Catsup.

BUCKET SHOP (N) A stock gambling place; a place where stocks are sold on a margin but never delivered.

BUCKET WORKER (N) A swindler.

BUD (N) A virgin; an adolescent girl.

BUDDY (N) Companion; fellowship.

BUDGE (N) A front trouser pocket.

BUFF (N) English slang for being charged with a crime.

BUFFALO (N) A male negro.

BUG (N-V) A woman lacking in neatness or appearance; a visible burglar alarm; a breast pin; an artificial sore; a lamp made by placing a wick in a can of grease; one committed to the insane asylum; a lunatic; to inject coal oil, tobacco juice, or some other substance, by a drug addict, with a view to causing a sufficient poisoning so that a shot of drugs may perhaps be obtained from a physician.

BUG DOCTOR (N) A psychiatrist.

BUGHOUSE (N) An insane asylum; a prison; a cheap lodging house; crazy; insane.

BUG JUICE (N) Opiate; knockout drops.

BUG TEST (N) A prisoner intelligence test.

BUG TRAP (N) A bed.

BUGGED CRIB (N) A safe equipped with a burglar alarm.

BUGGED JOINT (N) A place protected by burglar alarms; a place equipped with a burglar alarm.

BUGGER (V) To commit sodomy.

BUGGY (Adj-N) Insane; a wheelbarrow.

BUGGY BANDIT (N) An automobile thief.

BUGLE (N) The nose.

BUGS (N) Crazy; insane.

BUILD (N-V) Preparatory work; to work up a confidence, or pretended friendship.

BUILD-UP (N) A proposal for a sexual affair; preparatory work for a crime.

BUILD UP ONE'S HABIT (V) To increase one's dosage of narcotics.

BULL (N) A policeman; a plain cloth officer; a strong man; a package of smoking tobacco; a prison guard; a warden of a penitentiary; the keeper of a jail; false or worthless merchandise; a ration of meat (French slang).

BULL BUSTER (N) One with a hatred for police officers and who attacks them upon the least provocation; one who makes it a practice to assault policemen.

BULL CON (N) A convincing story; unreliable talk; a talk intended to deceive.

BULL COOK (N) A camp flunky; a cook's helper.

BULLDIKER (N) A masculine type woman.

BULLDOG (N) A brave person; a plucky person; a short barrel revolver or pistol.

BULL DOGGING A SAFE (N) Turning a safe upside down and blowing out the bottom.

BULL FIGHTER (N) An empty passenger coach.

BULL GUTS (N) Meat.

BULL HORRORS (N) A drug addict's delusions of being pursued by the law.

BULL MEAT (N) A criminal.

BULL PEN (N) A large room in a jail in which a large number of prisoners are kept; a police holdover tank; a flophouse for men.

BULL RING (N) The third degree; a severe examination of a prisoner to secure a confession; a severe treatment of a prisoner; the exercise area of a jail.

BULL'S EYE (N) A policeman with a retentive memory for faces; a plain cloth officer; a dark lantern.

BULL'S WOOL THIEF (N) A clothing store burglar.

BULLET BARON (N) A gangster.

BULLETS (N) Beans; a gun battle.

BULLETTE (N) A policewoman.

BULLY (N) A fighter; a black-jack made of a chunk of lead wrapped in cloth or leather.

BUM BEEF (N) False information lodged against a false accusation.

BUM CHUCK (V) To beg for food.

BUM DOGS (N) Sore feet.

BUM GINGO (N) A tramp who does not work.

BUM FACTORY (N) A relief station; a cheap lodging house.

BUM FODDER (N) Toilet paper.

BUM FINGER (N) False information.

BUM FLIPPER (N) A sore hand.

BUM GAM (N) A lame leg.

BUM GANG (N) Prisoners given the hardest jobs.

BUM HERMAN (N) An established tramp who does not voluntarily work.

BUM MOUTHPIECE (N) A poor lawyer or attorney.

BUM ON THE PLUSH (N) A member of the idle rich.

BUM PAPER ARTIST (N) One who makes or passes bogus money or checks.

BUM RAP (N-V) An unfair sentence; a murder sentence; to sentence or convict unjustly.

BUM ROCK (N) A diamond with a flaw; poor diamonds.

BUM SHAFT (N) A bad leg.

BUM STEER (N) Incorrect or false information; poor advice; wrong direction.

BUMMER (N) An established tramp who does not care to work; a beggar.

BUMSTICK (N) A train with a crew hostile to tramps.

BUMP (N-V) Death or murder; to kill; to die.

BUMP OFF (V) To kill; to assassinate; to terminate; to murder.

BUMPER (N) An assassin; one who slays treacherously.

BUM'S COMFORTS (N) Newspapers used as bedding by tramp.

BUN (N) A jag; a drunk.

BUNCO (V) To rob; to cheat; to swindle.

BUNCO MAN (N) A confidence man.

BUNCO STEERING (N) Luring a person to any place, then fraudulently compelling such person to lose money or value by means of a trick.

BUNDLE (N) A package of bills; a pickpocket; a woman; a newly born infant; a package sent to an inmate of a jail; plunder from robbery; a package from home; personal wealth.

BUNDLE BUM (N) A tramp who carries a bed roll.

BUNDLE STIFF (N) A tramp who carries a roll of bedding.

BUNDLE STIFF WILLIE (N) A tramp who carries a bed roll.

BUNDLE TOSSER (N) A grain thrashing worker.

BUNG (V) To strike.

BUNGER (N) A black eye; a shiner; a discolored eye.

BUNK (N-V) Poor liquor; no good; falsehood; lie; a hiding place; to conceal; synthetic liquor.

BUNK FATIGUE (V) To lie in bed.

BUNK HABIT (N) One who likes to lie around an opium den.

BUNKER (N) Sexual connection by the anus.

BUNKO (N) A swindling activity or trick; a confidential game.

BUNKY (N) A cell mate.

BUNNY (N) A small child or baby.

BURG (N) A town; a city; a village.

BURGLEE (N) The victim of a robbery.

BURIED (Adj) Convicted; cheated; held incommunicado by the police; imprisoned; detained by the police.

BURLAP SISTER (N) A prostitute.

BURN (V) To be electrocuted; to die in the electric chair; to electrocute.

BURN A PATH (V) To shoot one's way out of a tight place.

BURN IN THE CHAIR (N-V) Electrocute; to be electrocuted.

BURN JOB (N) A safe burglar who uses an acetylene torch.

BURN THE MIDNIGHT OIL (V) To smoke opium.

BURN UP (V) To be angry; to be excited; to shoot to death.

BURNED BEARING (N) An unresponsive or cold woman; an unresponsive prostitute.

BURNER (N) An electrocutioner.

BURNES (N) A form of cocaine.

BURNESE (N) A preparation of cocaine used for snuffing through the nostrils; crystallized cocaine.

BURNIE (N) Marihuana cigarette.

BURN'S SPECIAL (N) Stew.

BURNT (Adj) When a pickpocket action is detected by his victim.

BURRHEAD (N) A negro.

BURY (N-V) A sentence to prison; to produce convincing evidence; to be placed in solitary confinement.

BUS-BOY (N) A waiter's assistant.

BUS-GIRL (N) A waiter's assistant.

BUSH PAROLE (N) An escape from prison.

BUSHER (N) A new comer.

BUSHWA (N) An outsider who is unfriendly to the underworld element.

BUSINESS (N) Hypo device; opium den; the genitals of a female or male.

BUST (N) A burglary; a demolished stolen car; an escape from prison; a freight car burglary.

BUST A BROWNIE (V) To burglarize a box car.

BUST OUT (N) Escape from prison.

BUST THE JUG (V) To escape from prison.

BUST UP (N) A raid.

BUST WIDE OPEN (V) To secure a confession.

BUSTED (N) Divorced.
BUSTER (N) A burglar's tool; a jimmy used in safe
  cracking; a fighter; a weapon; a private watchman; a
  wooden club; a policeman's billy; a sledge hammer.
BUSTER AND SCREW MAN (N) A burglar.
BUSTERISH (N) One who is inclined to commit burg-
  lary.
BUSY (N) A detective (English slang) ; a plain cloth
  officer.
BUTCH (N) A peanut vendor on a train.
BUTCH KICK (N) Hip pocket of trousers.
BUTCHER (N-V) A surgeon; to kill; a sodomist; the
  captain of a prison guard.
BUTCHER CHOPPER (N) A machine gunner.
BUTT (N) A cigarette stub; a cigarette; a fraction of
  a year, month or week to serve in jail.
BUTTER BOX (N) A Dutchman.
BUTTERCUP (N) A female; a woman; an effeminate
  man.
BUTTERFLY (N) A driver who goes thru traffic cut-
  ting from left to right; a flighty girl; a delicate girl.
BUTTERFLY MAN (N) A forger.
BUTTER MILKER (N) A Pittsburg tramp.
BUTTON (N) The jaw; the point of the jaw; a police-
  man or detective badge; a policeman.
BUTTON CHOPPER (N) Laundry.
BUTTON UP YOUR FACE (V) To stop talking; to
  be quiet.
BUTTONS (N) A uniformed police officer; a small
  stolen article.
BUTT IN (V) To introduce your company or conver-
  sation where it is not wanted.
BUTT PEDDLER (N) A pimp; a prostitute.
BUTTS ON (N) Requesting to share or use something
  with which another is furnished, usually a cigarette.
BUTTS ON YOU (N) A request to share or use a cig-
  arette with which another is furnished.
BUTTY (N) A fellow workman.
BUY NEW SHOES (V) To jump bail; to flee while
  on bond.

BUZZ (V) To give confidential information; to whisper; to tell stories; to pilfer; to practice petty theft; to cross examine a prisoner.

BUZZARD (N) A Chief of Police; a mean person; a purse snatcher; a pickpocket.

BUZZER (N) A visible burglar alarm; a District Attorney; a door bell; a policeman's or detective badge.

BUZZING (N) Trying to buy narcotic.

BUZZMAN (N) An informer; a stool pigeon.

BY-BLOW (N) An illegitimate child.

C

C (N) Cocaine; a hundred.

C & A (N) A coat with large inner pockets for carrying loot or supplies; a large pocket; a country attorney.

CAB-JOINT (N) A whore house or brothel which gets its patronage thru taxicab drivers; a whore house or house of prostitution.

CAB MOLL (N) A prostitute; a prostitute in a Cab Joint.

CABBAGE (N-V) A dollar; to steal.

CACKLE (V) To turn states evidence; to confess.

CACKLEBERRY (N) An egg.

CACKLE PAPER (N) A bail bond.

CACKLER (N) A prison clerk.

CADDY (N) A hat.

CADET (N) A new drug addict; an abductor or enticer of young girls; one who prostitutes his wife or mistress; one who supplies girls for the white slave traffic.

CADGER (N) One who makes his living by trickery or begging.

CADY KATY (N) A hat.

CAGE (N) A caboose.

CAIN AND ABEL (N) A chair and table.

CAKE AND WINE (N) A prison fare of bread and water.

CAKE CUTTER (N) One who shortchanges.

CAKE HOUSE (N) A cheap lodging house.

CALABOOSE (N) A jail or prison.

CALENDAR (N) A case waiting trial.

CALF (N) An adolescent child; an overgrown girl.

CALF AROUND (V) To loaf.

CALICO (N) A woman; a female.

CALIFORNIA BLANKETS (N) Newspapers used as bedding by tramps.

CALIFORNIA COLLAR (N) The hangman's noose.

CALL A TURN (V) To identify a crook; to prove a criminal guilty.

CALL DOWN (N-V) A reprimand; to chide for a fault.

CALL HOUSE (N) An assignation house; a whore house; a house of prostitution.

CALL THE TURN (V) To identify a criminal, who refuses to talk, by an officer.

CALLING CARD (N) Finger print; bullet.

CAMEL BACK (N) A ridge under or in a gambling wheel.

CAMERA EYE (N) A retentive memory for faces; an officer with a good memory.

CAMISOLE (N) A strait jacket.

CAMP (N) A brothel or gathering place for male homosexuals.

CAMP DOG (N) A camp flunky; a flunky in a jungle.

CAMP EYE (N) A hobo camp watchman.

CAMP STRAWBERRIES (N) Beans.

CAN (N) A safe; a jail; a police station; the toilet; a bomb; a rest room; a cell in a jail; a house of detention; a chamber pot; an ounce of morphine.

CAN HEAT (N) A tear gas bomb.

CAN MAKER (N) A bomb maker.

CAN MOOCHER (N) A tramp who lives out of garbage cans.

CAN OPENER (N) A bail bond; a jimmy used for cracking safes.

CAN SHOOTER (N) A safe cracker.

CAN STIFF (N) A tramp who looks in garbage cans for food.

CAN UP (N-V) A hiding place; to cache or conceal.

CANAL (N) The urethra.

CANARY (N-V) A woman singer; a girl; a female; a woman; a prisoner or exconvict; a stool pigeon; an informer; to turn state's evidence.

CANARY BUD (N) A prisoner; an exconvict.

CANARY KID (N) A weakling; a coward.

CANDY (N) Cheap or imitation jewelry; cocaine.

CANDY JOB (N) A pleasant job.

CANDY KID (N) A lady's man; a pretty boy; a fair haired boy liked by women; a lucky fellow.

CANDY TRAIN (N) A train that transports jewelry.

CANISTER (N) A watch; a revolver; a safe; a steel compartment in a safe; a safe within a vault.

CANNED (N) A sodomite; one having sexual connection by the anus.

CANNED GOODS (N) A virgin; a young girl who has not been seduced.

CANNED HEAT (N) Inferior liquor.

CANNED HEATER (N) A drinker of canned heat; a drinker of solidified denatured alcohol.

CANNED MONKEY (N) Canned beef.

CANNED STUFF (N) Canned commercial smoking opium.

CANNON (N) A pickpocket; a revolver or pistol.

CANNON BALL (N) An important person; a gangster leader; a letter smuggled out of prison; a fast freight train.

CANNON BALL PETER (N) A cylindrical burglar proof safe, usually within a larger safe.

CANNON COPPER (N) A pickpocket detective.

CANNON GANG (N) A pickpocket gang.

CANNON WOMAN (N) An untidy woman; a prostitute.

CAN'T NEVER GET WELL (N) One who is marked for death.

CANUCK (N) A Canadian.

CANVAS (N) A strait jacket.

CAP (N) A capsule of narcotic.

CAPER (N) A criminal enterprise; a theft.

CAPPER (N) A go-between for gamblers; a go-between

for street fakirs; an outside man with swindlers; one
who brings in the suckers for a swindler or gambler.

CAPTAIN HICKS (N) Six on a pair of dice.

CAR (N) A stolen diamond stick pin or ring; a stolen
automobile.

CARBOLIC DIP (N) A prison bath in kerosene or
blue ointment.

CARD (N) A humorist.

CAROLINA NINE (N) Nine on a pair of dice.

CARPET RAGS (N) A mutilated person.

CARRION HUNTER (N) A gossip; an inquisitive person.

CARRY (V) To be supported by drug, after an injection.

CARRY A BALLOON (V) To carry a bedding roll.

CARRY IRON (V) To carry a gun.

CARRY THE MAIL (V) To go fast; to go in a
hurry.

CARRY THE STICK (V) To walk the streets all
night; to wander.

CARRYING A FLAG (N) Traveling under assumed
name.

CARRYING THE BANNER (N) Without the price of
a room and walking the streets at night.

CART WHEEL (N) A silver dollar; the act of throwing
a spasm by a narcotic user.

CASE (V) To look over; to survey the scene or place
to be taken before committing the crime; to check the
joint before the crime is committed; an investigation
before a crime is committed; a place to lie in ambush.

CASE A MARK (V) To select a victim.

CASE A MARK WITHOUT GETTING A RANK (V)
To plan a crime so well that no mistakes can occur
when it is committed.

CASE DOLLAR (N) One's last dollar.

CASE DOUGH (N) A very limited amount of money;
the last of one's money.

CASE NOTE (N) A dollar bill.

CASE A JOINT (N) To investigate a place prior to
committing the crime.

CASER (N) One who investigates a site in preparation for committing a crime; a guard; a watchman.

CASES (N) The last few dollars.

CASH A RUSH IN (N) A beggar collecting a percentage from a restaurant for a meal bought by a sucker.

CASH IN ONE'S CHECKS (V) To die.

CASHIER (V) To steal money.

CASTER (N) A hat.

CASTOR (N) A hat.

CASTOR-OIL ARTIST (N) A physician; a doctor.

CAT (N-V) A prostitute; a spiteful or disagreeable girl; a tramp; a stool pigeon; an informer; to ride on the outside of a train.

CAT AROUND (N-V) Looking for a female to entertain; to be entertained by a prostitute.

CAT BANDIT (N) A sneak thief; a purse snatcher; a female thief.

CAT BURGLAR (N) A female burglar.

CAT FLAT (N) A brothel; a house of prostitution; a whore house.

CAT HEADS (N) Biscuits.

CAT HOUSE (N) A brothel; a whore house; a cheap lodging house.

CAT-HOUSE CUTIE (N) A prostitute; a whore.

CAT MEAT (N) Scrap meat begged from a butcher by tramps.

CAT-NAPS (N) Short snatches of sleep which the addict may get during withdrawal.

CAT UP (N-V) The robbery of an itinerant worker; to rob at the point of a gun; to take the drug cure.

CAT-UP MAN (N) A robber of itinerant workers.

CAT WAGON (N) A brothel on wheels which travels from place to place.

CAT WORK (N) Robbery of itinerant workers.

CAT WORKER (N) One who robs itinerant workers.

CATCH (V) To become pregnant.

CATCH-COLT (N) An illegitimate child.

CATCH THE BUZZER (V) To discover a burglar alarm and escape before detection.

CATHOLIC (N) A pickpocket.

CATTER (N) A tramp who clings to the outside of railroad cars or rides the blind baggage.

CATTLE (N) Women; female.

CATTLE STIFF (N) A worker on cattle ranches.

CAUGHT (N) Pregnant.

CAUGHT IN THE SNOW STORM (Adj) Drugged with cocaine; under the influence of cocaine.

CAUGHT WITH A BISCUIT (Adj) Found with incriminating evidence.

CAUNFORT LODRAN (N) Head of a mob; a master thief.

CAVE (N) A hiding place.

CACIL (N) Cocaine; morphine.

CEE (N) Cocaine.

CEE-GEE (N) The coast guard.

CELL NINETY-NINE (N) The Coroner's office; unidentified; a mythical cell said to house unidentified dead.

CELLAR SMELLER (N) A prohibitionist; a liquor enforcement agent.

CEMENT (N) Any kind of narcotics as it passes into commerce rather than when it is used by the addict.

CEMENTED (N) Married.

CENTERAL OFFICE (N) Police headquarters.

CENTURY NOTE (N) A hundred dollar bill.

CESSPOOLS OF HATE (N) Girls dressing rooms.

C. G. (N) The Coast Guard.

CHAIN (V) To steal watches from the person by a pickpocket.

CHAIN BARNACLE (N) A loafer.

CHAIN GANG (N) A construction gang; a gang of convicts; prisoners working together in chain; a strict or brutal prison.

CHAIN MAN (N) A watch thief.

CHAIN ROCK (N) A chain gang on a rock pile.

CHAIN WORKER (N) A watch thief.

CHAIR CAR (N) A box car.

CHALK (N) A low grade beer; a convict sentenced unjustly; thin milk.

CHALKED (Adj) A mark placed on a cell door as a promise of punishment; detained by the police.

CHAMBER LYE (N) Urine.

CHAMBER OF COMMERCE (N) A brothel; a whore house.

CHAMOIS (N) Champagne.

CHANNEL (N) An addict who takes the drug intravenously.

CHANNEL LINE (N) The vein into which injections are made by addicts.

CHARACTER (N) An established tramp who does not work voluntarily.

CHARCOAL (N) A negro.

CHARCOAL LILY (N) A negress.

CHARGE (N) A narcotic injection.

CHARGE OUT (V) To leave to begin a criminal job.

CHARLEY (N) Cocaine; a gold watch.

CHARLEY COTTON (N) The cotton placed in an opium cooker as a filter.

CHARLEY PADDOCK (N) A hacksaw; a hacksaw blade.

CHARLIE ADAMS (N) The jail at East Cambridge, Mass. (Eastern slang.)

CHARLIE COKE (N) A cocaine addict.

CHARLIE ROLLAR (N) A collar.

CHARMING WIFE (N) A knife.

CHASER (N) A lascivious man.

CHAT (N-V) A house (French); to talk.

CHATTER BOX (N) A machine gun.

CHATTER GUN (N) A machine gun.

CHATTY (N) Dirty; lousy.

CHAW (N) An Irishman.

CHEAP (Adj) Mean; stingy.

CHEAP SHANTY MICK (N) A low-class Irishman.

CHEAP SKATE (N) One who refuses to pay his share.

CHEAP THIEF (N) One who steals from poor boxes.

CHEAT THE GALLOW (V) To escape hanging.

CHEATERS (N) Spectacles; eye-glasses.

CHEATING HUSSY (N) An untrue wife; an untrue sweetheart.

CHECK (N) A small amount of narcotic done up in a paper or capsule.

CHECK ARTIST (N) A forger of checks.

CHECK COP (N) A device for stealing poker chips.

CHECK KITING (N) Dating a check ahead with the expectation of having money to meet it when due.

CHECK OUT (N-V) Close; to give up; to die.

CHECKER (N) A detective or spy hired to watch workers.

CHECKERBOARD CREW (N) A mixed crew of white and dark workers.

CHEEPER (N) A stool pigeon; an informer.

CHEESE BOX (N) The Statesville, Ill., penitentiary.

CHEESE IT (N-V) Beat it; warning that an officer is coming; to stop.

CHEESY (Adj) Very bad; bad odor; dirty; lousy.

CHEF (N-V) The residue left in an opium pipe; an opium pillet after smoking; to prepare opium for smoking.

CHERRY (N) A virgin female; a toy balloon.

CHESTER (N) A pretty crook.

CHEV (N) A knife; a razor.

CHEV MAN (N) A knifer.

CHEVY (N) A knife.

CHEW (N) To eat; to feed.

CHEW THE BEEF (N-V) Small stolen articles; to complain.

CHEW THE RAG (V) To talk.

CHEWING (N) Food. (Used by tramps).

CHIC (N) Chicago, Ill.

CHICAGO AND ALTON COAT (N) A coat with large inner pockets for carrying loot or supplies; a large pocket.

CHICAGO AND ALTON POCKET (N) A large inner pocket of a coat used to carry loot or supplies.

CHICAGO MOWING MACHINE (N) A machine gun.

CHICAGO PILLS (N) Bullets.

CHICAGORILLA (N) A desperate character; a criminal; a gunman; a Chicago gorilla.

CHICK (N) A prison fare; a woman; a girl.

CHICKEN (N) A boy tramp; a catamite who travels with an older tramp; a woman; a female; an adolescent girl; a catamite.

CHICKEN BUTCHER (N) A ladies man.

CHICKEN COOP (N) A jail for women.

CHICKEN FEED (N) Small coins; small change.

CHICKEN HEART (N) A coward; one without courage.

CHICKEN LIVER (N) Cowardice; without courage.

CHICKEN-SHIT HABIT (N) An addict who uses a little bit of narcotic now and then.

CHICKEN STEALING (N) Petty theft.

CHICKEN THIEF (N) A petty thief.

CHIEF (N) A male Indian.

CHILI-EATER (N) A Mexican; a peon.

CHILI PICKER (N) A Mexican; a peon.

CHILL (V) To kill; to submit to arrest.

CHIN (V) To talk; to chat.

CHIN MUSIC (N) Talking; holding a conversation.

CHINAMAN (V) To have a drug habit; to be suffering withdrawal distress.

CHINESE NEEDLEWORK (N) Injecting narcotic.

CHING DOLL (N) A Chinese girl.

CHINK (N) A Chinaman; money.

CHINO (N) A Chinese dealer in narcotics.

CHIP (N) A cash register; a till; poker chips.

CHIP DAMPER (N) A money till.

CHIPPY (N) A prostitute; a street walker; a woman of easy morals; a lively or passionate woman; a young girl who goes with anyone; an untrue wife; an untrue sweetheart; a girl or woman; a mild narcotic; a user of drugs but not an addict to same.

CHIPPY HOUSE (N) A brothel; a whore house; a house in which prostitutes ply their trade.

CHIPPY USER (N) One who uses narcotics moderately.

CHIPPY WITH COKE (V) To use cocaine occasionally.

CHISEL (V) To cheat; to evade compliance with the law; to pilfer; to practice petty theft.

CHISEL IN (V) To obtain a share undeservedly or forcibly; to intrude or trespass on a rival's territory.

CHISELER (N) One who infringes on another's territory or profits; a petty thief; a borrower; a price cutter; a small operator.

CHIV (N) A knife.

CHIVY (N) A knife; a face.

CHOCOLATE BABY (N) A negro girl.

CHOCOLATE DROP (N) A negro.

CHOIR BOY (N) A novice at thievery.

CHOKER (N) A fur neckpiece; cheese; the hangman's noose.

CHOKER HOLES (N) Doughnuts.

CHOP (V) Shoot to death.

CHOP A LIMB N) Begging on the street.

CHOPPER (N) A machine gun; a gangster who acts as machine gunner for his confederates.

CHOPPIES CLAM (V) To stop talking.

CHORUS BOY (N) An effeminate young man.

CHOW (N) Food.

CHOW CHUCKER (N) A restaurant customer.

CHOW-MEIN (N) A Chinaman; a Chinese.

CHOW WAGON (N) A cooking wagon; a wheeled food carrier in prison.

CHRIST KID (N) A young boy with an angel face.

CHRISTMAS (N) A railroad guard; (English slang.)

CHRISTMAS CARD (N) A guard; a watchman.

CHRONIC (N) A drug addict.

CHRONICKER (N) An established beggar.

CHUCK (N) Food.

CHUCK AWAY (Adj) Imprisoned; placed in jail.

CHUCK DOUGH (N) Food money.

CHUCK-HORRORS (N) A state of the addict after quitting his habit when he cannot get enough to eat.

CHUCK WAGON (N) The caboose of a train.

CHUMP (N) A victim; a dupe; a person easily taken advantage of; a sucker.

CHUNK (N) Sexual intercourse.

CHUNK OF LEAD (N) An unresponsive woman; a cold woman.

CHUNK OF MEAT (N) A woman; a female.

CHURCH (N) A place where the identity of stolen jewelry is altered.

CHURCH HYPROCRITE (N) One who represents himself to be a church character, and while so steals.

CHURNS (N) Young girls of teen-age.

CIGARETTE PAPER (N) A bundle of heroin.

CINCIE (N) Cincinnati.

CINDER BULL (N) A railroad detective; a railroad watchman.

CINDER SIFTER (N) A tramp who walks the railroad tracks.

CINDER GRIFTER (N) A tramp who walks the railroad tracks.

CIPHER AROUND (V) To loaf.

CIRCUS (N-V) A narcotic addict who feigns spasm; a show staged by prostitutes and pimps; to drug a victim in order to get him to sign a blank check.

CIRCUS BEES (N) Body lice.

CITY COLLEGE (N) The Tombs Penitentiary, New York; a city jail.

CITY OF DEAD (N) A cemetery.

CLAIM (N) A stolen article.

CLAM (N-V) A sucker; a boob; a sap; a victim; refuse to talk; to keep from saying anything; to stop talking; an easy mark.

CLAM UP (V) To be quiet; to stop talking.

CLAMP (N) A kick.

CLAMP DOWN ON (V) To suppress crime.

CLAMP THE LID DOWN (V) To suppress crime.

CLAMPS (N) Handcuffs.

CLAPPER (N) A teasing woman; a troublesome woman.

CLARA (N) An all clear signal for an air alarm.

CLASS SLOUGH (N) A fine residence.

CLAW (N) A Federal enforcement officer; the Federal government; a policeman; the law of justice.

CLAW UP (N) A refusal to confess.

CLEAN (Adj) A pickpocket extracting all the money

from a stolen purse; no incriminating evidence against one; legal.

CLEAN DOUGH   (N)   Untainted money.

CLEAN ONE   (N)   An empty purse; a stolen car from which all identification has been removed.

CLEAN UP   (V)   To make a profit; to gain.

CLEANER   (N)   A go-between who restores articles won by a decoy.

CLEM   (N)   A circus fight with town hoodlums; a fight between several combatants.

CLERK   (N)   An employee of a gambling house.

CLIMB   (N)   Housebreaking through an upstairs window.

CLIMB A PORCH   (N)   To burglarize a dwelling through an upstairs window.

CLING THE DINGER   (V)   To beg from house to house.

CLINK   (N)   A jail.

CLINKERS   (N)   Handcuffs.

CLIP   (V)   To kill; to defeat; to cheat; to take money from a victim.

CLIP A MARK   (V)   To swindle; to cheat; to defraud.

CLIP ARTIST   (N)   A swindler.

CLIP GAME   (N)   A swindling trick; a confidence game; swindling activities.

CLIP JOINT   (N)   A low resort in which men are encouraged by women to participate in dishonestly conducted gambling games; a place where suckers are cheated.

CLIPPED   (Adj)   Arrested.

CLIPPER   (N)   A swindler.

CLOBBER   (N)   A suit.

CLOCK   (N-V)   A close scrutiny; to look at.

CLOCKER   (N)   A guard; a watchman.

CLOCKERS   (N)   The eyes.

CLOSE OUT   (V)   To close up a deal in margin gambling in which the sucker loses all.

CLOSE UP A JOINT   (V)   To watch a place until the owner closes up.

CLOUT   (N)   An explosion of nitroglycerine in a safe;

a lock easy to pick; a stolen object; a thief; a handker-chief.

CLOUT AND LAM (V) To steal and run.

CLOUTING (N) Stealing from stores and houses at night; assaulting; kidnapping.

CLOVER KICKER (N) A farmer.

CLOWN (N) A small town or village constable; a dis-honest or immoral person.

CLUB AND STICK (N) A detective; a plain cloth officer; a policeman.

CLUCK (N) Counterfeit money.

CLUCK TOWN (N) A small country town.

C NOTE (N) A hundred dollar bill.

COAL MINER'S STRAWBERRIES (N) Beans.

COAL-SHUTES (N) A very dark negro.

COAT MAN (N) A pickpocket confederate who lifts the victim's coat.

COASTING (N) An addict made cheerful from the use of narcotic drugs.

COCK (N) The male pudendum.

COCKEYED (Adj) Peculiar; eccentric; insane; in-toxicated.

COCONUT (N) Cocaine; the head; the skull.

COCKTAIL (N) A prostitute; a whore.

COD (N) A humorist; a droll person.

CODGER (N) A fellow; an old man.

CO-ED (N) A woman prisoner.

CO-ED PRISON (N) A prison in which both men and women are housed.

COFFEE AND (V) To give the price of a meal.

COFFEE BAG (N) A pocket.

COFFEE GRINDER (N) A machine gun.

COFFEE MILL (N) A machine gun.

COFFIN (N) A steel compartment in a safe; a safe within a vault; a cell.

COFFIN NAIL (N) A cigarette.

COFFIN NAILS (N) Smoking of too many cigarettes.

COFFIN VARNISH (N) Intoxicating liquor; bad whiskey.

COIN (N) Money.

COIN SNATCHER (N) A slot machine.
COKE (N) Cocaine, frequently used for any kind of narcotics.
COKE FIEND (N) A cocaine addict.
COKE HEAD (N) A user of cocaine; a user of other narcotics; a drug addict.
COKE-OVEN (N) A cocaine establishment.
COKE PARTY (N) A cocaine party.
COKIE (N) A person addicted to the use of narcotics; a person addicted to the use of cocaine; a user of drugs.
COKOMO (N) A cocaine user.
COLD BISCUIT (N) An unresponsive woman; a cold woman.
COLD BUG (N) A disconnected burglar alarm.
COLD COCK (N) A knockout blow; knock uncon- cious; knock senseless.
COLD DECK (N) A pack of cards prepared, by marks or otherwise, for dishonest play; a deck of stacked cards dishonestly introduced into a game.
COLD FEET (N-V) A failure of courage; an excess of fear; to lose courage at the critical moment; cowardice.
COLD HAND (N) A pickpocket.
COLD MEAT (N) A corpse.
COLD MEAT BLOCK (N) A dissecting table.
COLD MEAT BOX (N) A coffin.
COLD MEAT CART (N) A hearse.
COLD MEAT PARTY (N) A wide awake party; a funeral; watching of a dead body prior to burial.
COLD MEAT WAGON (N) A hearse.
COLD MITT (N) A welcome not wanted; a cold hand- shake.
COLD ONE (N) An empty purse. (A pickpocket slang.)
COLD PAN (N) An unresponsive woman; a cold wom- an.
COLD POKE (N) A wallet with no money in it. (A pickpocket expression.)
COLD PROWLER (N) A burglar who burglarizes houses while the tenants are absent.
COLD SLOUGH (N) A house or apartment where the tenants are not at home.

COLD SLOUGH JOB (N) A burglary of a house or apartment while the occupants are not home.

COLD SLOUGH PROWLER (N) One who burglarizes a deserted house.

COLD SLOUGH WORKER (N) A burglar who burglarizes a house or apartment while the tenants are away.

COLD STORAGE (N) The morgue; solitary confinement.

COLD STORAGE CHICKEN (N) An unresponsive woman; a cold woman.

COLD TURKEY (V) To speak frankly; to be arrested with the loot in one's possession; to quit using drugs without tapering off or without drugs to relieve the withdrawal.

COLLAR (N-V) A policeman; a necklace; to arrest.

COLLARED (Adj) When a pickpocket operator is apprehended.

COLLEEN (N) An Irish girl.

COLLEGE (N) Time spent in the penitentiary; a reformatory.

COLLEGE MAN (N) A prisoner; an exconvict.

COLLEGE WIDOW (N) A noncollege girl who goes with college students.

COM (N) The combination of a safe or vault.

COM SHOT (N) An explosive set off in the combination of a safe or vault.

COMACKER (N) A counterfeiter.

COMB (N) A combination lock; the combination of a safe or vault.

COMBO (N) A dish of several ingredients; a combination lock.

COME ACROSS (V) To pay; to confess; to tell the truth.

COME-ALONG (N) A device for pulling a lock out by the roots; a form of handcuffs; a tool for pulling the combination from a safe.

COME BACK (N-V) A quick detection; a forcible complaint; to make good; a victim resisting a hold up man.

COME BY CHANCE (N) An illegitimate child.

COME CLEAN (V) To confess; to tell the truth; to give in.

COME-ON (N-V) A confidence man; a person who is easily cheated; a sucker; sex attraction employed to entice or decoy; a decoy; to entice.

COME-ON DOUGH (N) Decoy money in a beggar's tray.

COME-ON GIRL (N) A female decoy.

COME-TO-JESUS COAT (N) A long coat worn by ministers and preachers.

COME-TO-JESUS COLLAR (N) The collar worn by a preacher or minister.

COME ON RACKET (N) Luring a victim; inveigling a victim.

COMET (N) A tramp who rides passenger trains.

COMING HOME (Adj) Just released from prison.

COMING OUT PARTY (N) Being discharged from prison.

COMM (N) A police commissioner.

COMMISH (N) A police commissioner.

COMMUNITY BO (N) A tramp who occasionally takes to the road.

CON (N) Confidence game used by pickpockets; a street car conductor; a combination lock; a lie; one who has consumption; an exconvict; a prisoner; a fluent talker; a convincing tale.

CON ARTISTS (N) Swindlers anxious to get something for nothing; any easy sucker.

CON CUT (V) To have the head shaved convict style; to have the hair cut convict style.

CON GAME (N) A swindle perpetrated by a confidence man; confidence trick; a swindling game.

CON JOB (N) Swindling.

CON MAN (N) A confidence man or worker; a prisoner; an exconvict.

CON MOLL (N) A female confidence worker.

CON QUEEN (N) A female detective.

CON TOWN (N) A small country town.

CONDUCER (N) A conductor.

CONEY ISLAND (N) A room in which the third degree is administered.

CONFIDENCE MAN (N) A swindler who gains the trust and confidence of his victim as a step in defrauding him.

CONK (V) To knock unconcious.

CONKED (Adj) Knocked senseless.

CONNECTING (N) Buying narcotics.

CONNECTING ROD (N) A go-between who adjusts differences with the law.

CONNECTION (N) One who sells narcotics; a narcotic trafficker; an understanding; an agreement; one on the outside who does favors for a prisoner; a guard or trusty who does favors for a prisoner.

CONNECTION-DOUGH (N) Money with which to buy narcotics.

CONNECTOR (N) One who acts as go-between, between the addict and the peddler, for a price.

CONNFIELD CLEMO (N) A prisoner who flees from a work gang.

CONNIE (N) A street car conductor.

CONNY (N) A conductor; a consumptive.

CONSENT (N) A theft committed with the consent of the victim.

CONTACT MAN (N) In a kidnapping case the go-between who handles the ransom money; the one who pays the ransom to the kidnappers.

CONTRABAND (N) Forbidden articles smuggled into prison.

CONVERT (N) A new drug addict.

CONVICT (N) A prisoner; one found guilty of a crime.

COOCH (N) A muscle dance.

COOK (N-V) Electrocute; electrocuted; to reclaim denatured alcohol; to distill liquor.

COOK THE RACKET (V) To spoil the game; to hinder the game.

COOK UP A PILL (V) To prepare opium for smoking.

COOK UP ONE (V) To prepare a pill for opium smoking.

COOKED (N) A sentence; convicted.

COOKED UP (Adj) Being under the influence of cocaine.

COOKER (N) The receptacle in which opium is cooked; a cocaine addict; an opium addict; a moonshiner.

COOKIE (N) An officer's badge; cocaine.

COOKING UP (N) Boiling nitroglycerine out of dynamite.

COOL CUCUMBER (N) A brave person; a plucky person.

COOL FISH (N) A brave person; a plucky person.

COOL OFF THE BUG (V) To disconnect a burglar alarm.

COOLER (N) A jail; a dark cell; a cell used for the solitary confinement of a prisoner; a deck of prepared cards; a chaperon; a gun silencer.

COOLIE MUD (N) Inferior opium.

COON (N) A negro.

COOP (N) A jail; a cell.

COOTIE CAGE (N) A bed.

COP (N-V) A policeman; a stolen object; a plain cloth officer; to steal.

COP A HEEL (V) To flee; to escape.

COP A PLEA (V) To plead guilty.

COP A SNEAK (V) To engage in sneak thievery.

COP BUSTER (N) One seized with a hatred for police officers and attacking them upon the least provocation.

COP DICK (N) A plain cloth officer.

COP DOCKET (N) A record of criminals kept by police department.

COP EYE (N) A plain cloth officer; a detective.

COP HER CHERRY (V) To take the virginity of a young female.

COP OUT (V) To escape; to confess.

COPPED OUT (Adj) Taken into custody; arrested.

COPPER (N) A policeman; a reduction of sentence.

COPPER HEART (N) Afraid; cowardice.

COPPER HEARTED (Adj) To be by nature a police informer; to cater towards police officers.

COPPER JOHN (N) A stool pigeon; Auburn Prison, New York.

COPPERS (N) Credits given to prisoners for good behavior while imprisoned; marks.

COPPESS (N) A policewoman.

COPPING (N) Stealing; theft; a stolen object.

CORKSCREW (N) The spine.

CORN (N) Whiskey; small coins.

CORN-EGGIE (N) Corn and eggs.

CORN-FED (N) Stout; robust.

CORN-HOLE (V) To have sexual relation by the anus.

CORN MULE (N) Whiskey made from corn; any spiritous liquor; raw corn whiskey.

CORNED WILLIES (N) Corned beef; corned beef hash.

CORNER (N) A fugitive; an equal division.

CORPSE (N) A skinny person.

CORSET (N) A bullet proof vest.

COTIES (N) Narcotics.

COTTON (N) A small piece of cotton used to strain the drug solution as it is drawn into the syringe of a narcotic addict.

COTTON BROTHERS (N) The cotton placed in an opium cooker as a filter.

COTTON HABIT (N) Addict who has a hypodermic outfit but too poor to afford a capsule, so clubs with another addict who has the price of a capsule.

COTTON PICKER (N) A negro.

COUGH UP (V) To pay; to pay by request or under pressure or threats.

COUNT (N) The population of a jail; the number of prisoners in a jail.

COUNTER (N) The bench in a court of law.

COUNTY HOTEL (N) A county jail.

COURAGE PILLS (N) Heroin in tablet form.

COURT CLASH (N) A court trial.

COURT PLASTER (N) A mortgage.

COUSIN JACK LANTERN (N) An improvised lamp made by placing a candle in a can of grease.

COVE (N) A fellow.

COVER (N) A hiding place.
COVER UP (N) One assisting a confederate.
COVER ONESELF WITH THE MOON (V) To sleep
  in the open without bedding.
COVER SHADE (N) An accomplice for a pickpocket.
COVER UP MAN (N) A pickpocket confederate.
COW (N) An old prostitute; milk; a jail.
COW FEED (N) Salad or greens.
COW GREASE (N) Butter.
COWTOWN (N) A town in a cattle district.
COWS AND KISSES (N) The wife.
CRAB (V) To interfere with; to complain.
CRACK (N) A burglary.
CRACK A CRIB (V) To be convicted of burglary.
CRACK IN (N) Burglary.
CRACKMAN (N) A burglary.
CRACK RACKET (N) Safe cracking.
CRACK SALESMAN (N) A pimp; a prostitute.
CRACK THE CLARET JUG (N-V) A nose bleed; to
  bleed.
CRACK WIDE OPEN (V) To give way under the
  third degree; to confess; to give in.
CRACKED (Adj) Mentally diseased.
CRACKED ICE (N) Unset diamonds.
CRACKER (N) A safe; a steel compartment in a safe;
  a safe within a vault; a poor southerner.
CRACKER BOX (N) A safe easy to open.
CRACKING (N) Breaking into a place or safe; forcing
  an entrance to a building; act of striking; speaking.
CRAP (N) The gallows; dung.
CRAP CAN (N) A toilet; privy; a rest room.
CRAP HOUSE (N) A toilet; a privy; a rest room.
CRAPPER (N) A toilet; a privy; a rest room.
CRAPS (N) A game in which the players gamble with
  two dice.
CRASH (V) To enter by force; to break into; to
  burglarize.
CRASH IN (N) Convicted of burglary.
CRASH OUT (V) To escape from prison.
CRASH THE BORDER (V) To flee the country.

CRATE (N) A jail; an old automobile.
CRAVAT (N) The hangman's noose.
CRAWLER (N) A legless cripple.
CRAZY ALLEY (N) The hospital for the criminally insane; the insane section of a jail.
CREAMPUFF (N) An effeminate man; a coward; a weakling; a female; a woman.
CREDITS (N) Given in jail for good behavior.
CREEP (N-V) A sneak thief; to engage in sneak thievery.
CREEP JOINT (N) Wherein two negro women operate, one takes her victim to bed and the other peeps through the door and at the psychological moment opens the door and takes purse from victim's trousers; a gambling house moving to a different place each night; a brothel or whore house in which patrons are robbed.
CREEPER (N) A prostitute who robs her patrons; a woman who steals from drunken man; a prostitute; a sneak thief; a bawdy house; one who robs sleeping or intoxicated persons; a garment thief; a man who invades another's marital rights; nervousness.
CREEPERS (N) Rubber soled shoes worn by burglars; a sneak thief; prison guards.
CREPE (N) A false beard.
CRIB (N) A safe; a saloon or gambling place; a hang-out where prostitutes ply their trade; a low resort; a money box.
CRIB CRACKER (N) A burglar.
CRIB CRACKING (N) House breaking.
CRIB JOB (N) A burglary job.
CRIBBAGE (N) A theft; a stolen article.
CRIBMAN (N) A safecracker.
CRIEPER (N) A garment thief.
CRIM-CON (N) A damage taken by a husband for the seduction of his wife.
CRIMP (N) A runner for sailor's boarding houses.
CRIMSON RAMBLERS (N) Bed bugs.
CRIP (N) A cripple.
CRIP FAKER (N) A beggar who pretends to be crippled.

CRIPPLE   (N)   An unprincipled criminal lawyer.
CROAK   (V)   To kill; to die; to murder; death.
CROAKED THE NECK   (Adj)   Hanging.
CROAKER   (N)   A doctor; a stool pigeon; an informer; a weapon; an assassin.
CROAKER JOINT   (N)   A hospital; a doctor's office.
CROCK   (N)   An opium pipe; the bowl of an opium pipe.
CROCKED ARM   (N)   A blow with the fist.
CROCKER NECK   (N)   A hangman.
CROCUS   (N)   A doctor.
CROOK   (N)   A criminal; a thief.
CROOK DOWN   (N)   The underworld outside of prison.
CROOK EYE   (N)   A deceitful look in a criminal's eye.
CROOKED RIB   (N)   A nagging wife.
CROOKED WORK   (N)   Mean thieving.
CROSS KID   (N)   A cross examination.
CROSS LOTS   (V)   To walk across country.
CROW BAIT   (N)   A corpse.
CROWLEY'S ANVIL   (N)   An ignorant worthless fellow who slanders people.
CROWN   (V)   To hit on top of the head.
CROWN SHEET   (N)   The seat of a trouser.
CRUISER   (N)   A police radio car; a homosexual who looks for patrons.
CRUM   (N)   A dirty tramp; one infested with lice.
CRUM BOSS   (N)   A rooming house janitor; a bunk house caretaker.
CRUM BOX   (N)   A bed; a bedroom.
CRUM JOINT   (N)   A cheap lodging house.
CRUM ROLL   (N)   A hobo's bed roll.
CRUMB   (N)   A dirty tramp; a tramp infested with lice.
CRUMB JOINT   (N)   A cheap lodging house.
CRUMB PAROLE   (V)   To forfeit parole.
CRUMB UP   (N-V)   A cleaning of the person; to clean up; to get rid of body lice.
CRUMBS   (N)   Fleas; mites; lice.

CRUMBY (N) A dirty tramp; a tramp infested with lice; a lousy person; a rooming house janitor; a bunk house caretaker; a vermin infested jail.

CRUMMY (Adj) Dishonest; cheap; unsatisfactory; dirty; lousy; the caboose of a train; a tramp infested with vermin; a bed room; a vermin infested jail; a rooming house janitor; a bunk house caretaker; any dirty person.

CRUSH (N-V) One forcing his attention on a woman; to crowd; to get away; to force.

CRUSH THE CAN (V) To escape prison.

CRUST (N) Impudence; forwardness; insolence.

CRY (V) To complain; to grumble.

CRY BABY (N) A tear gas bomb.

CUB (N) A young child; a young boy.

CUBE (N) A bindle of morphine; a cube pack of morphine.

CUBES (N) A pair of dice; morphine in cubes.

CUCKOO (Adj) Foolish; crazy; wild.

CUE BALL (N) One with no hair on his head.

CUFF (N-V) Handcuffs; to buy on credit.

CUFFS (N) Handcuffs.

CUPID (N) A small child; a small baby.

CUPID'S ITCH (N) Venereal disease.

CURBSTONE SAILOR (N) A prostitute; a whore.

CURE (N) Suicide.

CURTAINS (N) The end; death; murder.

CURTAINS FOR YOU (N) Death is your portion.

CURVE (N) A woman of easy morals; a loose woman or girl.

CUSH (N) Money; bribe money; pay.

CUSPIDOR (N) A low-bred person.

CUSTOMER (N) A new prisoner.

CUT (N-V) A share of stolen goods; a reduction of sentence; an equal division; to dilute liquor with water and alcohol; to give a share; to adulterate narcotics, such as morphine and heroin.

CUT A MELON (V) To divide or share large profits; to divide a large loot.

CUT CAKE   (N)   Shortchange.
CUT IN   (V)   To trespass in a rival's territory; to obtain
   a share undeservedly or by force; to give a share.
CUT LOOSE   (N)   A divorce.
CUT OFF   (Adj)   Dead.
CUT THE TAKE   (V)   To give a share.
CUT TWO WAYS   (V)   To give a share.
CUT UP   (V)   To divide.
CUTE LITTLE TRICK   (N)   A small child; a small
   baby; a beautiful young girl.
CUTER   (N)   A District Attorney.
CUTERED PILL   (N)   A strong unpalatable pill ob-
   tained when the bowel of the opium pipe becomes too
   hot or too full of yenshee.
CUTIE   (N)   A beautiful woman or girl.
CUTIES   (N)   Body lice.
CUTICLE GAME   (N)   A confidence game; a swindling
   activity; a swindling trick.
CUTOR   (N)   A District Attorney.
CUTTER   (N)   A District Attorney; a needle file; a
   gun man; an officer's badge; a pistol or revolver.
CUTTIE   (N)   A pretty young girl with a friendly man-
   ner.
CUTTING IRON   (N)   A pistol or revolver.
CUTTINGS   (N)   Division of spoils.
CYCLONE SHOT   (N)   A powerful charge in safe
   blowing.
CYMBAL   (N)   A watch.
CZAR   (N)   The principal keeper of a jail; a warden
   of a penitentiary.

D

DABBLE   (N)   When an addict has been off the drug
   and begins to use a little now and then.
DADDY   (N)   A girl's protector; a man who lives with
   his sweetheart.
DAFFY   (Adj)   Demented; crazy; insane.
DAFFY DAME   (N)   A fighting girl.
DAFFY DARTER   (N)   A fighting girl.

DAGO (N) An Italian; anyone of the Latin race.

DAGO BANDO GAME (N) A dishonest trick; a swindle game worked on Italians.

DAGO RED (N) A red wine of inferior quality.

DAISY CHAIN (N) A group of active sodomites; sexual variants.

DAISY ROOTS (N) Feet.

DASIES (N) Boots. (English slang.)

DAMAGED GOODS (N) A female no longer a virgin.

DAME (N) A female; a woman.

DAME-ENE (N) A whore house; a brothel.

DAMP POWDER (N) False alarms; bull con; a fake agitator; one who tells unconvincing tales.

DAMPER (N) A money-drawer; a cash register or till.

DAMPER GETTER (N) Burglary of a cash drawer; a thief who burglaries money drawers.

DAMPER PAD (N) A bank book.

DAMPER WORK (N) The burglary of cash registers.

DANCE (V) To die by hanging.

DANCE HALL (N) The execution chamber of a penetentiary in which capital punishment takes the form of hanging; the death house.

DANCE OF DEATH (N) Hanging.

DANCE ON A ROPE (V) To be hanged.

DANCER (N) One who dies by hanging.

DANCERS (N) The thirteen stairs of the gallow.

DANGER ARTICLES (N) Illicit goods.

DANGEROUS CURVES (N) A woman of easy morals.

DANGLER (N) A tramp who rides the rods of a train; a freight train.

DARB (N) An attractive young woman; money; goods.

DARBIES (N) Handcuffs.

DARK CLOUD (N) A negro.

DARK DAYS (N) Solitary confinement.

DARK HORSE (N) A night watchman; a woman; any female.

DARK MEAT (N) The exposed flesh of a negress.

DARKY (N) A negro.

DASHHOUND (N) Bibbed overalls.

DATE (N) An appointment.

DAUB (N) Material used to mark playing cards.

DAUBER (N) A painter who paints automobiles for car thieves; a forger.

DAUGHTER OF JOY (N) A prostitute; a whore.

DAY-OLDS (N) Stale bakery goods.

DEACON (N) The principal keeper of a jail; the warden of a penitentiary.

DEAD (Adj) Reformed; a beaten criminal; a criminal either discouraged or reformed.

DEAD BANG (N) Used when a pickpocket operator is apprehended.

DEAD BEAT (N) One who does not pay his bills.

DEAD EYE (N) A policeman with a retentive memory for faces; a good memory.

DEAD EYES (N) Poached eggs; a crack marksman; one with a good memory.

DEAD FREIGHT (N) A freight carrying articles too heavy to steal easily.

DEAD HEAD (N) A nonpaying passenger or spectator; a person who does not pay his way; an empty freight car; a tramp who steals train rides.

DEAD HEADING (N) Riding on trains without paying fare.

DEAD HORSE (N) Corned beef.

DEAD MAN'S SHIRT (N) A shirt issued to a discharged prisoner.

DEAD MARCH (N) A funeral.

DEAD MEAT (N) A corpse.

DEAD MONEY (N) Counterfeit monies.

DEAD ONE (N) A person who has ceased to be of any use; broke or incompetent; a reformed criminal; a retired tramp; a stingy person; an unoccupied house.

DEAD PAN (N) A face which shows no evidence of changing emotions or thoughts; a poker face without expression.

DEAD PLEDGE (N) A mortgage; a legal remedy.

DEAD PICKER (N) A prostitute who robs drunken patrons; a robber of intoxicated persons.

DEAD PICKING (N) Easy money; robbery of intoxicated persons.

DEAD PIGEON (N) An uninteresting person.

DEAD RAP (N) A death sentence; without any alibi.

DEAD RINGER (N) A double; alike.

DEAD ROOM (N) The death house.

DEAD-ROOM CHISELER (N) A professional mourner.

DEAD SNEAK (N) A stealthy escape.

DEAD SOLDIERS (N) Dung; empty beer bottles.

DEAD TO RIGHTS (Adj) Caught wth the stolen property; caught in the criminal act.

DEAD WAGON (N) A push-car used on railroads enabling track material etc. to be rolled out to work (Term used by hobos.); a hearse.

DEAD WOOD (N-V) Done for; having no chance; to be arrested by a narcotic agent directly and not with the intervention of the stool pigeon.

DEALER (N) Wholesaler of bogus money; a narcotic trafficker.

DEAN OF MEN (N) The principal keeper of a jail; a warden of a penitentiary.

DEATH WAGON (N) A machine gun.

DEB (N) A girl member of a mob, who by a willingness to fight alongside of the boys and, sometimes, sexual promiscuity has proved her worth.

DEB-GENERATE (N) A debutante of easy morals.

DEBUTART (N) A debutante of easy morals.

DECK (N) A small portion of narcotic; a package of cigarettes.

DECK HAND (N) A tramp who rides train roofs; a kitchen worker; a domestic; a camp flunky.

DECLARE IN (V) To obtain an interest by force or threat; to intrude or trespass in a rival's territory; to obtain a share undeservedly by force.

DECORATE THE PARLOR (V) To tip.

DECOY (N) A person employed to trap a suspect; a picture of a safe placed in front of a safe while it is being burglarized.

DEE-DEE (N) A deaf and dumb person.
DEEM (N) A ten-cent piece.
DEEMER (N) A dime; a ten cent piece.
DEEP-SEA CHEF (N) A dish washer.
DELIVER (V) Disburden of a child; to extract.
DEP (N) A deputy sheriff.
DEPRESSION STIFF (N) A tramp who takes to the road.
DERRICK (N) A shop lifter; a pickpocket who operates under the protection of an overcoat; a hangman.
DESIGNER (N) A counterfeiter.
DEUCER (N) A prisoner serving seven years.
DEVIL DODGER (N) A preacher.
DEW DROP (N) A night pleasure seeker.
DEW DROPS (N) Lumps of coal thrown at hoboes riding trains.
DEWEY (N) A revolver or pistol.
DEWIFE (V) Divorce.
DICE JOINT (N) A general store.
DICER (N) A derby hat; a hat; a doughnut; a fast train.
DICK (N) A detective; the male pudendum; a plain cloth officer.
DICK DAME (N) A female detective.
DICKEY (N) The male pudendum.
DIE IN A HORSE'S NIGHTCAP (V) To be hanged.
DIFFERENCE (N) Weapons.
DIG (N-V) A pickpocket; to stab.
DIG DEEP (V) To pay up.
DIG IN THE GRAVE (V) To shave.
DIGGER (N) A pickpocket; a prostitute; a whore.
DIGGING (N) A pickpocket operator working a crowd.
DIGGING IN (N) When a pickpocket operator is working in a crowd.
DIGGINGS (N) A gift to a beggar; a stolen object.
DIMBER (N) Attractive; excellent.
DINAH (N) Dynamite; nitroglycerine.
DINE (N) Dynamite.
DING (N-V) A beggar; a door-bell; to beg; to nag; to obtain by begging.

DINGALOO (N) A beggar.
DING BAT (N) A low-class tramp; a low beggar; a male pudendum.
DINGBATS (N) The male genitals.
DING-DONGER (N) A house to house beggar; a beggar.
DINGE (N) A negro.
DINGER (N) An alarm bell at the door of a bank; a door bell; a visible burglar alarm.
DINGHIYEN (N) An improvised hypodermic syringe made from a medicine dropper and used with a pin or nail.
DINGLE (N) The back room of a liquor establishment used as a criminal hangout.
DINGUS (N) An improvised hypodermic syringe made from a medicine dropper and used with a pin or nail; a male pudendum.
DINK (N) A lady's man; a dandy.
DINKY (N) A trolly car which has a very short run; very small.
DINKY DIRT (N) A shirt.
DINO (N) A railway section hand; an old beggar; an old tramp.
DIONAH (N) Nitroglycerine.
DIP (N-V) A pickpocket; to pick pockets.
DIP GANG (N) A pickpocket gang.
DIPPER (N) A pickpocket; an opium pipe.
DIPPING (N) Picking pockets by a pickpocket.
DIPPY (Adj) Crazy; mad; insane; demented.
DIPPY DAME (N) A flighty girl; a girl of easy morals.
DIPSEY (N) A sentence to the work house.
DIRT (N) Confidential information; money; sugar; gossip.
DIRT ROAD (N) The posterior; the rectum.
DIRTY (N) A treacherous person; a bad person.
DIRTY DAUGHTER (N) A girl of bad habits.
DIRTY-DISH (N) A person of unclean or dirty habits.
DIRTY DIG (N) An insult; a cutting remark.
DIRTY SPOT (N) A brothel; a whore house.
DIRTY TOWEL (N) A barber shop.

DISCARD ARTIST (N) A tramp who wears discarded clothes.

DISCHARGE (N) A member of a mob who breaks away from the mob before an arrest and by so doing avoids liability for a share of fall money; to resign from a gang.

DISTILLERY BUM (N) A drunkard tramp.

DISTILLERY STIFF (N) A drunkard tramp.

DITCH (V) To get rid of; to conceal; to throw away; to put away; to give the slip; to be put away.

DITCH THE LEATHER (V) To dispose of a stolen purse. (Pickpocket slang.)

DIVE (N) A low resort; a place in which girls are kept for immoral purposes; pocket picking (Pickpocket slang.)

DIVER (N) A pickpocket; a beggar or tramp who digs hungrily in garbage cans when a prospect is seen approaching.

DIVORCE (N) A pickpocket gang's loss of man by a jail sentence.

DIVORCE MILL (N) Divorce court.

DIVORCE MOLL (N) A woman with a husband or sweetheart in jail.

DIVORCED (Adj) Said of a girl who has lost her fellow by being sent to prison.

DIVVY (N-V) A share; a share of stolen goods; an equal division; to divide into shares.

DIVVY IN (V) To give one's share.

DIVVY UP (N) An equal division.

DIZZY (Adj) Silly; foolish; scatter-brained.

DO A BUNK (V) To run away; to escape.

DO A CRACK (V) To commit a burglary.

DO A DUST (V) To commit burglary.

DO A PENNY WEIGHT (V) To rob a jewelry store.

DO A SECOND STORY JOB (V) To burglarize a dwelling through an upstairs window.

DO A SOLO (V) To turn states evidence; to confess.

DO A TRICK (V) To serve a term in prison.

DO-RIGHT JOHNS (N) Non-addict; one not a drug addict.

DO-RIGHT PEOPLE (N) Non-addicts; one not a drug addict.

DOBE SHOT (N) A moderate charge of explosive in blowing a safe.

DOCK PIRATE (N) A wharf prowler.

DOE (N) A young child; an infant.

DOG (N-V) The feet; style; to turn coward; to get cold feet.

DOG EYE (V) To scan minutely.

DOG HOUSE (N) A storage place for stolen automobiles; a toilet; a privy; a caboose; in disfavor; a watch tower on the walls of a penitentiary.

DOG IT (V) To flee; to escape.

DOG NAP (N) The theft of a dog.

DOGNAPPER (N) One who steals dogs and then claims the reward offered.

DOGSHOW (N) Foot inspection in the army.

DOGGED (V) To follow; to trail; to shadow.

DOGS (N) The tumblers of a safe combination.

DOG'S EYE (N-V) A side long glance; a close scrutiny; a hostile look; to look at; to glare at.

DOG'S LIFE (N) An unhappy life; an unhappy marriage.

DOING A BIT (N) Serving a short prison sentence.

DOING IT ALL (N) Serving a life sentence.

DOING THE BOOK (N) Serving a penitentiary sentence for life.

DOLL (N) A pretty girl; a female.

DOME (N) The head.

DOMINOES (N) Dice.

DON (N) A Spaniard or Portuguese; dynamite.

DONG (N) A door bell.

DONGER (N) Trespassing on rival territory; a house to house beggar.

DONIGAN (N) A toilet; a privy; a rest room.

DONIGAN SLICKER (N) One who robs his victim in a rest room.

DONIGAN WORK (N-V) Robbery in a rest room; to rob one in a rest room.

DONKEY (N) A railway section hand.

DONKEY RIDE (N) A shortchange artist.

DONKEY'S BREAKFAST (N) A bed of straw.

DONNEKER (N) A wash room.

DOOLY (N) Dynamite; a revolver or pistol.

DO ONE'S HOUSE WORK (V) To burglarize a dwelling.

DOORMAT (N) A coward.

DOOR MATTER (N) A petty thief.

DOOR RAPPER (N) A house to house beggar.

DOOR SHAKER (N) A night watchman; a private patrol.

DOOZY (N) Attractive; excellent.

DOPE (N) Picking winner from past performance; narcotics; poison; medicine; morphine; cocaine; heroin; yen-shee; opium; a hypo needle; evidence; nitroglycerine; confidential information; a kept mistress; an inexperienced person.

DOPE DEN (N) An opium den.

DOPED UP (V) To be in a stupor from excessive use of drugs.

DOPE FIEND (N) A drug addict.

DOPE GUN (N) A hypodermic syringe.

DOPE HEAD (N) A user of drugs; a drug addict.

DOPE HOP (N) Exhilaration of narcotics.

DOPE PEDDLER (N) One who sells narcotics; a trafficker in narcotics.

DOPE RACKET (V) To deal in narcotics.

DOPE RING (N) A mob dealing in narcotics; a smuggler of narcotics; the illicit disposal of drugs.

DOPE RUNNER (N) A smuggler of narcotics; a trafficker in narcotics.

DOPE STICK (N) A cigarette; a stick for dipping narcotic.

DOPER (N) One who drives at a dangerously slow pace and holds up traffic behind him.

DOPEY (N-V) A dope; drugged by narcotics; stupid; slow-witted.

DO-RE-ME (N) Money.

DO RIGHT PEOPLE (N) Noncriminals.

DO THE CAN TRICK (V) To obtain food from garbage cans.

DO THE DRAG (V) To loiter about town; to walk the streets.

DO THE MERRY ALLEN (N) A pickpocket term for picking pockets.

DO THE SPLIT ACT (V) To give a share.

DO TIME (V) To serve a prison sentence.

DORF (N) A village.

DOSE (N) Venereal infection; a jail sentence.

DOSE OF CLAP (N) Gonorrhea.

DOSE OF HOT LEAD (N) Shooting.

DOSS (N-V) A bed room; to sleep.

DOSS HOUSE (N) A lodging house.

DOTTY (Adj) Crazy; mad; insane.

DOUBLE (N) A duplicate key.

DOUBLE CROSS (N-V) A betrayal; to betray confidence.

DOUBLE-FACED (Adj) Hypocritical; a false pretender; one who feigns to be other than he is.

DOUBLE FINN (N) A ten dollar bill; a ten year prison sentence.

DOUBLE HARNESS (V) To be married.

DOUBLE INSIDER (N) Pickpocket term for an inner vest pocket.

DOUBLE O (N-V) A glance; a curious and appraising glance; to examine; to stare at appraisingly; to spy.

DOUBLE SAW (N) A twenty year prison sentence.

DOUBLE SAWBUCK (N) A twenty year penitentiary sentence: a twenty dollar bill.

DOUBLE UP (V) To share a cell with another prisoner; to get married.

DOUBLED UP (Adj) Married; paired; two in a room.

DOUGH (N) Money; bread.

DOUGH BOXER   (N)   A cook; a kitchen worker; a prison.
DOUGH CHOPPER   (N)   An embezzler.
DOUGH GOD   (N)   Bread.
DOUGH-HEAD   (N)   A baker; a cook.
DOUGH-HEAVY   (N)   One having plenty of money.
DOUGH-NUT   (N)   An automobile tire.
DOUGH-NUT FACTORY   (N)   A restaurant.
DOUGH-NUT OPTIMIST   (N)   One satisfied with a hand-to-mouth existence.
DOUGH ROLLER   (N)   A cook; a kitchen worker; a camp.
DOUSE   (V)   To put out; to extinguish.
DOUSE GLIM   (V)   To put out light.
DOWN AND OUT   (Adj)   Without money; without any friends.
DOWN AND OUTER   (N)   One in needy circumstances; one financially at low ebb.
DOWN SOUTH   (N)   The U. S. Penitentiary at Atlanta, Georgia.
DOWN TO CASH DOUGH   (N)   Living on reserve fund; down to the last of one's money.
DOWN TO CASES   (N)   Living on reserve fund; down to the last of one's money.
DOWDY   (N)   A pickpocket who causes a crash or pushes his victim, in a crowd, in order to pick his pocket.
DOWDY-DOWDY   (N)   A pickpocket causing a crash or pushing his victim, in a crowd, in order to pick his pocket.
DRAG   (N-V)   The principal street in a town; a freight train; a tool for pulling the combination of a safe; a horse and wagon; a long tiresome ride; a loan; female costumes worn by a male homosexual; to puff from a cigarette.
DRAG A LONG HAND   (V)   To go a long distance.
DRAG IT   (V)   To flee; to escape.
DRAG MOOCHER   (N)   A street beggar.
DRAG THE PILES   (V)   To walk.
DRAG-WEED   (N)   Marihuana.
DRAGGING AN ANCHOR   (Adj)   Married.

DRAGNET (N) A wholesale police hunt for a criminal.

DRAIN (V) To urinate.

DRAW IRON (V) To draw a gun.

DREAM BOOK (N) A fortune teller's book used by Policy players.

DREAM SACK (N) A sleeping bag.

DREAM STICK (N) An opium pipe.

DREAM WAX (N) Opium.

DRESS A DOLL (V) To shortchange by placing bills of large denomination on the outside of a package of dollar bills.

DRESS GOODS (N) A woman; a female.

DRESS IN NUMBERS (V) To put on prison uniform upon entering prison; to be imprisoned.

DRESS SUIT BURGLAR (N) A lobbyist; a high-tone fixer; a slippery fellow.

DRESSED DOLL (N) A package of money with bills of larger denomination on the outside.

DRIFT (N) Divorce.

DRILL (V) To shoot; to cross examine.

DRILLER (N) A gunman.

DRIPPER (N) An improvised hypodermic syringe made from a medicine dropper and used with a pin.

DRIVE (N) The sensation derived from the use of narcotics.

DRIVE IN (V) To smuggle narcotic.

DROP (N-V) A fence; a place for receipt of stolen goods; a temporary cache for stolen goods; the gallows; to be caught with stolen goods.

DROP JOINTS (N) Places selected for depositing stolen goods temporarily.

DROPPED (Adj) Arrested.

DROPPER (N) A gun man; a professional killer; a machine gunner; a paid killer.

DROPPING THE PIGEON (N) Bunco game; finding envelope or wallet containing large amount of money, dropped by a confederate, the victim being made to believe it was really found. (Worked mostly by negroes.)

DRUID (N) An old tramp.

DRUM (N) A place where liquors are sold; a prison cell; a saloon; a vault.

DR. WHITE (N) Term used by narcotic addict to camouflage a reference to narcotics.

DRY COMDO (N) A dry meal of cheese and crackers.

DRY CROG (N) Narcotics.

DRY HOLE (N) A cold and unresponsive woman.

DRY LAND SAILOR (N) An old tramp who does not work.

DRY OUT (N) To secure a confession; to give in; to confess.

DRY UP (V) To stop talking.

DUB GAME (N) A "Gold Digger" sharing her earnings with a confederate.

DUCAT (N) A ticket; a warrant for arrest; a pardon; a dollar.

DUCE (N) A two dollar bill; a two year prison sentence; two.

DUCK (N-V) A tin pail in which beer is carried; to run away; to avoid; to leave.

DUCK OUT (V) To escape; to flee.

DUCK SOUP (N) An easy thing; something easily done.

DUCKET (N) A discharge certificate; a prison pardon.

DUCKEY (N) An effeminate man.

DUFFER (N) A name applied in contempt; a fool.

DUGOUT (N) The lowest type of a drug addict; an addict who has reached the bottom; a heavy eater.

DUKE (N) The keeper of a jail; the warden of a prison; the first.

DUKE IN (V) To give an initial confidence talk.

DUKE OF THE DUSTY ROAD (N) A tramp who is well established and does not have to work.

DUKES (N) The hands; the fists.

DUKIE BOOK (N) A meal ticket book.

DUMB DICK (N) A poor detective; a plain cloth officer.

DUM-DUMB (N) A shiftless no account drunkard.

DUMMY (N) A detective; a plain cloth officer; a pickpocket; a deaf and dumb person; false or worthless merchandise; a faint; the male pudendum.

DUMMY UP (N-V) A refusal to talk; a refusal to confess; to stop talking; to withhold information.

DUMP (N) A cheap rooming house; a restaurant; a jail; a place of concealment; a fence; a hangout; a railroad transfer or terminal point; a place where stolen goods are received.

DUMP-JOINT (N) A town.

DUNCE CAP (N) A backward person; a dull-witted person; one weak in intellect.

DURRY-NACKER (N) A female peddler; one who sells wares by crying them in the street.

DUST (N-V) Money; morphine; cocaine; heroin; to run; to flee; to escape.

DUST OFF (V) To administer a thorough beating to; to flee; to kill.

DUSTER (N) The inner door of a safe; a freight car burglar; a fugitive.

DUTCH ACT (V) To commit suicide.

DUTCH COURAGE (N) Narcotics.

DUTCH ROD (N) A Luger revolver.

DYNAMITE (N) Anything dangerous; a strong narcotic.

DYNAMITE JOB (N) A dangerous undertaking.

DYNAMITARD (N) A safe cracker who uses dynamite.

DYNO (N) One who handles dynamite on a construction job; the robbery of an intoxicated person; narcotics.

DYNO-ROUST (V) To rob an intoxicated person.

E

EARN BLOOD MONEY (V) To serve a jail sentence.

EASE A GAT (V) To draw a gun.

EASE ONE OF HIS DOUGH (V) To rob a person.

EAST AND WEST (N) A pickpocket's term for a vest.

EASTMAN (N) A pimp.

EASY (Adj) Dead.

EASY GRAFT (N) An easy way of making money.

EASY MARK (N) One who is easily cheated or deceived; a sucker; a fall guy; an easy victim.

EASY POWDER (N) Knockout drops; opiate.

EASY STREET (N) Financial security; wealth; having plenty money.

EASY TO TAKE (N) One who is easily victimized.

EDGE (N) An equal division.

EDUCATE (V) To pave the way for a swindle; to give an initial confidence talk to a prospective victim.

EGG (N) A bomb; a tear gas bomb.

EIGHTBALL (N) A negro; foolishness; one who acts queer.

EIGHT WHEELER (N) A freight car burglar.

ELASTIC PAPER (N) Bad checks.

ELBOW (N) A policeman; a plain cloth officer.

ELBOW SLINGER (N) A waiter or waitress.

ELECTRIC STOOL (N) The electric chair.

ELEPHANTEARS (N) A detective; a plain cloth officer.

ELEPHANTS TRUNK (N) A drunkard.

ELEVATE (V) To rob at the point of a gun.

ELEVATION JOB (N) Robbery at the point of a gun.

ELIMINATE (V) To kill; to assassinate.

EMBALMING FLUID (N) Coffee.

EMERGENCY GUN (N) A hypodermic syringe made from a medicine dropper and used with a pin.

EMMA GEE (N) A machine gun.

EMPTY CAN TRICK (N) Pretending to be out of gas in order to rob an autoist coming to assist.

ENAMEE (N) A beating.

ENAMEL (N) A heavy coat of face powder used by negro women alley workers.

END (N) A share; an equal division.

END OF THE ROPE (N) Dying.

ENFORCER (N) Weapons.

ENGINE (N) An opium smoker's outfit.

EPSOM SALTS (N) A doctor; a physician.

EQUALIZER (N) A pistol or revolver.

ERASE (V) To kill; to assassinate; to wipe out by shooting; to slay.

ERASER (N) A weapon; an assassin; a machine gun.

ERUIT (N) A new prostitute or whore.

EVE (N) Apple; a young female.

EVEN BREAK (N) An honest deal.

EVERY MOTHER'S SON (N) The entire mob; the entire group; everyone.

EX (N) A divorced wife or husband.

EX CON (N) An exconvict; one who has served a prison sentence.

EXPAND THE CHEST (V) To be talkative.

EXTRA GANG (N) A railway track gang.

EYE (N) Detective; a private detective; the Pinkerton Detective.

EYE DOCTOR (N) A sodomite; a beggar who holds a straight face while begging.

EYEDROPPER DOPE (N) An addict who uses an eye-dropper as a syringe.

EYE-OPENER (N) A drink of liquor; the first injection of narcotic of the day; a sodomite.

EYE SHUT (V) To sleep.

EYE TAPE (V) To make a close scrutiny; to look at.

F

FACE LACE (N) Whiskers; a beard.

FACE THE KNOCKER (V) To beg from house to house.

FACTORY (N) A hypodermic syringe.

FADE (V) To cover a dice wager; to escape; to flee; to rob at the point of a gun.

FADE OUT (N-V) Death; escape; to die.

FADED BOYEY (N) A negro informer.

FADING DICE (N) Dice loaded to bring up three and seven.

FAG (N) An effeminate man; a lawyer's clerk; a male homosexual.

FAG FACTORY (N) A gathering place or brothel of male homosexuals.

FAGAN   (N)   A narcotic informer; a thief who teaches others how to steal; an instructor of young thieves; a desperado or thug.

FAGGOT   (N)   A cigarette; a male homosexual.

FAGIN   (N)   One who instructs young thieves how to steal; an instructor of thieves.

FAIR DICE   (N)   Honest dice.

FAIR SEX   ·(N)   A female.

FAIRY   (N)   An effeminate man; a male homosexual; a man having the characteristics of a woman.

FAKE   (N-V)   An imposer; a fraud; to cover up defects in deceptive falsehood.

FAKE ALOO   (N)   A hypodermic syringe made from a medicine dropper.

FAKE CRIP   (N)   A beggar who pretends to be crippled.

FAKELOO   (N)   False worthless merchandise; a hard luck story.

FAKER   (N)   A street vender or person who sells fake notions.

FAKIR   (N)   A structural iron-worker.

FALL   (N-V)   An arrest; a conviction in court; to be arrested.

FALL AND WINTER MARRIAGE   (N)   Where one of the persons is much older than the other.

FALL BACK   (N)   A friend in need.

FALL DOUGH   (N)   Money for bail or court defense.

FALL GUY   (N)   One who serves sentence for another; an innocent person who deliberately takes the blame for another's misdeeds and serves a prison sentence; a victim; a sucker; a dope.

FALL MONEY   (N)   Money used to secure bail after arrest.

FALL TOGS   (N)   Dude clothes worn at a trial to create a favorable impression on the court.

FALSE ALARM   (N)   A fraud; an imposter; a divorced woman; the arms.

FALSE CUT   (N)   A pretense at cutting cards.

FALSE TRIAL   (N)   Inability to think properly.

FAMILY MAN   (N)   A receiver of stolen goods.

FAN (N-V) A pickpocket; to locate a pocket book; to search a prisoner for a weapon.

FAN A SUCKER (V) To search a victim's clothing for loot.

FANCY (N) A pimp supported by a prostitute.

FANCY FRAIL (N) An attractive young woman.

FANCY FREE (N) Not married.

FANCY MAN (N) One supported by a prostitute.

FANCY WOMAN (N) A mistress; a kept woman.

FAN INSIDE PIECE (N) Pickpocket term for a vest.

FANNER (N) Searcher of the person.

FANNING (N) Attempt by a pickpocket operator to locate a poke; locating the purse; speaking.

FANNING BEE (N) A mob conference; the discussion between a mob gang.

FANNING A SUCKER (N) A pickpocket's trying to locate what pocket victim's money is in.

FANNY (N) The buttocks.

FANS (N) The hands.

FAR AND NEAR (N) Beer.

FARE TRADE (N) Smuggling.

FAREWELL MAN (N) Welfare worker.

FARM (N) The hospital for the criminally insane.

FARM HAND (N) A bootlegger's customer who has his liquor analyzed by a pharmacy.

FARMER'S DAUGHTER (N) A woman of easy morals.

FAST COUNT (V) To short change.

FAST FINGER BOY (N) A gun man fast on the trigger.

FAST FINGER WORK (N) An expert gunman.

FAST HOUSE (N) A brothel; a whore house.

FAST ONE (N) A trick; a trick devised for dishonest purposes; a clever swindler; a prostitute.

FAST RATTLER (N) A passenger train.

FAT CHANCE (N) No expectation.

FATHER TIME (N) A judge; the principal keeper of a jail; the warden of a penitentiary; an old man; a prison court.

FATIGUE (N) A prison worker.

FATTIE   (N)   A policeman; a very fat person.
FAUNTLEROY   (N)   A clerical worker.
FAWNEY   (N)   A ring.
FAWNEY MAN   (N)   A peddler of bogus jewelry.
FEATHER   (N-V)   A bed; to plunder; to fleece.
FEATHER BED   (N)   A padded prison cell.
FEATHEREDGE   (N)   New tire which has never been
on the ground.
FED   (N)   A Federal law enforcement officer.
FED PEN   (N)   A Federal penitentiary.
FED RAP   (N)   A sentence to be served in a Federal
prison.
FEEBLO   (N)   An addict; a dunce; a prison intelligence
test.
FEED A STRETCH   (V)   To sentence to prison.
FEED ONE'S FACE   (V)   To eat.
FEED THE STICK   (V)   To club.
FEELER   (N)   A lock pin; a cross examination.
FEELERS   (N)   The cross examination of a prisoner.
FEKE   (N)   A lock pin.
FEMME   (N)   A young woman; a young girl.
FEMME FINGER   (N)   A policewoman.
FENCE   (N-V)   One who buys and disposes of stolen
property; a professional dealer in stolen goods; a re-
ceiver of stolen goods; to deal in stolen goods.
FEW   (N)   A prison sentence of less than fifteen days;
a short sentence.
FIB   (V)   To strike; to lie; to tell an untrue story.
FIDDLE   (N)   Pickpocket term for coat.
FIDDLE AND FLUTE   (N)   A suit of cloth.
FIDO   (N)   A jail trusty.
FIELD OF WHEAT   (N)   The principal street of a
town.
FIELD WORKER   (N)   One of a mob who does the
actual stealing for the gang.
FIFTY-FIFTY CLOWN   (N)   A town constable on duty
until midnight.
FIG   (N)   A pickpocket.
FIGURE-EIGHT   (N)   An addict pretending to be suf-

fering from some pain or disease, in an effort to get drugs.

FILE (N) A pickpocket.

FILE EM OFF (V) To shove.

FILL A BLANKET (V) To roll a cigarette.

FILL IN (N-V) A gambler's term for going in a game; to become one of a party.

FILL OUT (V) To obtain information through diplomacy; to locate places of worth or value for a burglary.

FILLED BLANKET (N) A rolled cigarette; a married couple.

FILLING STATION (N) A small town; a water tank.

FILLY (N) A woman; a young girl.

FIN (N) A five dollar bill; a five year prison sentence.

FINAGLE (V) To manipulate a situation to one's own advantage.

FINAL STEP (N) Marriage.

FINE AS SILK (Adj) In good condition.

FINGER (N-V) One who acts as informer to police; to call to the attention of the police; to inform upon; an officer; a spotter; to accuse; to select a victim.

FINGER FATTY (N) A policeman; an officer.

FINGER LOUSE (N) A stool pigeon; an informer.

FINGER MAN (N) A reconnoiterer for thieves; one who points out the victim for a killing or kidnapping; a person who obtains detailed information; one who lines up victims for a gang killing.

FINGER MOB (N) A gang that operates under the protection of the police.

FINGER OF STUFF (N) A rubber condom of narcotics which is swallowed or concealed in the rectum by an addict.

FINGER PRINT (N) The finger impression of a criminal used for identification.

FINGER SMITH (N) A pickpocket.

FINGER STIFF (N) An obstetrician.

FINGER THE LAY (V) To investigate prior to committing a crime.

FINGERS (N) A pickpocket.

FINGER'S END   (N)   A ten per cent cut of the loot; ten per cent of the proceeds of the loot.

FINGY   (N)   One who has lost one or more fingers.

FINIF   (N)   A five year prison sentence.

FINISHING SCHOOL   (N)   A jail for women.

FINK   (N)   A begging hobo; one who works or acts as a strike breaker; a traitor; an addict informer; a detective.

FINN   (N)   A five dollar bill; five; a five year prison sentence.

FIRE   (V)   To inject narcotics hypodermically.

FIRE ALARM   (N)   A divorced woman.

FIREBUG   (N)   One who commits arson; a pyromaniac; one who unlawfully sets fires.

FIRE DICK   (N)   An arson investigator.

FIRE EATER   (N)   A brave person; a plucky person; a fireman.

FIRE EXTINGUISHER   (N)   A chaperon.

FIRE PLUG   (N)   A large ration of opium.

FIREPROOF PETER   (N)   A fireproof safe.

FIRE WATER   (N)   Intoxicating liquor.

FIREWORKS   (N)   Shooting; disturbance; gunfire, firearms.

FISH   (N-V)   A new prisoner in jail; a victim; a dope; an innocent person indicted or sentenced for another; a fifty cent piece; tapioca pudding; to steal through windows with a stick.

FISH AND SHRIMP   (N)   A pimp; a pander.

FISH-BACK   (N)   A marked deck of cards.

FISH TANK   (N)   The main compartment of a jail where prisoners are first received.

FISH FOR SUCKER   (V)   To look for a victim.

FISH OIL   (N)   Cod liver oil.

FISH STORY   (N)   Lies; falsehood.

FIRST FRIEND   (N)   The person to whom a prisoner is paroled.

FIT HOUSE   (N)   The hospital for the criminally insane.

FITTER   (N)   The locksmith of a burglar mob.

FIVE CENTURIES   (N)   Five hundred dollars.

FIVE-FINGER (N) A thief.
FIVE C NOTE (N) A five hundred dollar bill.
FIVE SPOT (N) A five dollar bill; a five year sentence.
FIX (V) To bribe; to settle illegally by a money payment.
FIX-UP (N) An injection taken by a drug addict.
FIXED (Adj) Injured; bribed.
FIXER (N) A dishonest lawyer; a person who intercedes with the police on behalf of a criminal; the one who looks after the man arrested and squares the sucker; a claim agent.
FIXING DOUGH (N) Bribe money.
FIXING MONEY (N) Bribe money.
FLAG (N-V) An effeminate man; a criminal lookout; to allow a prospective victim to go unmolested; to accost a prostitute; to halt a person; to order an undesirable to leave town.
FLAGMAN (N) A criminal lookout.
FLAG RAG (N) Paper money.
FLAGGED (Adj) Released from prison; allowed to go one's way unmolested by the officer.
FLAME CHAIR (N) The electric chair; electrocution.
FLANNEL MOUTH (N) An Irishman.
FLAPPER (N) A lively and frivolous girl; a flighty girl.
FLASH (N-V) A quick show or expose; showy; imitation jewelry; anything worn for show; to exhibit.
FLASH GUN (V) To show a gun.
FLASH DOUGH (N) Counterfeit money.
FLASH HOUSE (N) A dive frequented by criminals, tramps, prostitutes and low type persons.
FLASH MAN (N) A dishonest gambler.
FLASH MOB (N) A gang of imposing thieves; confidence workers.
FLASH NOTES (N) Counterfeit bills.
FLASH ROLL (N) Money carried by confidence man, merely for display; counterfeit bills.
FLAT (Adj) Without funds; broke; an innocent person sentenced for a crime committed by another.

FLAT CARS   (N)   Pancakes.
FLAT CATCHER   (N)   A swindler.
FLAT DOG   (N)   Bologna sausage.
FLAT FLOOSIE   (N)   A prostitute; a prostitute who operates in a room or flat.
FLAT FOOT   (N)   A policeman who walks the beat.
FLAT JOINT   (N)   A gambling joint; a crooked gambling house; a house of prostitution; a brothel; a whore house.
FLAT MOUTH   (N)   A criminal lawyer.
FLAT WHEEL   (N)   A slow person; a cheap skate; a stupid person; a cripple; a lame person.
FLAT WORKER   (N)   A thief who makes a specialty of stealing from dwelling houses; a house breaker; a house burglar; a burglar of apartment houses.
FLATS   (N)   Pancakes.
FLATTEN OUT   (V)   To hide; to kill.
FLATTER   (N)   A detective; a plain cloth officer.
FLATTIE   (N)   A detective.
FLATTY   (N)   A detective.
FLEA   (N)   An annoying person; a restless person.
FLEA BAG   (N)   A hobo's bed roll.
FLEA BOX   (N)   A cheap lodging house; a bed room.
FLEA TRAP   (N)   A cheap lodging house; a bed room.
FLEAS AND ANTS   (N)   Pants.
FLEECE   (N)   A theft.
FLEECER   (N)   One who commits theft.
FLESH FACTORY   (N)   A house of prostitution; a whore house.
FLESH MARKET   (N)   A house of prostitution; a whore house.
FLESH PEDDLER   (N)   A theatrical agent; a prostitute; a whore.
FLESH SESSION   (N)   Sexual intercourse.
FLICKER   (N)   A feint to go out; a beggar who pretends to faint in order to create sympathy.
FLICKER OUT   (V)   To die.
FLIER   (N)   A drug addict.
FLIGHT FRILL   (N)   A flighty girl; a lively and frivolous girl.

FLIM-FLAM (V) To trick; to defraud; to deceive; to steal with cleverness.

FLIM-FLAM WORKER (N) A till tapper; a short change artist; a swindler.

FLIM-FLAMMER (N) A swindler.

FLIMP (N) A pickpocket; one who robs persons.

FLIP (Adj-V) Too outspoken; to be knocked unconscious with an overdose of narcotic; to board a moving train.

FLIRT (N) A woman; a female; a lewd female; one who plays at courtship.

FLIT (N) A male homosexual.

FLOAT (N) A coat.

FLOATER (N) A tramp; a suspended sentence with order of court to leave town; an order to leave town within a given time; a tramp who does not voluntarily work.

FLOATING (Adj) Drugged from an overdose of narcotic.

FLOATING ROOMER (N) A tramp who will not work unless compelled to.

FLOATING PAROLE (N) A parole with permission to travel.

FLOCK OF BUZZARDS (N) A gang of pickpockets.

FLOGGER (N) An overcoat.

FLOGGER STIFF (N) An overcoat thief.

FLOOR DICK (N) A store detective.

FLOORLESS JIG (N) Hanging.

FLOOSEY (N) A woman or young girl.

FLOP (N-V) A place of shelter; a bed; an arrest; failure to receive a parole; to sleep.

FLOP DOUGH (N) Lodging money.

FLOP GAME (N) A swindle by means of an exchange of envelopes, the victim getting an empty one; a blank envelope swindle.

FLOP HOUSE (N) A cheap lodging-house; a rooming house; a jail.

FLOP IN THE HAY (V) To go to bed.

FLOP JOINT (N) A cheap lodging-house; a rooming house; a jail.

FLOP OUT (V) To sleep in the open.
FLOP RACKET (N) Professional tumbler in insurance frauds.
FLOP ROOM (N) The bedroom.
FLOP SHOW (N) An all night theatre.
FLOP WORK (N) The robbery of sleeping persons.
FLOPPER (N) A tramp who steals train rides; a beggar who pretends to be deformed or crippled; a legless cripple.
FLOPPER SITTER (N) A one-legged or legless beggar who sits on the sidewalk and begs.
FLOOSIE (N) A woman; a young girl; a prostitute; a whore.
FLOOSY (N) A woman; a young girl; a prostitute; a whore.
FLOUNDER (N) A Newfoundlander.
FLUNK (N) A camp flunky; the steel inner compartment of a safe.
FLUNKY (N) A male servant; a cook helper.
FLUSH (Adj) Having plenty of money; well heeled.
FLUSHED (Adj) Being supplied with plenty of money.
FLUTTER (N) A degenerate; a sodomite.
FLUZIE (N) A prostitute; a whore.
FLY (N) A second story burglar.
FLY A KITE (V) To smuggle a letter in or out of prison; to obtain money by means of worthless or forged negotiable paper.
FLY AWAY (N) A fugitive.
FLY BULL (N) A plain cloth officer; a detective.
FLY BY NIGHT (N) One who seeks pleasure during the nighttime.
FLY COP (N) A detective; a pickpocket detective.
FLY LIGHT (V) To travel without a bundle; to go hungry.
FLY MOLL (N) A female detective.
FLY SPECK (N) A very small person.
FLY SPECKS (N) Black pepper.
FLY THE COOP (V) To escape from prison.
FLY THE RED FLAG (V) To menstruate.

FLYER (N) A drug addict.
FLYING IN THE CLOUDS (Adj) Under the influence of narcotic; drugged.
FLYING JIB (N) A talkative drunk.
FOB (N-V) The trouser change or watch pocket; to steal a watch from a person (Pickpocket slang).
FOB MAN (N) A watch thief; a pickpocket who steals watches.
FODDER (N) Salad or greens.
FOG (N-V) Shooting; to shoot; to kill.
FOG FAG (N) An effeminate man.
FLOGGED (Adj) Drugged from the use of narcotics.
FOGLE (N) A silk handkerchief; a pickpocket.
FOLD UP (V) To take the drug cure.
FOLLOW UP MAN (N) An undertaker.
FOO FOO DUST (N) Morphine; cocaine; heroin.
FOOLISH POWDER (N) Morphine; cocaine; heroin.
FOON (N) A ration of opium prepared for smoking.
FOOT-BALL (N) A tear gas bomb.
FOOT-LOOSE (Adj) Unmarried; single.
FORBIDDEN FRUIT (N) Pork; a young virgin.
FORBIDDEN FRUIT EATER (N) A lascivious man.
FORCED LANDING (N) A tramp being compelled to leap from a moving train.
FORD CHILD (N) The illegitimate child of a Ford family.
FORD FAMILY (N) A destitute family, not married and traveling in an old car.
FORD MARRIAGE (N) The common-law marriage of motor itinerants.
FORD MOTHER (N) An itinerant mother of an illegitimate child.
FORD WIFE (N) The unmarried female companion of a Ford family.
FORE AND AFTER STIFF (N) A tramp who carries his bedding on his back and his cooking utensils in front.
FOREIGNER (N) One serving a sentence for sexual or impulsive crime.

FORGOTTEN WOMAN (N) A prostitute; a whore.

FORK (N) A pickpocket using his fingers to pick a pocket.

FORK OVER (V) To pay; to hand over.

FORTY-FIVE (N) Beans.

FORTY THIEVES (N) Those who take advantage of bankruptcies by holding fake fire sales.

FOUNDRY (N) A maternity hospital.

FOUR BITS (N) Fifty cents.

FOUR-FLUSHER (N) An unreliable person; a boaster; a welcher; a piker; one who poses for effect; one who pretends to have and has not; a bluffer; a braggart.

FOUR LETTER MAN (N) A male homosexual.

FOUR STRING (N) A gang of four men; four people.

FOURTH OF JULY (N) A gun battle.

FOX (N) A fugitive; a stool pigeon; an informer; a tramp who rides inside passenger trains.

FRAIL (N) A young girl; a woman.

FRAME (N-V) A conviction on false evidence; the position of the pickpocket while working; to trump up charges against; to cause to be unjustly punished; to conspire to incriminate an innocent person.

FRAME A TWISTER (N) An effort on the part of an addict to get narcotics by feigning spasm of some kind.

FRAME UP (N-V) A conspiracy; a plot to injure some one; a false indictment; a false arrest; false information; the fallows; to sentence or convict unjustly.

FRAME UPON (V) To accuse falsely.

FRAMED (Adj. Convicted unjustly.

FRAMED IN STEEL (N) Imprisoned; placed in prison.

FRATERNITY BROTHER (N) A fellow inmate.

FREE AND EASY (N) A woman of easy morals; a prostitute; a whore.

FREE HOLDER (N) A man supported by a prostitute or whore.

FREE HOTEL (N) A jail.

FREE LANCE (N) An habitual adultress.

FREE LANCER (N) An unmarried man.

FREEMAN (N) A married woman's lover.

FREE TICKET (N) A killing; murder.

FREE WHEELER (N) A woman of easy morals; a prostitute; a whore.

FREEZE (V) To retain; to keep; to buy and sell stolen goods.

FREEZE ON TO (V) To steal.

FREEZE OUT (V) To force victim out of gainful partnership.

FREEZE UP (V) To refuse to talk.

FREEZER (N) A refrigerator car; false or worthless merchandise.

FREIGHT (N) Bribe money; goods in transit; liquor in transit across the border.

FRENCH DISEASE (N) Venereal disease.

FRESH BULL (N) An industrious policeman.

FRESH CAT (N) A tenderfoot tramp.

FRESH COW (N) One with a newly developed case of gonorrhea.

FRESH FISH (N) A new prisoner.

FRESH GUY (N) One too cocksure.

FRESH ONE (N) A new prisoner.

FRIE (V) To be electrocuted.

FRIED CHICKEN (N) A passionate young woman.

FRIENDS TO STAY (N) A female menstruation period.

FRIG (N) Sexual union.

FRIGIDARE (N) A cold and unresponsive woman.

FRIGLANDER (N) A Dutchman.

FRILL (N) A young girl.

FRISK (N-V) The searching of a prisoner for weapons; pocket picking; to search; to search for weapons.

FRISK A DRAG (V) To search a train.

FRISK THE JOINT (V) To search a place; to commit burglary.

FRISKER (N) A pickpocket.

FRITZ (N) A German.

FRITZED (Adj) Out of business; ruined.

FRITZER (Adj) Not good.

FROCK (N) A suit of cloth.

FROG   (N)   A dollar bill; a freshman; one who's voice is changing.

FROG EATER   (N)   A Frenchman.

FROG LEGS   (N)   A French girl.

FROGGY   (N)   A Frenchman.

FROLIC   (N)   A theft; a criminal enterprise.

FROM NOW ON   (N)   A life sentence.

FRONT   (N-V)   A disguise; a suit of cloth; a watch and chain; a good appearance; counterfeit money made from onionskin paper and printed on one side; to print counterfeit money.

FRONT AND BACK MAN   (N)   One who carries advertising board on his back; a walking advertisement.

FRONT AND BACK STIFF   (N)   A tramp who carries his bedding on his back and his cooking utensils in front.

FRONT FOR   (V)   To recommend; to go to one's aid.

FRONT GEE   (N)   A pickpocket confederate.

FRONT GUY   (N)   A man with good personality and appearance.

FRONT JOB   (N)   The act of assisting a confederate; the robbery of a bank cashier's cage only.

FRONT MAN   (N)   A criminal lawyer; one who operates a legitimate business as a screen for criminal activity.

FRONT OFFICE   (N)   A police station; police headquarters.

FRY   (V)   To be electrocuted; to electrocute; to die in the electric chair.

FRY IN THE CHAIR   (V)   To be electrocuted; to electrocute.

FRYING OF FAT   (N)   Extortion for political purpose.

FRUIT   (N)   A woman of easy morals.

FRUIT TRAMP   (N)   A tramp who follows the fruit harvest and works only when in need.

FRUITER   (N)   A male homosexual.

FRUMP   (N)   A prim old woman.

FRYER   (N)   An adolescent girl.

FUDGER   (N)   A motorist who stopped by a red light, keeps edging forward into the pedestrian crossing.

FULL OF HOPS   (N)   Insane; crazy.

FULL OF JUNK (N) Drugged by the use of narcotics.
FULL OF LARCENY (N) Criminally inclined.
FULL OF LEAD (Adj) Riddled with bullets.
FULL OF POISON (Adj) Full of narcotics.
FULL TIME (N) A life sentence.
FUN (N) A ration of opium prepared for smoking.
FUNERAL DIP (N) A pickpocket who operates in funeral crowds.
FUNNY MONEY (N) Counterfeit coins.
FURS (N) A woman; a female.
FUSSED UP (Adj) Passionate; a female of sexual desire.
FUTURE HOME (N) A cemetery.
FUZZ (N) Thieves; a guard or watchman.
FUZZY (N) An industrious policeman; one with an adolescent beard.
FUZZY FACE (N) One with an adolescent beard; a boy; a boy tramp; a catamite.
FUZZYTAIL (N) An ill natured person.

G

G (N) A thousand dollars.
GAB (N-V) The mouth; to talk; to talk freely.
GABBY (N-Adj) A gossip; a tale bearer; talkative; inclined to talk too much.
GABOON (N) A cuspidor.
GAB ROOM (N) A ladies' rest room.
GAD THE HOOF (V) To walk.
GAFF (N-V) The means by which gambling device is controlled; to punish; to cheat.
GAFF WHEEL (N) A crooked gambling wheel controlled by the operator.
GAFFER (N) A tramp who is criminally inclined, and works only when his courage fails him.
GAFFLE ON TO (V) To seize; to steal.
GAG (N) A trick or scheme; any begging trick.
GAGER (N) A middle man; a person who disposes of stolen goods.
GAGGER (N) The receiver of stolen goods; a fence; a man who prostitutes his wife or mistress.

GALAWAY (N) A Catholic priest.

GALL (N) Unlimited assurance; brazenness.

GALLON DISTEMPER (N) Delirum tremens.

GALLOPING DOMINOES (N) Dice.

GALLOW BIRD (N) A prisoner sentenced to capital punishment; a prisoner sentenced to be hanged.

GALLOW CHEATER (N) One who escapes hanging.

GALLOWS BIRD (N) An unprincipled person who deserves to be hanged.

GALWAY (N) A Catholic priest.

GAM (N) The leg.

GAME (Adj) Courageous; crippled; plucky; a stolen object.

GAMP (N) A midwife.

GANDER (N) A glance; a view of; a divorced man; a searcher; look at; close scrutiny.

GANDERER (N) A guard; a watchman.

GANDY (N) A tamping bar.

GANDY DANCER (N) A laborer who works with pick and shovel; a railway section hand; a petty crook.

GANG BANGING (N) When teen-age girls are forced by teen-age males to have sexual relation.

GANG BUSTER (N) Officer engaged in breaking up organized crime.

GANGLAND (N) The underworld outside of prison walls.

GANG PUSHER (N) A foreman.

GANG UP (V) To gather; to combine against.

GANG UP WITH (V) To become a member of the same gang.

GANGRENOUS (N) Relating to gangsters.

GANOV (N) A thief; a fool.

GAP (V) To witness a crime but not participate in it.

GAPPER (N) A witness to a crime; an addict who is desperate for narcotics; a mirror.

GAPPER'S BIT (N) An amount given to one who witnessed the crime but did not participate in it.

GARBAGE (N) A term used by tramps and hobos for food.

GARBAGE CAN (N) Inferior food; a low or unclean prostitute or whore; a dirty hobo camp.

GARBAGE HOUND (N) A restaurant customer.

GARBAGE JOINT (N) A cheap restaurant.

GARGLE (N-V) A drink; to drink.

GARNISH (N) Handcuffs.

GARROTER (N) A robber; a strong arm man; a strangler.

GARTER (N) An unfixed sentence.

GARTERS (N) Leg irons.

GAS BEGGAR (N) One who travels with a family in a cheap automobile.

GAS HOUND (N) A drinker of adulterated liquor; a fast driver of an automobile.

GAS METER (N) A leather valise.

GASED (Adj) Being executed in a gas chamber.

GASH (N) The mouth; a cut; a prostitute; a whore; the female pudendum.

GASH HOUND (N) One who runs after women; a lascivious man.

GASSY (Adj) Talkative.

GAT (N-Adj) A revolver or pistol; gun crazy.

GAT UP (V) To rob at the point of a gun.

GATE LIFTER (N) The snout of a pig.

GAVEL POUNDER (N) A judge.

GAVEL WIELDER (N) A judge.

GAY CAT (N) A criminal tramp; a tramp who works occasionally; one who commits sabotage; one who goes ahead seeking information for a mob; a safe cracker.

GAY HOUSE (N) A brothel; a whore house.

GAZER (N) A Federal officer; a Federal narcotic agent.

GAZOOK (N) A boy; a young tramp; a fool; a flunky in a jungle hobo camp; a boy kept for unnatural purpose by a tramp; an inexperienced youth.

GAZOONY (N) A boy; a young tramp; a flunky in a jungle hobo camp; a boy kept for unnatural purpose by a tramp; an inexperienced youth.

GEASE (V) To pay for protection.

GEE (N) A man; a narcotic drug; opium.

GEE A JIG (V) To rob a negro.

GEE BAG (N) The strainer at base of opium pipe bowl; the packing used in making the connection between the stem and bowl of an opium pipe airtight.

GEE-CHEE (N) A Charleston negro.

GEE-FAT (N) Narcotics.

GEE-GEE (N) A race horse.

GEE-RAGS (N) The packing used in making the connection between the stem and bowl of an opium pipe airtight.

GEE STICK (N) An opium pipe.

GEE-YEN (N) The residue left in an opium pipe; an opium pellet after cooking.

GEED UP (Adj) Under the influence of narcotics; drugged.

GEEHUNCLE (N) A cripple; a lame person.

GEEK (N) A snake charmer; the performer in the cannibal show of a circus; any disliked person.

GEESER (N) A small amount of narcotic.

GEEZE (N) A fellow.

GEEZER (N) An injection of narcotic.

GEEZO (N) A prisoner; a convict.

GENERAL PRINCIPLES (N) Arresting one for no reasons.

GENTLEMAN OF THE ROAD (N) A highway robber; a tramp who does not voluntarily work.

GERMAN FLUTES (N) Boots.

GERVER (N) A safe blower.

GET A LOAD OFF (V) To listen to; to take a look at; to talk one's belief.

GET A RANK (V) To have something go wrong with a criminal job.

GET A RUMBLE (V) To have something go wrong with a criminal job; to get information ahead of certain facts.

GET AWAY (N) An escape; a successful retreat with the stolen articles.

GETAWAY CAR (N) A car, used in making the escape, after a crime has been committed.

GET CANNON (V) To get drunk.

GET CAUGHT   (V)   To become pregnant.

GET HEELED   (V)   To arm oneself.

GET HEP   (V)   To become wise to certain facts; to become informed.

GET PAINTED UP   (V)   To have the number stencilled on a prisoner's uniform.

GET THE GATE   (V)   To be dismissed; to be discharged from prison.

GET THE HABIT OFF   (V)   To lighten the withdrawal of narcotics.

GET THE KEY   (V)   To be imprisoned.

GET THE LAY   (V)   To make an investigation before a crime is committed.

GET THE ROPE   (V)   To be hanged.

GET THE SHORT   (V)   To run short of money.

GET THE SPRINGS   (V)   To be discharged from prison.

GET THE WORKS   (V)   To be sentenced to death; to be killed.

GET TO   (V)   To bribe.

GET UP   (V)   To finish a prison sentence.

GETTING BY   (N)   Living without doing any hard work.

G HEAT   (N)   Being wanted by the Federal officers.

GHOST TOWN   (N)   A has been desert town.

GHOST WITNESS   (N)   A witness who appears in another's stead.

GHOUL   (N)   One who blackmails a woman attendant of a house of prostitution; a blackmailer of women.

GHOW   (N)   An opium pipe.

GIFFER   (N)   A pickpocket.

GIG   (N)   A dance hall sheik; one supported by a woman as her lover.

GIGGLE SOUP   (N)   Intoxicating liquor.

GIGGLE WATER   (N)   Intoxicating liquor; champagne.

GIGOLO   (N)   A young man supported by a woman as her lover.

GILLIGAN HITCH   (N)   A strangle hold.

GIMICK (N)   A tool; the device by which a dishonest
gambling apparatus is controlled; a device to trick
someone; a secret device by which a swindler controls
a prize wheel; a cripple.

GIMMICK (N)   A secret device by which a swindler
controls a prize wheel; a device by which a roulette
wheel is controlled; a catch bolt on a lock; a tool.

GIMP (N)   A cripple; a lame person.

GIN (N)   A negro prostitute.

GINGERBREAD DOOR (N)   A safe door with artistic
trimmings.

GINK (N)   A migratory worker; a country bumpkin; a
countryman.

GINNY (N)   An Italian.

GIRAFFE (N)   An inquisitive person.

GIRL AT EASE (N)   A prostitute; a whore.

GIRL BELOW THE LINE (N)   A prostitute; a whore.

GIRL ON THE TURF (N)   A prostitute; a whore.

GIRL SCOUT (N)   A female reconnoiterer for a criminal mob.

GIVE A CUT (V)   To give a share.

GIVE A DOSE (V)   To infect one with a venereal
disease.

GIVE A FANNER (N-V)   Quickly search a prisoner
for weapons; park sleepers hit on the soles by policeman; to order one to move on.

GIVE A FLOATER (V)   To order an undesirable to
leave town.

GIVE A HOT HOUSE (V)   To be provided a passionate time by a prostitute.

GIVE A JOB (V)   To sentence or convict unjustly.

GIVE A LINGO (V)   To tell a hard luck story.

GIVE A PERMANENT WAVE (V)   To be electrocuted; to electrocute.

GIVE A REANK (V)   To recognize; to notice.

GIVE A ROUST (V)   To cause a crush in a crowd or
push against a victim in order to be able to pick his
pocket.

GIVE A STEER (V)   To give confidential information.

GIVE A TICKET (V) Sentence to prison.

GIVE A WORKING OVER (V) To cross examine; to give the third degree.

GIVE AN OAK TOWEL RUBDOWN (V) To club a victim.

GIVE AND TAKE GIRL (N) A prostitute; a whore.

GIVE HER A DRINK (V) To put a charge of nitroglycerine in a safe.

GIVE HER A PAST (V) To unite in sexual intercourse.

GIVE HOURS (V) To order an undesirable to leave town.

GIVE IT A CASE (V) To make an investigation prior to committing a crime.

GIVE ME BUTTS (N) A request to share something which another has; a request to share a cigarette being smoked by another.

GIVE THE BUM'S RUSH (V) To oust bodily.

GIVE THE BUZZ (V) To cross examine.

GIVE THE CHAIR (V) To electrocute; to be electrocuted; to sentence.

GIVE THE ELECTRIC CURE (V) To electrocute; to be electrocuted.

GIVE THE FINGER (V) To swindle; to cheat; to defraud; to identify.

GIVE THE GATE (V) To put an end to friendly relations; to dismiss; to put out.

GIVE THE HEIST (V) To increase a price.

GIVE THE JERRY (V) To knock unconcious.

GIVE THE LUMPS (V) To strike.

GIVE THE NEEDLE (V) To persecute; to give an injection of narcotic.

GIVE THE NOOSE (V) To sentence to hang.

GIVE THE PRICE (V) To give a beggar the price for a meal.

GIVE THE ROPE (V) To sentence to hang.

GIVE THE RUSH ACT (V) To pick pockets fast in a crowd.

GIVE THE WEEPS (V) To attack with tear bombs.

GIVE THE WORKING OVER (V) To cross examine; to give the third degree.

GIVE THE WORKS (V) To pronounce a death sentence; to kill; to beat up; to assault; to give the third degree.

GIVE UP (V) To turn informer; to surrender.

GIVE A HOLE (V) To place in solitary confinement.

GIVE A HOT FOOT (V) To hit on the soles a park sleeper.

GIVING UP (N) Paying for protection; giving information.

GLAD MITT (N-V) A warm welcome; a hearty hand shake; to welcome.

GLASS (N) Diamonds.

GLASS CHIN (N) A weakling; a coward.

GLASS-EYE (N) A drug addict.

GLASS-GUN (N) A hypodermic syringe.

GLASS HAND (N) A handshake without real friendship behind it; a cold handshake.

GLASS HOOP (N) A diamond ring.

GLASS JAW (N) A sensitive jaw; a coward; a weakling; a prize fighter who can be knocked out easily; an easy victim.

GLASSY EYE (N) A drug addict.

GLAUM (V) To employ violence; to employ fear or force; to steal.

GLAUM THE GRAPEVINE (V) To steal from a clothesline.

GLEAMER (N) A thief.

GLETUS (N) Money; a bank roll.

GLIM (N) A light; a match; an eye; an eyeglass; a flashlight.

GLIM WORKER (N) An eyeglass peddler.

GLIMS (N) Spectacles; the eye.

GLIMMER (N) A black eye.

GLITTERS (N) Cheap or imitation jewelry.

GLOAT GETTER (N) A person easily annoyed; a person provoked to anger or displeasure by small infliction of irritation.

GLOM (V) To steal; to take; to grab; to employ violence; to employ fear.

GLOM ON TO (V) To take; to seize; to steal; to snatch; to hold on to.

GLOOMER (N) An undertaker.

GLUE-NECK (N) A untidy woman; a low prostitute; a low whore.

GLUE-POT (N) A post office.

GLUED (N) Married.

G-MAN (N) An operative of the Federal Bureau of Investigation; a Federal officer.

G-NOTE (N) A thousand dollar bill.

GO (N-V) A small amount of narcotic sufficient for an injection; to come to terms; to agree.

GO ABOUT (N) An established tramp who does not have to work.

GO ABROAD (V) To be imprisoned.

GO AROUND THE HORN (V) To prevent release of a prisoner on Habeas Corpus, until first questioned by the officers.

GO BAIL (V) To pay bail charges for another.

GO BEFORE THE MAN (V) To appear in prison court; to be interviewed by the warden.

GO-BETWEEN (N) One who acts as middleman between two groups, as merchants and racketeers.

GO BOILER PLATE (V) To wear formal attire; to wear a bullet proof vest.

GO-BY (V) To snub; to pass up.

GO DOWN ON (V) To commit sodomy; to have sexual connection by the anus.

GO FOR (N-V) A dupe; to have unquestioning confidence in another.

GO FOR A RIDE (V) To be taken for a death ride.

GO HAYWIRE (V) To go insane; to lose one's mind; nervousness.

GO HOLLYWOOD (V) To commit sodomy.

GO HOME (V) To be discharged from prison.

GO ON THE BEND (V) To engage in thievery.

GO ON THE BIG GREEN CARPET (V) To make

an appearance in prison court; to be brought before the warden for an interview.

GO ON THE GRIFT   (V)   To commit a crime.

GO ON THE OWL   (V)   To commit a crime at night.

GO ON THE PROWL   (V)   To engage in sneak thievery.

GO OUT   (V)   To engage in thievery.

GO OUT IN THE COUNTRY   (V)   To be taken for a death ride; to be taken for a killing.

GO OUT OF CIRCULATION   (V)   To be arrested and imprisoned.

GO OVER THE HILL   (V)   To escape from prison.

GO OVER THE ROAD   (V)   To go to prison; to be imprisoned.

GO OVER THE WALL   (V)   To escape from prison.

GO THROUGH   (V)   Searching a pickpocket's victim to locate his purse.

GO SOUTH   (V)   To steal an object and hide it.

GO STIR-BUG   (V)   To go crazy while in prison; to become insane while in a penitentiary.

GO TO BAT   (V)   To stand trial.

GO TO CHURCH   (V)   To sleep in a church.

GO TO SCHOOL   (V)   To sleep in a schoolhouse.

GO UP   (V)   To stand trial; to be sentenced to penitentiary.

GO UP A TREE   (V)   To be hanged.

GO UP FRONT   (V)   To be interviewed by a prison warden; to appear in court.

GO UP THE GOLDEN STAIRS   (V)   To go before the trial board.

GO WITH THE BIRDS   (N)   A tramp who travels to the West Coast for the winter.

GO WRONG   (V)   To turn informer.

GOAT   (V)   To anger; to inflame; to irritate.

GOBBLE UP   (V)   To steal.

GOBBLER   (N)   A type who has sexual connection by the anus; a male homosexual.

GOD-HOPPER   (N)   A religious person.

GOD'S MEDICINE   (N)   Narcotics.

GOGGLER   (N)   A motorist who pokes along at a snail's

pace looking at everything but the highway and holding up traffic.

GOING IN THE SKIN (N) The act of injecting narcotic beneath the skin.

GOING OUT (N) Leaving prison; a prisoner expecting a release.

GOING OVER (N) A cross examination; the third degree; a severe examination given a prisoner to secure a confession.

GOLD BRICK (N) A fraud; a trick; a swindler.

GOLD DIGGER (N) A woman who gets as much as possible from men and gives little or nothing in return; a young woman who accepts a man's attention for the sake of his gifts.

GOLD DUST (N) Cocaine.

GOLD FISH (N) A prisoner in the inspection line up; the third degree; a police beating; an exhibit of suspects to victims for purpose of identification; a wealthy victim.

GOLD FISH BOWL (N) A room in which the third degree is given.

GOLD MINE (N) A profitable venture.

GOLD MINER (N) A young woman who accepts a man's attention for the sake of the gifts he gives her.

GOLF BALLS (N) Dice.

GONDOLA (N) A flat-bottom steel coal car.

GONER (N) Dead; one who has been convicted of a crime; one sent to prison; a prisoner; an exconvict; one who cannot be saved from disaster or death.

GONG (N) Opium; an opium pipe.

GONG KICKER (N) An opium addict.

GONGER (N) Opium stick.

GONGOLA (N) An opium pipe.

GONIFF (N) Jewish word for thief.

GONSEL (N) A boy kept for unnatural purpose.

GONSIL (N) An inexperienced youth; a stupid person; an unsophisticated youth.

GOOBY (N) Leaving for prison after being given a sentence.

GOOD (N) Dead.

GOOD DOG   (N)   A likeable person; a trusted person.
GOOD FELLOW   (N)   A man or woman crook who pays their bills.
GOOD HEAD   (N)   A trustworthy person; a person of good judgement.
GOOD LAY   (N)   An easy victim; a good place for a robbery; a satisfying and passionate woman.
GOOD PEOPLE TALENT   (N)   Clever crooks.
GOOD SPORT   (N)   A plucky person; a brave person; a person who meets more than his share.
GOOD TIME   (N)   The reduction of sentence gained by good behavior.
GOODS   (N)   Stolen articles; evidence; drugs; narcotics.
GOOF   (N)   A man; a fellow; a fool; a slightly unbalanced person.
GOOF BALL   (N)   A user of narcotic; marihuana cigarette.
GOOF BUTTS   (N)   Marihuana cigarettes.
GOOFER   (N)   A desperado; a thug; a victim; a dupe.
GOOFY   (N)   Gun-crazy.
GOO-GONGS   (N)   Spectacles.
GOO-GOO   (N)   A Filipino.
GOO-GONS   (N)   Spectacles.
GOOGS   (N)   Glasses; spectacles.
GOOH   (N)   A prostitute: a whore.
GOOK   (N)   A low untidy prostitute or whore.
GOON   (N)   A strike breaker's guard.
GOOSE   (N-V)   Sexual variants; a Hebrew; to commit sodomy.
GOOSEBERRY   (N)   Clothes on a line; a clothesline.
GOOSEBERRY BUSH   (N)   A clothesline.
GOOSEBERRY PICKER   (N)   A thief who steals from clotheslines.
GOOSEBERRY PICKING   (N)   Easy stealing; the theft of clothes from a clothesline.
GOOSEBERRY PUDDING   (N)   A woman of loose morals; a woman who is easy to make for sexual purpose.
GOOSEBERRY TRICK   (N)   One who steals clothes from a clothesline.

GOOSING RANCH (N) A brothel; a house of prostitution; a whore house.

GOOZLUM (N) Gravy.

GOPHER (N) A burglar; a safe blower; a yeggman; a safe with a time lock; an iron safe; a safe or vault cracker who tunnels underground to reach same; a boy used to gain entrance to a building; a thug; a desperado.

GOPHER GANG (N) A gang of vault tunnelers.

GOPHER IN (V) To blow a safe; to tunnel into a vault.

GOPHER MAN (N) A safe blower; a safe cracker; a vault tunneler.

GOPHER MOB (N) A gang of vault tunnelers.

GOPHER RACKET (N) Safe cracking; vault tunneling.

GOPHER WORKER (N) A safe cracker; a vault tunneler; a safe burglar.

GORILLA (N) A thug; an assassin; a man serving as bodyguard for a gangster; a thief who uses violence in committing a crime; a gun man; a desperado.

GOSPEL FOWL (N) Chicken.

GOSPEL GRINDER (N) A preacher.

GOULASH (N) A Hungarian.

GOVERNMENT SECURITIES (N) Handcuffs.

GOVERNMENT'S STIFF (N) A pardon issued by the governor.

GOW (V) To remove the residue from an opium pipe.

GOW HEAD (N) An opium addict.

GOWED UP (N) Under the influence of narcotics.

GOWSTER (N) A drug addict.

GOY (N) A Gentile; a Christian.

GOYNK (N) Opium.

GOZUNG (N) A flunky in a jungle camp.

GRAB (N) A stolen article; a theft; a kidnap.

GRAB A HANDFUL OF RODS (V) To catch a freight train.

GRAB JOINT (N) A cheap restaurant.

GRAB OFF (V) To steal.

GRADUATE (N-V) A discharge on completion of a

sentence; an exconvict; to leave prison at the end of one's sentence.

GRAFT (N) A legal or illegal method of obtaining money unfairly; obtaining money easily; something easy.

GRAFTER (N) A thief; a cheat; a pickpocket; a tramp who begs from different charity organizations.

GRAND (N) One thousand dollars; a thousand-dollar bill.

GRANDMA (N) An old woman.

GRANDY (N) A midwife.

GRAPE (N) Champagne.

GRAPE EYE (N) One with small piercing eyes.

GRAPEVINE (N) News that travels secretly through the underworld; rumor; confidential gossip; underworld news; a clothesline.

GRAPEVINE TROLLY (N) Secret channels through which narcotics are distributed.

GRAPPA (N) Brandy made from distilled wine or mash.

GRASS (N) Salad; greens.

GRASS SKIRT (N) A grass widow.

GRASS WIDOW (N) A divorced woman; a married woman who is separated from her husband.

GRAVEL (N) Sugar.

GRAVEL TRAIN (N) The go-between of lobbyists who buys up legislators.

GRAVEYARD STEW (N) Milk toast.

GRAVY (N) Money easily obtained.

GRAVY HOUND (N) A prison hospital patient.

GRAVY TRAIN (V) To have comfort and luxury.

GRAY BACKS (N) Lice; mites.

GRAY HOUSE (N) A jail.

GRAY MARE (V) A hag.

GRAYSTONE COLLEGE (N) A jail.

GREASE (N-V) Expression used by safe crackers for nitroglycerine; bribe money; protection money; a poor cook; a poor prison cook; to pay a bribe; to pay for protection; to put a charge of nitroglycerine in a safe.

GREASE BALL (N) A dirty hobo; a disliked person; a person of unclean habits; a kitchen worker.

GREASEBALL GRUNT (N) A cook's helper.

GREASE JOB (N) A bribe.

GREASE JOINT (N) A restaurant.

GREASE MAN (N) Safe burglar who uses explosive to open a safe.

GREASE POT (N) A cook; a kitchen worker; a camp or prison cook.

GREASE SPOT (N) A dirty kitchen; a dirty restaurant.

GREASETAIL (N) A dirty tramp who is infested with lice.

GREASE THE TRACK (V) To fall under a moving train.

GREASER (N) A Mexican.

GREASY (N) A cook; a kitchen worker; a prison camp cook.

GREASY COAT THIEVES (N) Vagrant pickpockets who steal for beer money.

GREASY SPOON (N) A cheap dirty restaurant.

GREEFO (N) Marihuana.

GREEN ASHES (N) The residue left in an opium pipe after smoking; an opium pellet after cooking.

GREEN BAG (N) A lawyer.

GREEN GOODS (N) Counterfeit bills; a counterfeiter.

GREEN GOODS GAME (N) Counterfeiting.

GREEN GOODS MAN (N) One who sells worthless securities to farmers and swindles poor people; one who passes bogus money.

GREEN GOODS WORKER (N) One who sells false securities.

GREEN HORN (N) A sucker; a sap; one new and performing for the first time.

GREEN LIGHT (N) A police station.

GREEN WORK (N) Bile.

GREEN MUD (N) Bile; the residue left in an opium pipe; an opium pellet after smoking.

GREENIES (N) Money.

GREENS   (N)   Paper money; bills.
GRETA   (N)   Marihuana.
GRETCHEN   (N)   An unsophisticated German girl.
GRIDALE   (N)   Begging on the street by singing hymns.
GRIDDLER   (N)   An English street singer.
GRIFO   (N)   Marihuana.
GRIFFA   (N)   Marihuana.
GRIFFING   (N)   When a pickpocket operator is work-
ing in a crowd.
GRIFT   (V)   To steal; to graft; to work a racket.
GRIFFER   (N)   A grafter; a confidence man; a grafter
with a circus; a pickpocket.
GRILL   (V)   To question; to give the third degree.
GRIND ORGAN   (N)   A machine gun.
GRINDSTONE   (N)   One who poses as a victim for
a pickpocket to practice upon.
GROCERY BOY   (N)   A hungry addict.
GROUCH BAG   (N)   A money bag carried next to the
body.
GROUND HOG   (N)   A worker of underground tun-
nel or caisson.
GROWLER   (N)   A beer can; a bucket; a wrestler; a
chamber pot used in a cell.
GUFF   (N)   A witless conversation; a senseless talk.
GUGU   (N)   A Filipino.
GUIFF   (N)   A low dirty prostitute or whore.
GULF   (N)   Term used of man impersonating officers;
a public rest room.
GULL   (N)   A victim; a sucker; a victim of thieves.
GULLY MINE   (N)   A slick promoter who fleeces poor
people.
GUM   (N-V)   Opium; to spoil; to harm.
GUMBOOT   (N)   A detective; a plain clothes officer.
GUMFOOT   (V)   To go quickly; to sneak; to spy for the
police.
GUM GAME   (N)   A confidential game; a swindling
activity.
GUM MOB   (N)   A pickpocket trio.
GUM SHOE   (N)   A detective; a spy; a plain clothes

officer; a sneak thief; one who sneaks; a spy for the police; a prowler.

GUMSHOE MAN (N)   A detective; a shadow man; a spotter; a prowler.

GUMSHOE WORKER (N)   A private detective; a spotter; a prowler; a shadow man.

GUMBO (N)   Soup.

GUNNERS (N)   Suspenders; a soft rubber sole shoe worn by sneak thief.

GUMMY (N)   Sticky; glue.

GUMP (N)   Chicken.

GUMP GLOOMER (N)   A chicken thief.

GUMP GUNNING (N)   Chicken stealing.

GUMS (N)   Shoes with rubber soles worn by burglars.

GUN (N)   A criminal; a pickpocket; a gunman; a dope addict's hypodermic needle; a thief who does not use force.

GUNBOAT (N)   A tin can used by tramps to cook in; a steel freight car.

GUN BULL (N)   An armed guard.

GUN COPPER (N)   A detective who works pickpockets.

GUN FEAST (N)   A gun battle.

GUN MAKER (N)   An instructor of young thieves; a Fagin; an instructor of novice pickpockets how to steal.

GUN MOB (N)   A mob of expert pickpockets.

GUN MOLL (N)   A woman who accompanies, or carries a gun, for a gangster; a woman pickpocket; a female thief.

GUN PLAY (N-V)   Gunfire; to become involved in a gun fight; to discharge a gun.

GUNNEL STIFF (N)   A tramp who rides the rods.

GUNNER (N)   An Irishman from Galway; one going around carrying a gun.

GUNNING (N)   Looking for an enemy with a gun.

GUNNY-SACK CHARGE (N)   One arrested as a suspicious character.

GUNSEL (N)   A stupid or treacherous person; an inexperienced youth.

GUNSMITH (N)   One who trains novice pickpockets how to steal.

GUNTZEL (N)   A stupid inexperienced youth.

GUNZEL (N)   A boy; a young tramp; a fool.

GUT BUCKET (N)   A chamber pot used in a prison cell.

GUT BURGLAR (N)   A poor cook; a poor prison cook.

GUT HAMMER (N)   A dinner gong.

GUT RAPPER (N)   A rubber hose used in administering the third degree.

GUT REAMER (N)   A sodomite.

GUT SHOP (N)   A butcher shop.

GUTS (N)   Sausage; daring; courage; the combination of a safe; the under bracing of a freight car.

GUTTER HYPE (N)   A very low user of cocaine.

GUTTER RAT (N)   A street urchin.

GUTTER SLUT (N)   A low dirty prostitute or whore.

GUTTERSNIPE (N)   A petty thief; a lowbred person; a tramp who picks cigarette or cigar butts from the gutter.

GRUB (N)   Food.

GRUB SLINGER (N)   A waiter; a waitress.

GRUBBER (N)   A beggar.

GRUMBLE (V)   To pay an obligation.

GRUMBLING (N)   Praying.

GRUNT (N)   A helper.

GRUNTER (N)   A wrestler.

GUY (N)   A man; a boy; a fellow; too familiar; a dark lantern.

GUZZLE (N)   Third degree questioning; applying the strangle hold.

GYP (V)   To defraud; to cheat; to swindle; to steal; a gypsy.

GYPACT (N)   Swindling.

GYP ARTIST (N)   A swindler; a cheat; a defrauder.

GYP JOINT (N)   A place of business in which the customers are cheated.

GYP MOLL (N)   A female swindler.

GYP RACKET (N) A confidence game; swindling activity.
GYPO CONTRACTOR (N) A contractor who furnishes poor accommodations.
GYPSTER (N) A swindler.

H

H (N) Heroin; hypo device; opium pipe.
HABIT (N) One addicted to narcotics; sickness of a narcotic addict who is deprived of drugs.
HABITUAL (N) A criminal whose habit is to commit crimes.
HACK (N) A constable; a prison guard; the caboose of a train; a white person.
HAG (N) An old woman; a witch.
HAIRPIN (N) A woman; a girl.
HAIR POUNDER (N) A teamster.
HAIRY (N) A he man.
HALF-A-BUCK (N) Fifty cents; a fifty-cent piece.
HALF A C (N) Fifty.
HALF A CASE (N) Fifty cents.
HALF A CENTURY (N) Fifty dollars; a fifty dollar bill.
HALF A G (N) Five hundred.
HALF A GRAND (N) Five hundred dollars.
HALF A NED (N) A five dollar gold piece.
HALF-BAKED (Adj) Foolish; incomplete.
HALF COOKED (Adj) Not ready; mildly intoxicated.
HALF HITCH (N) The combination of a safe half turned.
HALF NED (N) A five dollar gold piece.
HALF PIECE (N) A half ounce of narcotic.
HALF PINT (N) A small person.
HALF SAW (N) Five.
HALF SHOT (Adj) Mildly intoxicated.
HALFY (N) A legless cripple.
HALLELUJAH LASS (N) A Salvation Army girl.
HALLELUJAH PEDLER (N) A Salvation Army preacher.

HALO   (N)   The colored circle about a female nipple.
HALTER   (N)   The hangman's rope; the nose.
HAM DONNY   (N)   A third rate pugilist.
HAMLET   (N)   A police captain.
HAMMER AND TACK   (N)   The back.
HAND A LINE   (V)   To tell a hard luck story.
HANDCUFF   (N)   An engagement ring; marriage; a wife.
HANDOUT   (N)   An easy job; a gift to a beggar.
HANDFUL   (N)   A five year sentence.
HAND-PAINTED SHOESTRING   (N)   A braggart and bluff; a four-flusher.
HANDICAP   (N)   Handcuffs.
HANDLE   (N)   A name; the nose.
HANGER   (N)   A woman's purse.
HANGING BEE   (N)   A lynching.
HANG-OUT   (N)   A residence; a meal given a beggar; a criminal headquarters.
HANG PAPER   (V)   To forge checks; to obtain money by worthless or forged checks.
HANG SOMETHING ON   (V)   To convict on false evidence.
HANG THE JURY   (V)   To bring about a disagreement in an endeavor to invalidate the trial.
HANG THE SLUG   (V)   To club.
HANG UP   (V)   To buy on credit.
HANK OF HAIR   (N)   A woman; a girl.
HAPPY DUST   (N-V)   Cocaine; heroin; to inhale cocaine.
HAPPY POWDER   (N)   Morphine; cocaine; heroin.
HARD BOILED   (Adj)   Harsh; heartless; rough; a thug.
HARD BOILED BABY   (N)   A burglar proof safe.
HARD BOILED MOLL   (N)   A woman of easy morals who is heartless and rough; a heartless prostitute or whore.
HARD HEAD   (N)   A safe burglar who uses explosive to open a safe.
HARD MONEY   (N)   Counterfeit money.
HARD NICKED   (Adj)   Robbed of everything.

HARD OIL (N) Butter.

HARD ON (N-Adj) Passionate; passionate lust; having a grievance against an individual.

HARD RAPPER (N) A severe judge.

HARD ROCKS (N) Diamonds.

HARD ROCK BOY (N) A diamond smuggler; a diamond thief.

HARD STUFF (N) Money; coin; gold or silver money.

HARD TACKS (N) Commissary candy.

HARD UP (N-Adj) Passion; sexual desire; passionate.

HARDWARE (N) Weapons; tools; cheap jewelry; a revolver or pistol; money.

HARNESS (N) The re-enforcement on the outside of a safe; a mounting for jewelry; a policeman's uniform; a revolver holster.

HARNESS BULL (N) A policeman; a uniform officer.

HARNESSED BOX (N) A safe with extra bars and levers covering the front as a protection.

HARP (N-V) An Irishman; a woman; a girl; to challenge; to complain.

HARPER'S WEDDING RINGS (N) Brass knuckles.

HARPIE (N) A prostitute.

HARPOON (N) A hypodermic syringe.

HARVEST (N-V) A wholesale arrest; to rob one of his earning.

HARVEST BUZZARD (N) A robber of harvesters who travels from place to place.

HASH (N) An intoxicating preparation made from the sprouts of Indian hemp.

HASH BURNER (N) A poor prison cook.

HASH CARRIER (N) A waitress.

HASH HITTER (N) A restaurant customer.

HASH HOUSE (N) A cheap restaurant.

HASH SLINGER (N) A waitress in a cheap restaurant.

HASH STIFF (N) A tramp cook.

HASHER (N) A waitress; a waiter.

HATCHET MAN (N) A Chinese tong war assassin.

HAUL (N) Stolen property; a good burglary.

HAUL A FISH (N) A wholesale arrest.

HAVE A BUN ON (V) To be intoxicated.

HAVE A CHINAMAN ON ONE'S BACK   (V)   To have
a drug habit; to be suffering withdrawal distress.
HAVE A CRUST   (V)   To be overbold.
HAVE A FRIEND   (V)   To menstruate.
HAVE A FULL HOUSE   (V)   To have all the venereal
diseases at one time.
HAVE A HEMORRHAGE   (V)   To be very angry.
HAVE AN IRISH SHAVE   (V)   To go to the toilet.
HAVE AN OUT   (V)   To have an alibi; to have an
excuse.
HAVE ANTS IN THE PANTS   (V)   To be nervous; to
be restless or jumpy.
HAVE TAKING WAYS   (V)   To be given to petty
thievery; to be easily made.
HAVE THE DROP ON ONE   (V)   To have one cov-
ered with a gun.
HAVE THE HOT GOODS ON   (V)   To be caught with
stolen goods.
HAVE WHAT IT TAKES   (N)   Passionate; passionate
lust.
HAWK   (N)   A detective; a guard; a watchman.
HAWKSHAW   (N-V)   A detective; to perform the work
of a detective.
HAY   (N)   Marihuana; salad or greens.
HAY BAG   (N)   A female tramp; a low dirty prostitute
or whore.
HAY BURNER   (N)   A pipe; a marihuana smoker;
a horse.
HAY BUTTS   (N)   Marihuana cigarettes.
HAY HEAD   (N)   A marihuana smoker.
HAY KICKER   (N)   A farmer.
HAYMAKER   (N)   A knockout blow.
HAYWIRE   (Adj)   Crazy; insane.
HAZEL   (N)   Heroin.
HEADACHE   (N)   A troublesome person.
HEADLIGHT   (N)   An egg; a mulatto.
HEADLIGHTS   (N)   Fried eggs.
HEAD OF LETTUCE   (N)   A package of greenbacks;
a bundle of bills.
HEAD OF THE HOUSE   (N)   A husband.

HEALER (N) A criminal lawyer; one who adjusts differences with the law; a go-between.

HEAR THE BIRDIES SING (V) To be knocked unconscious.

HEARSE (N) A caboose.

HEARSE MAN (N) A convicted murderer.

HEART BALM (N) Alimony; breach of promise.

HEART BREAKER (N) A ladies' man.

HEAT (N) Trouble; trouble with the police; trouble with gangsters; pressure placed against certain individuals.

HEATER (N) A revolver or pistol; firearms; an overcoat; a cigar.

HEATROLA (N) A revolver or pistol.

HEAVEN DUST (N) Morphine; cocaine; heroin.

HEAVEN REACHER (N) A prison chaplain.

HEAVY DOUGH (N) A large amount of money; wealth.

HEAVY DOUGH BOY (N) A wealthy person.

HEAVY FOOT (N) A policeman.

HEAVY GUN (N) A gang leader.

HEAVY GUY (N) A gang leader.

HEAVY HAND (N) A Federal law enforcement officer; the Federal Government.

HEAVY MAN (N) A specialist in bank safe or vault; a gambling house armed watcher.

HEAVY MONEY (N) Counterfeit coins.

HEAVY MUSIC (N) A machine gun.

HEAVY SONG (N) A machine gun.

HEAVY SUGAR (N) A great deal of money; a wealthy person.

HEAVY WORKER (N) A specialist in bank safe or vault.

HEEB (N) A Jew.

HEEBEE (N) A Jewess.

HEEBY-HEEBIES (N) Nervousness.

HEEL (N-V) A thief; a betrayer; an unworthy person; a despised person; a parasite; a stool pigeon; an informer; to furnish money to; to spy for the police; to supply.

HEEL AND TOE (V) To walk.

HEEL IN (V) To intrude as in a rival's territory.

HEELED (Adj) Armed with a weapon; having plenty of money; armed.

HEELER (N) A smallway politician; a bouncer; a hanger on; a prowler; a shadow man.

HEIFER (N) A young girl.

HEIFER BARN (N) A whorehouse; a brothel.

HEIFER DEN (N) A whorehouse; a brothel.

HEIFER DUST (N) Snuff; a cross examination of prisoners.

HEINE (N) A German.

HEIST (N-V) A holdup; an increase in price; to hijack; to oust bodily.

HEIST A JUG (V) To rob a bank.

HEISTMAN (N) A holdup man.

HEISTED (Adj) Robbed; hijacked.

HELL CAT (N) A furious woman; a spiteful woman; a hag.

HELL SHOUTER (N) A preacher.

HELL'S HALF ACRE (N) A cemetery.

HELLO DEARIE (N) A prostitute; a whore.

HE-MADAME (N) A male brothel manager.

HEMORRHAGE (N) Catsup.

HEMP-SEED (N) A dishonest person who deserves to be hanged.

HEMPEN COLLAR (N) The hangman's noose.

HEMPEN FEVER (N) Death by hanging.

HEMPEN WIDOW (N) The widow of a hanged criminal; a widow whose husband has been hanged for a crime.

HEN FRUIT (N) Eggs.

HEN HOUSE (N) Women's quarters of a penitentiary.

HEN HUSSY (N) A woman.

HEN MEDIC (N) A woman doctor.

HEN-PECKER (N) A nagging wife.

HEN SNATCHER (N) A chicken thief.

HERDER (N) A guard in a penal institution; a prison guard; a foreman.

HERRING (N) An incorruptible girl; a virgin; a burglar proof safe; a person from England.

HERRING CHOKER (N) A Scandinavian.
HERRING SNAPPER (N) A Scandinavian.
HEP (Adj) Wise.
HEP TO (Adj) Informed about; acquainted with the fact.
HI-BINDER (N) A tong war assassin.
HICK (N) A farmer.
HICK COP (N) A small town constable.
HICK TOWN (N) A small country town.
HICKORY (N) A wooden club; a policeman's billy.
HIDE (N) A fur; a pocket book.
HIDE AWAY (N) A small country town.
HIDE GO SEEKER (N) A purse snatcher.
HIDE OUT (N) Whiskers; a hiding place; a criminal resort: a criminal in hiding.
HIGH (Adj) Under the influence of narcotics.
HIGHBALL (V) To leave in haste; to go fast; to go in a hurry.
HIGHBINDER (N) A Chinese assassin; a desperado; a thug.
HIGH DIVER (N) A pickpocket; picking a pocket.
HIGH GRADE (N) A theft; a steal.
HIGH-HAT (N-V) A snob; a large pill of smoking opium; a vulgar person; to pass one by.
HIGH IRON (N) The main track.
HIGHJACK (N-V) A highway robbery of a fellow criminal; to waylay on the road and rob vehicles belonging to racketeers; to rob smugglers of their stock.
HIGHJACKER (N) A drug trafficker.
HIGH-PRESSURE (V) To give an initial confidence talk; to extort.
HIGH-ROLLER (N) A big gambler; a tramp who has plenty of money.
HIGHSIGN (V) To give a warning.
HIGH STEPPER (N) Pepper.
HIGH-STEPPING MAMA (N) A female of easy morals; a lively woman; a prostitute; a whore.
HIGHTAIL (V) To leave hurriedly; to travel swiftly.
HIGHTOBY (V) To commit highway robbery.

HIGH VOLTAGE   (N)   A passionate woman; a woman of lust; passion.

HIGH VOLTAGE MAMA   (N)   A passionate young woman.

HIGHWAY   (N)   A robbery committed on the highway.

HIGHWAY MOPERY   (N)   A robbery committed on the highway.

HIGH YELLOW   (N)   A mulatto.

HIJACK   (N)   Same as Highjacker; a person who robs fellow criminals; a robber of traffickers.

HIKER   (N)   A town constable.

HINGES   (N)   The joints.

HINHTY   (N)   Suspicious.

HINKY-DINK   (N)   Clark Street, Chicago, known to tramps.

HIP   (N)   Confidential information.

HIP GEE   (N)   Gambling money placed on a hot tip.

HIP DOUGH   (N)   Money gained by shortchanging.

HIP PEDDLER   (N)   A prostitute; a whore.

HIPE   (N)   Money gained by shortchanging.

HIPER   (N)   A swindler.

HIPPED   (Adj)   Without funds; broke; a tramp who is cold and hungry and without any funds.

HIS HONOR   (N)   A judge.

HIS NIBS   (N)   A judge; a Chief of Police.

HISSER   (N)   The mouth; the face.

HIST   (V)   To hold up; to hijack; to increase a price.

HISTER   (N)   A drunkard.

HIT   (N)   A prison term; an almost new tire.

HIT AND RUN MARRIAGE   (N)   A marriage of short duration.

HIT IT UP   (V)   To travel fast; to celebrate.

HIT THE FLOP   (V)   To go to bed; to go to sleep.

HIT THE GONG   (V)   To smoke opium.

HIT THE GOW   (V)   To smoke opium.

HIT THE HAY   (V)   To go to bed; to go to sleep.

HIT THE HIGH SPOTS   (V)   To move swiftly.

HIT THE HUMP   (V)   To attempt to escape.

HIT THE PIPE   (V)   To smoke opium.

HIT THE ROAD   (V)   To travel.

HIT THE ROCKS   (N)   To be discharged from prison.
HIT THE STEM   (V)   To smoke opium.
HIT THE TIES   (V)   To walk along the railroad track.
HITCH   (N)   A term in jail.
HITCH-HIKE   (V)   To journey by walking and begging rides.
HITCH UP THE REINDEERS   (V)   To make ready to use cocaine.
HITCHED   (Adj)   Married.
HITTING JUNK   (V)   To be using narcotics.
HITTING THE SPOT   (N)   Excessive drinking.
HITTING THE STUFF   (N)   Excessive use of narcotics.
HIXER HINEY   (N)   A German.
HEY RUBE   (Excl)   The circus signal for a free for all fight.
HIZZONER   (N)   A judge.
HOBO BELT   (N)   Southern California.
HOBO CAGE   (N)   The compartment of a jail where tramps are confined.
HOBO LIMIT   (N)   A freight train whose crew is friendly to tramps.
HOBO SHORT LINE   (N)   A tramp whose death was caused by being run over by a train; a tramp who committed suicide by throwing himself under a train.
HOBO'S DELIGHT   (N)   A cigarette stub.
HOBOBO   (N)   A boy tramp; a boy tramp kept for unnatural purpose by an older tramp.
HOBOETTE   (N)   A female tramp.
HOBONN   (N)   A tramp; a tramp who is willing to work for food and lodging; a vagabond.
HOCK   (V)   To pawn.
HOCK SHOP   (N)   A pawnbroker's office; a pawnbroker's place of business.
HOCUS   (N)   A pickpocket.
HOG   (N)   A locomotive; a greedy person.
HOG BOX   (N)   A crooked faro box.
HOG-EYE   (N)   A patent lock.
HOG-HEAD   (N)   A locomotive engineer.
HOG LEG   (N)   A six shooter; a revolver; a pistol.

HOG SCRAPER   (N)   A barber.

HOGGER   (N)   A locomotive engineer.

HOIST   (N)   A night watchman who was held up; a robbery at the point of a gun.

HOISTER   (N)   A shoplifter; one who steals from shops; a thief who operates under the protection of an overcoat.

HOISTS   (N-V)   A stickup man; to raise; to rob.

HOKUM   (N)   A line of nonsense talk; talk that is not true.

HOKUS   (N)   Opium.

HOLD   (N)   To have narcotics for sale.

HOLD HEAVY   (V)   To have plenty of money.

HOLD OUT   (N-V)   A dishonest gambling device for holding out cards; to keep an unfair amount; to keep something secret; to withhold a share; to profit by short-changing.

HOLD THE BAG   (V)   To be dope; to be scapegoat.

HOLD THE LADY DOWN   (V)   To ride the draw rods of a freight car.

HOLD THE SACK   (V)   To be deserted and left to face the charge; to take all the blame.

HOLDUP   (N)   Robbery at the point of a gun.

HOLDUPEE   (N)   The victim of a robbery.

HOLE   (N)   Dungeon; solitary confinement; the subway; a hiding place.

HOLE UP   (N-V)   Hiding in one place for awhile; a hiding place; to hide.

HOLLER   (N)   The complaint of a victim.

HOLLIGAN HUSTLER   (N)   A robber who administers knockout drops.

HOLY BEDLOCK   (N)   A common-law marriage; an illicit love affair.

HOLY JOE   (N)   A chaplain.

HOLY KNOT   (N)   Married.

HOLY AND HOLLIES   (N)   The bed room.

HOME   (N)   A jail.

HOME BARNACLE   (N)   A worker who sticks to one place for some time.

HOME GUARD   (N)   A tramp who does not migrate.

HOME PORT (N) Criminal's headquarters.
HOMIE (N) A homosexual.
HONEY (N) An attractive girl; a colored female; a negro prostitute or whore.
HONEY DIPPING (N) A discharge from the alimentary canal of a female.
HONEY MAN (N) A young man supported by a woman lover or prostitute.
HONEY TRAIN (N) A fruit train.
HONG YEN (N) Heroin put up in red pills.
HONKY-TONK (N) A cheap amusement place.
HOOCH (N) Intoxicating liquor.
HOOD (N) A hoodlum; a petty gangster; a thief; a criminal.
HOODLUM (N) A young rowdy; a lawless person.
HOOF (N) A ring; the foot.
HOOFER (N) A dancer.
HOOK (N-V) A pickpocket; a knife; to marry; to steal; to handcuff a man to a girder with his toes barely touching the floor.
HOOK A SUCKER (V) To defraud a person; to swindle a person; to cheat.
HOOK NOSE (N) A Jew.
HOOK SHOP (N) A whorehouse; a brothel.
HOOK UP THE REINDEERS (V) To inhale cocaine.
HOOKED (Adj) Addicted to narcotics.
HOOKER (N) A prostitute; a whore; a warrant of arrest.
HOOKS (N) The hands.
HOOLIGAN (N) An English term for hoodlum.
HOOLIGAN HUSTLING (V) To give a victim knockout drops and then rob him.
HOOP (N) A ring; a bait; a stolen diamond pin or ring.
HOOP UP (N) Marry.
HOOPS (N) Handcuffs.
HOOSEGOW (N) A jail; a prison; a public toilet.
HOOSIER (N) A prison visitor.
HOOSIER FIEND (N) An inexperienced drug fiend.
HOOTCH (N) Liquor.

HOOTCHIE (N) A whore or prostitute monger.
HOP (N) A narcotic, especially opium; a legless cripple.
HOP-A-LONG (N) A cripple.
HOP GUN (N) A hypodermic syringe.
HOPHEAD (N) An opium addict; a user of narcotics.
HOP JOINT (N) An opium den; a place where opium is smoked.
HOP LAY OUT (N) An opium smoker's outfit.
HOP PARTY (N) An opium party.
HOP PEDDLER (N) A narcotic trafficker.
HOP STICK (N) An opium pipe.
HOPTALK (N) A talk intended to deceive; bragging.
HOP TOY (N) A container for smoking opium.
HOPPY (N) A drug addict; a cripple; a lame person.
HOPPY DUST (N) Cocaine.
HOPPED UP (Adj) Intoxicated on opium; under the influence of opium or drugs.
HOPPERS (N) Hotel bell boys.
HOPS (N) Tea.
HORN (N) The nose.
HORN IN (V) To enter without invitation; to interfere; to intrude.
HORNSWOGGLE (V) To cheat; to swindle; to defraud.
HORSE (N) Corned beef; an awkward person of large bones.
HORSE COP (N) A mounted policeman.
HORSEMAN (N) A policeman who collects protection money; a collector of protection money.
HOSE (N) Sexual union; copulation.
HOT (N) Wanted by the police; stolen goods; a wanted criminal; illicit goods.
HOT AIR (N) Senseless talk.
HOT BALONEY (N) A stolen automobile tire.
HOT BANG (N) Confidential information; a female of passionate lust.
HOT BOX (N) A passionate young woman.
HOT CANDY (N) Stolen jewelry.
HOT CAR (N) A stolen automobile.

HOT CAR HUSTLER (N) A thief who deals in stolen automobiles.

HOT CHAIR (N) The electric chair used for electrocution.

HOT CHOCOLATE (N) A passionate negress.

HOT COAT (N) A stolen coat.

HOT DISH (N) A passionate young woman.

HOT DODGER (N) A person wanted by the law; a wanted circular or poster.

HOT DOUGH (N) Stolen money; counterfeit coins.

HOT DOUGHNUT (N) A stolen automobile tire.

HOT DREAM (N) An opium dream.

HOT FOOT (N-V) A method used to make a victim talk by burning his bare feet with a hot poker or matches; to walk swiftly; to hurry; to run.

HOT GAMBLER (N) A lucky one.

HOT GOODS (N) Stolen goods; loot; illicit goods.

HOT GREASE (V) Being troubled.

HOT HEAD (N) A Burn's detective; a plain cloth officer.

HOT HEAVY (N) A wanted criminal.

HOT HOLE (N) A whore house; a brothel.

HOT HONEY (N) A passionate young woman.

HOT HOUSE (N) A brothel; a whore house; the room in which an electrocution takes place.

HOTHOUSE PLANT (N) A carefully reared young girl.

HOT ICE (N) Stolen diamonds; diamonds to be gotten rid of quickly.

HOT JOINT (N) An illegitimate establishment under criminal suspicion.

HOT LAY (N) A woman of easy morals; a passionate sexual union.

HOT LEAD (N) Bullets.

HOT MAMA (N) A pretty and sexually attractive young woman; a passionate young woman.

HOT MEAT (N) Exposed female flesh.

HOT MEMBER (N) A passionate young woman.

HOT MESS (N) A stolen object; trouble.

HOT NUMBER   (N)   A wanted criminal; a young wo-
man of loose morals.
HOT NUTS   (N-Adj)   A lascivious   man;   desirous;
eager; passionate.
HOT ONE   (N)   A stolen automobile.
HOT PAPERS   (N)   Stolen bonds.
HOT PANTS   (N)   A young girl desirous for sexual
union; a passionate woman; lust.
HOT PROWLER   (N)   A burglar who enters a house
while the tenants are home.
HOT PEPPER   (N)   A passionate young woman; lust.
HOT PIECE OF DARK MEAT   (N)   A   passionate
young negress.
HOT PLATE   (N)   The electric chair; electrocution.
HOT ROCK   (N)   A prostitute; a whore.
HOT ROCKS   (N)   Stolen jewelry; stolen diamonds.
HOT ROD   (N)   A hopped up automobile; a gun man.
HOT ROLL   (N)   A roll of blankets.
HOT SCORE   (N)   Stolen goods.
HOT SEAT   (N)   The electric chair.
HOT SHEET   (N)   A police list of stolen automobiles;
a police record.
HOT SHORT   (N)   A stolen automobile.
HOT SHOT   (N)   A fast freight train; a sure bet; a big
money man; a well known gangster; a night club; a
police patrol car; a petty crook; an injection of poison
in place of the drug.
HOT SLOUGH   (N-V)   A house or apartment the
tenants of which are home; an occupied dwelling; to
burglarize a house while the tenants are home.
HOT SLOUGH WORKER   (N)   A burglar who burglarizes a house while the tenants are at home.
HOT SLUG   (N)   A wanted criminal; a bullet.
HOT SPARK   (N)   Stolen diamonds; a stolen diamond
stick pin.
HOT SPOT   (N)   The electric chair; a whore house; a
brothel.
HOT STIFF   (N)   A bad check.
HOT STUFF   (N)   Anything stolen; a passionate wo-
man; lust.

HOT SQUAT (N) The electric chair; death in the electric chair; a sentence to be electrocuted.

HOT TAMALE (N) A passionate Mexican girl.

HOT TEARS (N) Stolen pearls.

HOT TIP (N) An important piece of inside information.

HOT TONGUE (N) A passionate young girl.

HOTEL (N) A jail.

HOTEL HOTSY (N) A prostitute; a whore.

HOTSY (N) A young girl.

HOTSY-TOTSY (N) A pretty young girl.

HOUND (N) A plain cloth officer; a detective.

HOUNDED (Adj) Persecuted; watched by officers.

HOUDINI (N) A clever escape.

HOURS (N) Time given a convict or person to leave town; the hour set for an electrocution or hanging.

HOUSE DICK (N) A hotel detective.

HOUSE DOG (N) A tramp who goes from house to house doing odd jobs for meals or what little money he can get.

HOUSEKEEPER (N) A brothel hostess; a prostitute; a whore.

HOUSE MAN (N) A prowler; a burglar.

HOUSE OF CALL (N) A brothel; a whore house.

HOUSE OF JOY (N) A brothel; a whore house.

HOUSE OF ILL DELIGHT (N) A brothel; a whore house.

HOUSE PAROLE (N) A trusty who acts as house orderly to a prison official.

HOUSE PROWL (N) One who makes an investigation prior to committing a burglary.

HOUSE PROWLER (N) A house burglar.

HOUSE PROWLING (N) A burglar who works flat surveying the locality previous to committing a burglary.

HOUSE WORK (N) A peddler who goes from house to house.

HOUSE WORKER (N) A house to house beggar.

HOW STRONG ARE YOU (Intg) How much money have you.

HOZZONER (N) A judge.

H. Q. (N) Detective headquarters.
HUMBUG (N) A skin game.
HUMMER (N) A false arrest.
HUMMING-GEE BOWL (N) The bowl of an opium pipe.
HUMP (N) A hunchback; a criminal lookout; half a prison term.
HUN (N) A German.
HUNCH (N) Suspicion; an intuitive feeling; a tip; a presentiment; a hunch back.
HUNGER LANE (N) A railway running through a poor and inhospitable district.
HUNK (N-V) Revenge; to get even.
HUNK OF GLASS (N) A diamond.
HUNK OF HEAVEN (N) A pretty young girl.
HUNK OF ICE (N) A diamond.
HUNK OF LEAD (N) A doughnut.
HUNK OF MEAT (N) The male pudendum.
HUNK OF SKIRT (N) A female; copulation.
HUNK OF TAIL (N) A prostitute; a whore; a woman of easy morals.
HUNKY (N) A common laborer.
HUNTER (N) A pickpocket.
HURRY BUGGY (N) A police patrol car.
HUSH (N) A gun with a silencer; a silencer; bribe money used to silence a victim.
HUSH DOUGH (N) Bribe money given to avoid exposure.
HUSH-EM (N) A gun silencer.
HUSH-HUSH (N) A machine gun with a silencer.
HUSH MONEY (N) Bribe money given to insure the keeping of a secret; protection money to quiet a scandal or crime.
HUSKEY (N) An Eskimo.
HUSTLE (N) A prostitute who looks for trade on the street; a pickpocket who operates on street cars; an accomplice who distracts a victim or places him in a position for a pickpocket.
HUSTLE JOB (N) A crime requiring speed in completing same.

HUSTLE SHEETS (V) To sell newspapers on the street.

HUSTLER (N) A petty thief; a pimp; a prostitute; a whore; a woman of the street; a night walker.

HUSTLING (N) A prostitute's walking the street at night looking for trade.

HUSTLING BROAD (N) A prostitute; a whore; a woman of easy morals.

HUSTLING HUSSY (N) A prostitute; a whore; a woman of easy morals.

HUT (N) A cell in a jail.

HYGELO (N) A drug addict.

HYPE (N) A drug addict; a narcotic injection; a hypodermic syringe.

HYPE RACKET (N) Short change.

HYPESTICK (N) A hypodermic syringe.

HYSTER (N) A shoplifter; a drunkard.

I

ICE (N) A diamond; diamonds.

ICEBERG (N) A cold unemotional woman; a large diamond; an unresponsive woman in sexual union.

ICEBOX (N) A safe; a morgue; a life penitentiary sentence; a cell used for solitary confinement of a prisoner; the coroner's office; a diamond safe box.

ICE CREAM HABIT (N) The use of drugs for a day or two a week or irregularly without becoming addicted.

ICEHOUSE (N) A jewelry store.

ICE-MAN (N) A diamond smuggler; a diamond thief.

ICE PALACE (N) An elegantly furnished whore house or brothel.

ICE TONG DOCTOR (N) A doctor who illegally practices medicine; a doctor who sells narcotics illegally.

ICE WAGON (N) An unresponsive or cold woman; a hearse.

ICER (N) A refrigerator car.

ICY MITT (N) Being turned down by your best girl; a cold hand shake.

IDIOT STICK (N) A shovel.

I DON'T CARE   (N)   A chair.

IKEY   (N)   A Jew.

IN   (N)   A place or means of entrance; on the inside of a deal; influence; confidential information.

IN A FIX   (Adj)   Pregnant.

IN A HUDDLE   (N)   In a conference.

IN A JAM   (Adj)   Wanted by the police.

IN BAD   (Adj)   In trouble; in unfavorable circumstances; wanted by the police.

IN BAD SHAPE   (Adj)   Pregnant.

IN CAMERA   (N)   Court cases from which the public is excluded.

IN DUTCH   (Adj)   In a bad way; in trouble with the law; in disgrace; in trouble.

IN HOCK   (Adj)   Pawned; in prison.

IN HOSPITAL   (Adj)   In jail.

IN LIMBO   (Adj)   In jail; doing time.

IN LINE   (Adj)   In accord with the prevailing standard or code; amenable.

IN OUT   (N)   A door.

IN RIGHT   (Adj)   Getting an easy living by political method; getting a protection from the authorities.

IN THE AIR   (Adj)   Nervous; in a tension of fear.

IN THE BAG   (Adj)   Certain; sure; as good as in one's possession; taken care of; fixed; arranged in alliance.

IN THE BENNY   (Adj)   Wearing a complete clothing outfit.

IN THE BIG-TIME   (Adj)   Engaged in major crime.

IN THE BUCKET   (Adj)   In jail.

IN THE CAN   (Adj)   In jail.

IN THE CLEAR   (Adj)   Safe; free from suspicion; net proceeds.

IN THE DOG HOUSE   (Adj)   In some one's bad grace.

IN THE DOUGH   (Adj)   Wealthy; rich; having plenty of money.

IN THE HEAT   (Adj)   In bad predicament; in bad with the law.

IN THE MONEY   (Adj)   Winning; well supplied with money.

IN THE PUSH   (Adj)   Part of the gang.

IN THE RACKET (Adj) Engaged in crime.

INDIAN HAY (N) Marihuana.

INDORSER (N) A sadist who mistreats a prostitute or whore.

INK (N) Coffee.

INK FACE (N) A negro.

INNOCENT STUFF (N) A talk intended to deceive.

INSECT (N) A small person.

INSIDE (Adj) Incarcerated.

INSIDE DOPE (N) Confidential or exclusive information.

INSIDE JOB (N) Information given for the committing of a crime by one who is in the confidence of the victim.

INSIDE MAN (N) Term used in bunco to designate party to whom the steer introduces the victim; the one who does the actual stealing for a gang.

INSIDER (N) An inside pocket of a coat or vest; a pickpocket getting into the inside pocket of his victim.

INSPECTOR OF PAVEMENT (N) A tramp who does not have to work.

INTIMATE (N) A skirt; a female.

IN QUOD (Adj) In jail.

INCORRIGIBLE (N) The prison ward where unruly are kept.

INCORRIGIBLE ROGUE (N) A no good vagabond; a no good tramp.

INFORMATION FENCE (N) A criminal who sells information to crooks.

INK POT (N) A resort where low characters hang out.

IRISH APPLE (N) An onion; potato.

IRISH BABY BUGGY (N) A wheelbarrow.

IRISH CLUBHOUSE (N) The police station.

IRISH GANDY DANCER (N) A section hand; a laborer on a railroad section gang.

IRISH MUTTON (N) Syphilis.

IRISH PASTURE (N) A pretended faint.

IRISH SHAVE (V) To become clean; purify.

IRISH SLUM (N) Cheap jewelry that turns green.

IRISH TURKEY (N) Corned beef.

IRON (N) Handcuffs.
IRON BRACELETS (N) Handcuffs; nippers.
IRON BEN (N) A bullet-proof vest.
IRON CURE (N) Voluntary narcotic cure.
IRON HOUSE (N) A jail.
IRON MAN (N) A silver dollar.
IRON MIKE (N) Brass knuckles.
IRON OUT (V) To shoot to death.
IRON SKULL (N) A boiler maker.
IRON WORKER (N) A safecracker.
IT (N) Death.
ITALIAN FOOTBALL (N) A tear gas bomb; a bomb.
ITALIAN PERFUME (N) Garlic.
ITCHING FEET (N) A wonderlust.
ITCHY FEET (N) The driver of a car who endangers
every car and pedestrian on the street by speed.
IVORIES (N) Piano keys; teeth; dice; billiard balls.
IVORY (N) A coat.
IZZY (N) A Jew.

J

JAB (N) A hypodermic shot; a hypodermic injection.
JAB OFF (N) A narcotic injection.
JAB POP (N) A narcotic injection.
JABBER (N) A prize fighter; talking; a hypodermic
syringe.
JACK (N) Money; a tramp; pipe tobacco.
JACK AND JILL (N) A cash register; a money till.
JACKASS (N) Raw corn whiskey.
JACK GAGGER (N) A man who prostitutes his wife
or mistress.
JACK HORNER (N) A corner.
JACK LANTERN (N) A lamp made by placing a
candle in a can.
JACKLEG (N) A dishonest gambler.
JACK ROLL (V) To rob a drunk; to rob a sleeping
man.
JACK ROLLER (N) One who robs sleeping or drunk-
en persons; a prostitute or whore who robs her patrons.

JACKET (N) A jacket in which unruly prisoners are laced up.

JACKING (N) A beating given a prisoner with a blackjack.

JACOB (N) A ladder.

JADED JENNY (N) A prostitute or whore.

JAG (N-V) A state of drunkenness; to be under a narcotic spree.

JAGGED (Adj) Intoxicated.

JAIL ARITHMETIC (N) Making up a false list of expenses to conceal an embezzlement; the measure of time in jail.

JAIL BAIT (N) A girl under age.

JAIL BREAK (N) An escape from prison.

JAIL BIRD (N) A prisoner; an exconvict.

JAKE (Adj) All right; O.K.; money.

JAKE HOUND (N) One who gets drunk on Jamaica ginger.

JAKEY (N) Jamaica ginger.

JALOPPY (N) An old broken down automobile.

JAM (N-V) A small stolen article; an overdose of narcotic; to be in trouble.

JAM CLOUT (N) A shoplifting job.

JAM CLOUTER (N) A shoplifter who operates under the protection of an overcoat.

JAM SHOT (N) Method of shooting off a safe door; safe burglar's method of shooting off safe door by inserting explosive in jamb; a moderate charge of explosive in safe blowing.

JAM SNATCH (N-V) A shoplifting job; to shop lift.

JAMAKE (N) Jamaica ginger.

JAMES (N) A burglar's jimmy.

JAMMED (Adj) Suffering from an overdose of narcotics; in a bad predicament.

JAMMED UP (Adj) In custody of the law.

JAMOCHE (N) Coffee.

JANE (N) A young girl; a woman.

JAP (N) A Japanese; a negro.

JAR (N) Surprise; a shock; a petty dispute.

JARRED (Adj) Arrested.

JAVA (N)   Coffee.
JAWBONE (N-V)   Credit; to buy on credit.
JAWBONE TIME (N)   The time in jail before sentence is pronounced.
JAYPEE (N)   Justice of the Peace.
JAZZ (N)   Sexual union; a lively time.
JAZZ BABY (N)   A woman of easy morals; a passionate woman; a prostitute or whore.
JAZZED UP JANE (N)   A female no longer a virgin.
J.B. (N)   A Stetson hat.
JEANS (N)   Trousers.
JELLY (N)   Easily acquired money; a girl easily made.
JELLY BEAN (N)   A weakling; a coward.
JELLY FISH (N)   A weakling; a coward.
JENNY LINDA (N)   A widow.
JERK OF JESUS (N)   Hanging.
JERRIED (Adj)   Hurt; injured.
JERRY (N-V)   A railway section hand; a small pistol that can be secreted up the sleeve; to knock unconscious.
JERSEY LIGHTNING (N)   Bad whiskey.
JERV (N)   A vest pocket.
JEWELRY (N)   Handcuffs; a woman's genitals.
JIG (N)   A negro; a colored person.
JIG CHASER (N)   A white person who seeks the company of negresses.
JIG SHOP (N)   A blacksmith shop.
JIGALOO (N)   A negro.
JIGGABOO (N)   A negro.
JIGGAROO (N)   A warning that a policeman is approaching.
JIGGER (N)   An artificial sore.
JIGGERMAN (N)   A lookout; a spotter; a criminal lookout.
JIGGER MOLL (N)   A female criminal lookout.
JIGGERS (Excl)   A warning; warning of the approach of a policeman; fleas; lice; mites.
JIGGLER (N)   A lock pick.
JIGS (N)   A key.
JIM CROW (N)   A negro.

JIM CROW CAR (N) A car used exclusively for negroes in the south.

JIM HOW (N) The head rest used in smoking opium.

JIMMY (N) A tool used in forcing locks; a bar used by burglars to produce a leverage in forcing an entrance to a building.

JIMMY BAR (N) A burglar's jimmy.

JIMMY HOPE (N) Soap.

JIMMY IN (V) To trespass or intrude on a rival's territory.

JIMMY VALENTINE (N) A safe cracker; a peterman; a criminal tramp.

JINNY (N) A blind pig; a chisel with a bent end used by burglars.

JIP (V) To cheat; to swindle; to defraud.

JIP OF THE OLD BLOCK (N) The child of a crook.

JIT (N) Five cents.

JITNEY (N) A nickle; a negro; a five cent piece.

JITTER BUG (N) Air gun used as tie tamper by railroads.

JITTERS (N-V) Nervousness; to be uneasy.

JIVE (N) Small talk; marihuana.

JUNK BOX (N) The money box in a safe.

JOB (N) A crime; a theft.

JOB A MAN (V) To convict unjustly; to railroad a suspect.

JOB WITH A NOSE (V) To give a confidential talk.

JOBBED (Adj) Persecuted; convicted by perjured testimony.

JOCK (N) The male penis; a tramp who takes a young boy under his care, usually for perverted reasons.

JOCKER (N) A tramp of the sodomite type.

JOCKEY (N) A horse thief; a rider of a race horse; a tramp of a sodomite type.

JOE (N) Coffee.

JOE BELOW (N) A musician who plays very bass notes.

JOE POP (N) An occasional shot.

JOEY (N) A hypocrite; a religious hypocrite.

JOGGY (N) A hacksaw; a hacksaw blade.

JOHN (N) Safe burglars use this expression to inden-
tify themselves only to other safe crackers in jail, as a
safe cracker who uses explosives; a sucker; a lavatory; a
toilet; a Chineseman; a Chinese farmer.

JOHN B. (N) A Stetson hat.

JOHN FARMER (N) A farmer.

JOHN HANCOCK (N) A signature.

JOHN HENRY (N) A signature.

JOHN HOOSIER (N) A farmer.

JOHN LAW (N) An officer of the law; a policeman.

JOHN YEGG (N) A safe blower who travels in the
disguise of a tramp; a tramp safe-blower.

JOHNNIE (N) An Englishman; the penis; a lady's
man; a person who enjoys the company of ballet girls.

JOHNNIE BATES (N) A greenhorn; a sucker; a sap;
a victim; a dope; one who can be easily tricked.

JOHNNY LAW (N) An officer of the law; a policeman.

JOHNNY O'BRIEN (N) A box car.

JOHNSON (N) Coffee.

JOINT (N) An opium den; any low resort; a speakeasy; a house of prostitution; a brothel; a meeting place
for thieves; a hypodermic syringe.

JOINT BUSTER (N) A burglar.

JOINT CASER (N) One who makes preparation for a
burglary.

JOKER (N) An exconvict.

JOLLIER (N) A flatterer; one of good nature.

JOLLY (N) A good person.

JOLLY ROWSERS (N) The trousers.

JOLT (N) A term in jail; an injection of narcotic; a
convict.

JOLT IN STIR (N) A term in penitentiary.

JOMER (N) A kept mistress.

JOSH (N-V) A country man; a joke.

JOSKIN (N) A green country man.

JOY FLAKES (N) Morphine; cocaine; heroin.

JOY HOUSE (N) A whore house; a house of prostitution; a brothel.

JOY LADIES (N) Prostitutes; whores; women of easy morals.

JOY PROP (N) An occasional shot of narcotic.

JOY POWDER (N) Morphine; cocaine; heroin.

JOY PRONG (N) The male pudendum.

JOY RIDE (N) Sexual union; a narcotic exhilaration.

JOY RIDER (N) A legless cripple who goes about on a board on rollers.

JOY SISTERS (N) A prostitute; a whore.

JOY STICK (N) An opium pipe; the male pudendum.

JOY SPOT (N) A whore house; a brothel.

J.P. (N) Justice of the Peace.

JUDGE LYNCH (N) A lynching.

JUG (N) A pickpocket who operates in a bank; a jail; a lockup; a bank.

JUG BREAKING (N) Bank robbery.

JUG HEAVY (N) A criminal who makes a specialty of bank safe and vault.

JUG HEISTER (N) A bank robber.

JUG HOCK (N) A bank guard.

JUG HOISTER (N) A bank robber.

JUG JOB (N) Expression used by safe burglar, which means bank; burglary of a bank safe or vault.

JUG RAP (N) A sentence for bank robbery.

JUG WORK (N) Bank robbery.

JUGGED (Adj) Arrested; placed in jail.

JUGGER (N) A bank robber.

JUICE CHAIR (N) The electric chair; electrocution.

JUMP (N) An unlawful seizure.

JUMP THE FENCE (V) To escape and forget bail; to flee while on bond.

JUMPER (N) A device for defeating ignition locks; an absconder.

JUMPER TRAMP (N) A tramp who steals train rides.

JUNGLE (N) A wooded spot where safe crackers meet; a hobo camp; a district in which tramps and hoboes camp.

JUNGLE BUM (N) A tramp who frequents jungles.

JUNGLE BUZZARD (N) One who preys upon tramps

in jungle; a tramp who begs from his fellow tramps; hoboes.

JUNGLE STIFF   (N)   A tramp who frequents jungles.

JUNGLE UP   (V)   To spend the night in a camp.

JUNIPER   (N)   A wire used to deflect a burglar alarm circuit.

JUNK   (N)   Narcotics; morphine; plated jewelry; stolen articles; money; money in a safe; imitation or cheap jewelry.

JUNK HOG   (N)   A drug addict.

JUNK GRAFT   (N)   A narcotic trafficker.

JUNK MAN   (N)   A narcotic trafficker.

JUNK PEDDLER   (N)   A narcotic trafficker.

JUNKER   (N)   A drug addict; one addicted to the use of narcotics.

JURY FIXER   (N)   One who bribes a juryman.

K

KABITZ   (N)   Unwanted advice.

KACK   (N)   A refined person.

KALE   (N)   Money.

KANGAROO   (N-V)   A mock court conducted by prisoners; to convict unjustly; to sentence unjustly.

KANGAROO COURT   (N)   A mock court conducted by prisoners.

KANGAROO POCKET   (N)   A large pocket; a coat with a large inner pocket used by shoplifters for carrying loot.

KATE   (N)   An attractive prostitute or whore.

KEEK   (N)   A detective hired to spy on workers.

KEENO GAME   (N)   A swindling activity; a confidential game.

KEEP ONE'S NOSE CLEAN   (V)   To stay within the law; to avoid suspicion.

KEEP THE MEET   (V)   To keep an appointment with an addict or peddler of narcotics.

KEEP UNDER COVER   (V)   To hide.

KEESTER   (N)   A suitcase; a valise; a traveling bag;

a baggage theft; a safe; a safe within a vault; a woman's genitals.

KEESTER WORK (N) A baggage theft.

KEISTER (N) A baggage thief; a safe; a suitcase; female genitals.

KEISTER HACK (N) A baggage car guard.

KEISTER PLANT (N) Narcotics secreted in the rectum.

KEIPTER (N) A steel compartment within a vault.

KELLY (N) A hat; a derby hat.

KELLY STICK (N) A stick with a can attached used by tramps in washing clothes.

KELT (N) A white person.

KEPT WOMAN (N) A mistress.

KEPTIE (N) A mistress.

KETTLE (N) A locomotive; a watch.

KEWIE (N) A red headed woman.

KEWPIE (N) An infant; a child.

KEY HOLE (N) An informer for the police.

KEY RACKET (N) Dropping key in toilet asking victim to return same, victim stoops to find key, suspect takes purse out of pocket of coat which victim has hung up in toilet.

KEY STONE (N) A district attorney; a detective.

KEY TICKET (N) A lottery ticket with marking indicating the winner.

KEYSTER (N) The female pudendum; a suit case.

KEYSTER GETTER PETERMAN (N) A luggage or baggage thief.

KEYSTER PLANT (N) Narcotic concealed in the rectum; narcotic concealed in the female pudendum.

KEYSTER WORK (N) A baggage theft.

KEBBETS IT (N) A term used between fence and thief to charge it.

KICK (N-V) A pocket; a trouser pocket; a pocket book; the sensation derived from the use of narcotics; to protect; to complain.

KICK AWAY (V) To break away from the use of narcotics.

KICK BACK (N-V) A return of money; a boomerang;

to make restoration to a victim of that of which he had
been robbed; to relapse into his habit after a period of
abstinence by an addict.

KICK IN   (N-V)   A gift to a beggar; to contribute; to
pay a share; to confess; to crack a safe; to give in; to
pay an obligation.

KICK OFF   (N-V)   Death; to die.

KICK OVER   (N-V)   A burglary; a theft; to steal from;
to rob.

KICK THE AIR   (V)   To be hanged.

KICK THE BUCKET   (V)   To die.

KICK THE GONG   (V)   To smoke opium.

KICKING THE HABIT   (N)   The drug cure; withdrawal from the use of narcotics.

KICKS   (N)   Shoes.

KID   (N-V)   A young expert; an infant; a boy tramp;
to joke.

KID GLOVE   (N)   A high brow tramp; a high class
crook.

KID LAMB   (N)   A boy kept by a tramp for unnatural
purpose.

KID PEN   (N)   A reformatory.

KIDDER   (N)   A joker.

KIDDIE   (N)   A young thief.

KIDNAPEE   (N)   A kidnapped person.

KIDNAPER   (N)   A child stealer; a wife abductor.

KIKE   (N)   A no good Jew thief.

KILL OR CURE   (N)   The Kelly cure.

KILLER   (N)   A professional murderer.

KILLING   (N)   A good haul of stolen objects; a theft.

KILTY   (N)   A Scotchman.

KINDERGARTEN   (N)   A reformatory.

KING PIN   (N)   The principal keeper of a jail; the
warden of a penitentiary.

KING SCREW   (N)   The chief jailer of a prison; the
warden of a penitentiary.

KING SNIPE   (N)   A railway section foreman.

KINKY   (N)   A stolen automobile; a stolen object; a
criminal; a negro.

KINKY GOODS   (N)   Stolen goods; illicit goods.

KIP (N-V) A bed; a bedroom; a night watchman; to sleep.
KIP BAG (N) A hobo's bed roll.
KIPP (N) A lodging house.
KIRK (N) A church.
KISS IN (V) To curry favors.
KISS OFF (N-V) A sexual variant; to discharge; to commit sodomy.
KISS THE BOOK (V) To take an oath.
KISS THE DOG (N) A pickpocket having to face the victim.
KISSER (N) The mouth; the face.
KITCHEN BIDDY (N) A female kitchen worker.
KITCHEN DERBY (N) The belly.
KITCHEN MECHANIC (N) A cook.
KITCHEN MYSTERY (N) Hash.
KITE (N) A narcotic purchase of one ounce; a begging letter; an immoral woman; a prostitute; a whore; a note smuggled in or out of prison.
KITE A CHANCE (V) To forge.
KITE FLYER (N) A passer of counterfeit money; a passer of bad checks.
KIT THE CINDERS (N) A tramp who walks along the railroad tracks.
KITTEN (N) A small child; a small baby; an adolescent girl.
KLINK (N-V) A jail; to hit with a blackjack; to hit with the butt of a gun.
KLINK STIFF (N) A tramp who carries bedding and cooking utensils.
KLINKITY (N) A tramp who carries bedding and cooking utensils.
KLUCK (N) A boob; a no good person.
KNEEL AT THE ALTAR (V) To commit sodomy.
KNIGHT OF REST (N) A tramp who does not have to work.
KNIGHT OF THE ROAD (N) A tramp or hobo.
KNOB (N) The head.
KNOB KNOCKER (N) A safe burglar who knocks off

the combination of a safe and uses a punch to knock the lock; a safe cracker who uses a hammer.

KNOB-KNOCKING (V)   To use a hammer in knocking the combination off a safe.

KNOCK (V)   To squeal; to betray a friend; to accuse another.

KNOCK AT THE DOOR (V)   To take the drug cure.

KNOCK DOWN (N-V)   Stealing a railroad fare; to give an introduction; to embezzle; to give confidential information.

KNOCK OFF (V)   To arrest; to raid.

KNOCK OVER (V)   To arrest; to raid; to commit burglary or robbery.

KNOCK OFF A BANK (V)   To rob a bank.

KNOCK OUT DROPS (N)   Drugs placed in a drink to stupefy a victim.

KNOCK OVER A JOINT (V)   To commit burglary or robbery.

KNOCKER (N-V)   A fulminate cap; a person opposed to the use of drugs; to speak ill of another.

KNOWLEDGE BOX (N)   A school; a schoolhouse.

KNUCKLES (N)   Brass knuckles.

KNUCKLE DUSTER (N)   One who uses brass knuckles.

KNUCKLE HAPPY (N)   One always ready to fight.

KNUCKS (N)   Brass knuckles.

KOSHER (Adj)   Not guilty of; above reproach; clean; without incriminating evidence.

KOSHER CUTIE (N)   A Jewess.

KUDOS (V)   To applause; to recognize; to acclaim; to honor.

KUTER (N)   Twenty-five cents.

L

LABOR SHARK (N)   An employment agent.

LABOR SKATE (N)   An official of a labor union.

LACED MUTTON (N)   A prostitute; a whore.

LADY BIRD (N)   A kept woman; a mistress.

LADY FINGER (N)   A weakling; a coward.

LADY FOR HIRE   (N)   A prostitute; a whore.

LADY IN WAITING   (N)   An old maid; an unmarried woman somewhat advanced in years.

LADY KILLER   (N)   A young man who stands strong with the women.

LADY NICOTINE   (N)   Tobacco.

LADY OF LEISURE   (N)   A prostitute; a whore; a woman of easy morals.

LADY OF PLEASURE   (N)   A prostitute; a whore.

LADY OF THE EVENING   (N)   A prostitute; a whore.

LAG   (N)   A convict; an exconvict; a penitentiary sentence.

LAGGER   (N)   An exconvict.

LAM   (V)   To beat; to make an escape; to flee; to jump bail.

LAM THE JOINT   (V)   To escape from prison.

LAMASTER   (N)   A fugitive from justice; a forfeiter of bail bond; one hiding from the law.

LAMB   (N)   An innocent victim indicted for a crime committed by another; a weakling; a coward; a swindler's victim; a dupe; a boy tramp who travels with older tramps.

LAMB'S FRY   (N)   A tie.

LAMB'S TONGUE   (N)   A dollar bill.

LAME   (N)   One easily victimized.

LAMMISTER   (N)   An escaped prisoner.

LAMP   (N-V)   An eye; a close scrutiny; to see; to leer at.

LAMP HABIT   (N)   User of opium.

LAMOAS   (N)   Harmless.

LAMPOST   (N)   A tall lanky person.

LAMSTER   (N)   A fugitive.

LAND BROKER   (N)   An undertaker.

LAND RAT   (N)   A petty thief who works on land.

LAPPER   (N)   A sodomite.

LARCENY   (N)   Dishonest cupidity.

LARD BALL   (N)   A very fat person.

LAST CALL   (N)   Death.

LAST HOME   (N)   The cemetery.

LAST HOPE (N) An old maid; an unmarried woman somewhat advanced in years.

LAST RATTLER (N) Death.

LAST ROUND UP (N) Death.

LAST WALTZ (V) To move a body to the death house.

LATCH (V) To get hold of one's self.

LEATHERED UP (Adj) The cracks of a safe being soaped and ready for the nitroglycerine.

LAUGH AND SCRATCH (V) To inject narcotics.

LAUGHING JAG (N) A fit of laughter while under the influence of narcotics; a fit of laughter while intoxicated.

LAUNDRY QUEEN (N) A negress.

LAVENDER BOY (N) A male homosexual.

LAW (N) A prison guard; a chance to escape.

LAW GHOST (N) A lawyer who works for another but does not actually plead the case; a lawyer who seldom appears in court but prepares the cases for trial.

LAWFUL BLANKET (N) A wife.

LAWN MOWER (N) A machine gun.

LAY (N-V) The scene of a proposed robbery of a person; the act of smoking opium; to survey a prospective place to rob or burglarize; to have sexual union with a female.

LAY A GOLDEN EGG (V) To extort money from a wealthy person.

LAY A HIP (V) To smoke opium; to have sexual union.

LAY AN EGG (V) To drop a bomb.

LAY DOWN (V) To quiet; to give up; to have sexual union.

LAY DOWN JOINT (N) An opium den; a brothel; a whore house.

LAY IN LAVENDER (V) To serve a jail sentence.

LAY LOW (V) To hide for the time being.

LAY PAPER (V) To pass worthless checks.

LAY THE LEG (V) To have sexual union.

LAY THE HIP (V) To smoke opium; to have sexual union.

LAY THE HOOKS ON (V) To steal.

LAYING ON THE HIP (N) The act of smoking opium.

LAYING OUT (N) Assaulting.

LAYOUT (N) The circumstances in which a proposed crime is to be committed; the plan for a proposed crime; a gambling outfit; narcotic tools; opium smoking oufit.

LAZY (N) A prison guard.

LEAD COCKTAIL (N) Gunfire; discharging a gun; bullet.

LEAD MEDICINE (N) Bullets.

LEAD PIPE CINCH (N) Something done without difficulty.

LEAD POISONING (N) A bullet wound.

LEAD SEALS (N) Counterfeit coins.

LEAD SLUGS (N) Bullets.

LEAF (N) A dollar bill; narcotics.

LEAF GUM (N) Narcotics.

LEAPIN (N) An addict full of narcotics.

LEAK (N-V) Urine; to urinate.

LEAN (V) To strike with the fist.

LEAN AND FAT (N) A hat.

LEAN AND LINGER (N) The finger.

LEAP (N) A marriage.

LEARY (Adj) Scared; timid; suspicious; worthless merchandise.

LEATHER (N) A pickpocket term for a wallet; a purse; a pocketbook.

LEATHER LIFTER (N) A pickpocket.

LEATHER POKE (N) A pocketbook.

LEATHER SNATCHER (N) One who steals purses by snatching them away from the victim.

LEAVES (N) Paper money; bills.

LEERY (Adj) Afraid; suspicious.

LEFT BRITCH (N) Left front trouser pocket; a term used by pickpockets.

LEFT HAND DAUGHTER (N) An illegitimate child.

LEFT HAND SON (N) An illegitimate child.

LEFT HAND MISTRESS (N) A mistress; a kept woman.

LEFT PRATT (N)   Left trouser pocket, a term used by pickpockets.

LEFT TURN (N)   A blunder.

LEFTY (N)   One with a left leg or arm missing.

LEG (V)   To walk.

LEG BAIL (V)   To escape from prison.

LEG CUFFS (N)   Leg irons.

LEG PULLING (N)   Blackmail.

LEGALLY LASSOED (Adj)   Hanged; married.

LEGS (N)   Race track crooks.

LEGIT (N)   Goods acquired honestly.

LEGIT ROCKS (N)   Genuine rocks; genuine diamonds.

LEM-KEE (N)   Gum opium.

LEMON (N)   No good; a witness who turns state evidence; one who is easily victimized by criminals or tramps.

LEMON BOWL (N)   An opium pipe fitted with a lemon rind.

LEMON GAME (N)   Cheating a sucker at a pool game; a swindle scheme at a pool game.

LEMON POOL (N)   Two playing one game of pool.

LET HAVE IT (V)   To assault; to kill.

LET LOOSE THE POWDER (V)   To set off an explosive.

LET OFF (N)   Acquitted.

LETTER CARRIER (N)   A tramp who writes home his experiences.

LETTUCE (N)   Paper money; bills.

LEUR (N)   A hypodermic syringe.

LEVI (N)   A Jew.

LEVI STRAUSES (N)   Bib overalls.

LEVIS (N)   Bibless overalls.

LIBRARY BIRD (N)   One who spends most of his time loafing in a library.

LICK-BOX (N)   A sodomite.

LID (N)   A hat; a complete clothing outfit; criminal supression.

LIE IN STATE (V)   To serve a jail sentence.

LIFEBOAT (N)   A parole; a commutation of sentence.

LIFE LINE LINER   (N)   A release from prison; a pardon.

LIFE ON THE INSTALLMENT PLAN   (N)   A series of prison sentences.

LIFE PRESERVER   (N)   Weapons.

LIFE SAVER   (N)   A parole.

LIFER   (N)   A prisoner serving the remainder of his living days in penitentiary; a life sentence.

LIFT   (N-V)   A pickpocket; a shop lifter; a sneak theft; being cheerful under the effect of narcotic; to steal; to pilfer.

LIFTER   (N)   A shoplifter; a petty thief; a prowler.

LIFTING   (N)   Kidnapping.

LIFTING A LEATHER   (N)   Stealing a purse.

LIG ROBBER   (N)   One who hides in a bed room waiting to rob or assault the victim.

LIGHT   (V)   To steal.

LIGHT ARTILLERY   (N)   A hypodermic syringe; an addict using a hypodermic needle.

LIGHT BROWN   (N)   A mulatto.

LIGHT FINGERED   (Adj)   Thieving.

LIGHT-HOUSE   (N)   A criminal lookout who is always able to recognize a detective; a procurer for a brothel or whore house.

LIGHT INFANTRY   (N)   A tramp term for fleas, mites or lice.

LIGHT PIECE   (N)   A small coin.

LIGHT WEIGHT   (N)   A judge who knows very little about the law.

LIGHTNING SLINGER   (N)   A telegraph operator.

LIKKERED UP   (V)   To get drunk.

LILLIES   (N)   The female hands.

LILY   (N)   An easy victim.

LILY LIVER   (N)   A coward.

LIMB OF THE LAW   (N)   A lawyer.

LIMBER   (V)   To get ready to fight.

LIMBO   (N)   A jail.

LIME-JUICER   (N)   An Englishman.

LIMEY   (N)   An Englishman.

LIMIT   (N)   The maximum sentence.
LIMPY   (N)   A cripple; a lame person.
LINE   (N)   Nitroglycerine.
LINE UP   (N-V)   An exhibition of suspects to victims for the purpose of identification; to make an investigation prior to committing a burglary.
LINE UP A PLANT   (N)   An investigation made by criminals prior to committing a burglary or robbery.
LINE UP SESSION   (N)   An exhibition of suspects to victims for the purpose of identification.
LIP   (N-V)   A lawyer; an attorney; insolence; to talk.
LIP BURNER   (N)   A cigarette stub.
LIP IN   (V)   To intrude in a conversation.
LIPPIE CHASER   (N)   A male negro who prefers white women.
LIPPING THE DIPPER   (V)   To test the eye or medicine dropper by sucking the air out.
LIQUIDATE   (V)   To kill; to assassinate.
LIQUOR PLUG   (N)   A drunkard.
LIT UP   (V)   To be excessively full of narcotics.
LITTLE ACCIDENT   (N)   A new born baby.
LITTLE ANGEL   (N)   A small child.
LITTLE BLACK BOOK   (N)   Secret police records.
LITTLE HOUSE   (N)   A reformatory.
LITTLE MONKEY   (N)   A small child.
LITTLE PACKAGE   (N)   A baby.
LITTLE RED WAGON   (N)   A dump wagon.
LITTLE SCHOOL   (N)   A reformatory.
LITTLE SHAVER   (N)   A small child.
LITTLE SOUVENIR   (N)   A new born baby.
LITTLE STRANGER   (N)   A new born baby.
LITTLE TRAMP   (N)   A dirty child.
LIVE CLOSE TO ONE'S BELLY   (V)   To be poor.
LIVE ONE   (N)   A dwelling occupied by good prospective victims; a young girl who will step out.
LIVE WIRE   (N)   A spendthrift; a smart crook; a good victim.
LIVELY LETTUCE   (N)   Easy money.
LI-YUEN   (N)   Opium of high quality.
LIZARD SCORCHER   (N)   A camp cook.

LIZZIE LOUSE (N) A police patrol car.

LOAD (N-V) A narcotic injection; to victimize.

LOADED (Adj) Under the influence of narcotic; under the influence of liquor.

LOAN SHARK (N) A money lender.

LOB (N) A sap; a loafer in an opium den; a cash register.

LOBBY GON (N) A loafer in an opium den; a heeler for a big shot.

LOBSTER (N) A victim; a slow person; a person with little intelligence.

LOCAL RIDER (N) A tramp who occasionally takes to the road.

LOCK (N) A fence; a place where stolen goods are received.

LOCK PICKER (N) An abortionist; one using a pin to commit abortion.

LOCK SHOT (N) A safe burglar who loads his nitro-glycerine in the lock of the safe.

LOCK UP (N) A jail; a key.

LOCKER (N) A safe; a steel compartment in a safe or vault.

LOCO (Adj) Insane; crazy.

LOCO DUDS (N) A strait jacket.

LOCO SUIT (N) A strait jacket.

LOCO WEED (N) Marihuana cigarette; marihuana.

LOCUS (N) Narcotics.

LOCUST (N) A wooden club; a policeman's billy; knock out drops.

LOFT LIFTER (N) A cloth factory burglar; a warehouse burglar.

LOFT WORK (V) To burglarize cloth factories or warehouses.

LOFT WORKER (N) A cloth factory burglar; a warehouse burglar.

LOG (N) An exconvict; an opium pipe.

LONE WOLF (N) A criminal who operates alone; an unmarried man; a thief who works without a confederate.

LONER (N) A pickpocket who works without a confederate.

LONEY GUN (N) A machine gun.

LONG ARM (N) The Federal Government; a Federal law enforcement officer; a policeman.

LONG BIT (N) Fifteen dollars.

LONG DROP (N) The gallows.

LONG END (N) The larger share of a cut.

LONG KNIFE (N) A white person.

LONG ROD (N) A rifle.

LONG STRAW BELT (N) A tramp term for the Northwest.

LONG TIMER (N) A prisoner with a long sentence to serve.

LOOEY (N) A police lieutenant.

LOOGAN (N) A minor hoodlum; a helper.

LOOKER (N) One who makes a preliminary survey for thieves.

LOOKING (N) Trying to buy narcotics.

LOOKOUT (N) A jiggerman; one who watches while his confederate commits a burglary.

LOOSE LOVE CENTER (N) A house of prostitution; a whore house.

LOOSE LOVE LADY (N) A prostitute; a whore.

LOOSENER (N) A laxative food.

LOOSENERS (N) Prunes.

LOOT (N) Stolen goods.

LORD AND MASTER (N) A husband.

LORD'S SUPPER (N) A prison fare of bread and water.

LOSE ONE'S NERVE (V) To lose courage.

LOSER (N) Sent to prison; an exconvict; having served time in prison.

LOSS OF A MAN (N) Arrest of one of the members of a mob while they are in the act of committing a crime.

LOST (N) Murdered.

LOST LADY (N) A prostitute; a whore; a woman of easy morals.

LOT OF BEE AND HONEY (N) Wealthy; in possession of a lot of money.

LOUD SPEAKER (N) A wife.
LOUSE AROUND (V) To loaf.
LOUSE BAG (N) A sore.
LOUSE HOUSE (N) A lodging house.
LOUSE CAGE (N) A hat; a bed; a cheap lodging house; a vermin infected jail; a bedroom.
LOVE APPLE (N) A tear gas bomb.
LOVE CHILD (N) An illegitimate child.
LOVE LETTER (N) Bullet.
LOVE PEDDLER (N) A prostitute; a whore; a lascivious man.
LOVE PIRATE (N) A whore monger.
LOVER (N) A pimp; one who receives support from a prostitute or whore.
LOWER BERTH (N) The under bracing of a freight car used by tramps in stealing rides.
LOWER DECKER (N) The under bracing of a freight car used by tramps in stealing rides.
LUBRICATED (Adj) Intoxicated.
LUCKY BOY (N) A young man supported by a woman as her lover; a lover of a prostitute or whore; a man kept by a prostitute or whore.
LUER (N) The hypodermic needle used by drug addicts.
LUG (N-V) A stupid person; a hanger on; to make a loan.
LUGGER (N) A beggar.
LUMMY (N-V) An atractive female; to be attractive.
LUMP (N) Lunch.
LUMP OF LEAD (N) The head.
LUMPER (N) A river thief.
LUMPY (N) Worthless merchandise.
LUNG DUSTER (N) A cigarette.
LUSH (N-V) A sodomite; a drunkard; strong beer; inferior liquor; to rob an intoxicated person.
LUSH DIVER (N) One who robs intoxicated persons.
LUSH JOB (V) To rob intoxicated persons.
LUSH TOUCHER (N) One who robs intoxicated persons.
LUSH WORKER (N) A thief who robs drunken men;

a prostitute; a prostitute who robs her drunken patrons; a pickpocket who works trains.

LUSHER   (N)   A prostitute; a whore.

LYE BUG   (N)   An artificial sore made by using lye.

LYNCHER   (N)   The illegal hanging of another.

M

M   (N)   Morphine.

MACARONI   (N)   An Italian.

MACE   (N)   A blackjack; a lover of a prostitute or whore; a man kept by a prostitute or whore; a procurer.

MACGIMPER   (N)   A lover of a prostitute or whore; a procurer.

MACHINE GAT   (N)   A machine gun.

MACHINERY   (N)   A hypodermic syringe used by a drug addict.

MACK   (N)   A lover of a prostitute or whore; a man kept by a prostitute or whore; a pimp.

MACKED UP   (N)   Dressed up.

MACKEREL   (N)   A pimp; a procurer; a lover of a prostitute or whore.

MAD MONEY   (N)   Money for carfare home which a young girl keeps in case of fight with her date.

MADAM   (N)   A hostess of a brothel; a prostitute; a whore; a handkerchief.

MADAME   (N)   The keeper of a brothel or house of prostitution.

MADE   (Adj)   Detected by the victim. (A pickpocket term.)

MADE WOMAN   (N)   A female no longer a virgin.

MADHOUSE   (N)   A brutal person; an asylum for insane; excitement.

MAGAZINE   (N)   A six month sentence.

MAGDALENE   (N)   A reformed prostitute; a reformed whore.

MAGGIE   (N)   A revolver or pistol.

MAHOGANY   (N)   A mulatto.

MAHOGANY FLATS   (N)   Bed bugs.

MAHULA (V) To become bankrupt; to have no money.

MAIDEN-HEAD (N) A virgin female.

MAIN BULL (N) A chief of Police; a Chief of Detectives.

MAIN DRAG (N) A main street; the principal street of a town.

MAIN GUY (N) The boss; a gang leader; the head person.

MAIN LINE (N) The median or middle vein; the main dining room.

MAINLINER (N) An addict who injects in the middle vein; prisoners who eat in the main dining room of a jail.

MAIN MAN (N) A highjacker.

MAIN SPRING (N) The work house.

MAIN STEM (N) The head person; the principal street of a town.

MAIN SCREW (N) A warden of a penitentiary; principal keeper of a jail.

MAIN SQUEEZE (N) A leader; a chief of a gang mob; a gang mob; a foreman; a head fellow.

MAKE (N-V) Detecting of pickpocket operator by the victim; to recognize; to obtain; to steal; to identify.

MAKE A BIRD'S NEST (V) To put putty in the combination of a safe after a hole is drilled in it.

MAKE A BOAST (V) To secure freedom.

MAKE A BREAK (V) To attempt an escape from prison.

MAKE A CONNECTION (V) To make a purchase of narcotic from a peddler.

MAKE A GETAWAY (V) To effect an escape.

MAKE A JOINT (V) To commit a burglary or robbery.

MAKE A KILLING (V) To make a steal of greater value than expected.

MAKE A RIFFLE (V) To beg on the street.

MAKE A SPREAD (V) To get narcotic lay-out ready to use.

MAKE A SUCKER (V) To defraud; to cheat; to swindle.

MAKE A TOUCH (V) To lift a purse; to beg on the street.

MAKE ONE (V) To identify a person.

MAKE ONE SING (V) To make or secure a confession from a criminal.

MAKE THE BOAST (V) To be released by order of the parole board; receive a pardon.

MAKE THE FLOP (V) To sit on the sidewalk and beg.

MAKE THE MAN (V) To make a purchase of narcotic from a peddler.

MAKE THE RIFFLE (V) To win.

MAKE THE QUEER (V) To make counterfeit coins.

MAKE TIME (V) To date a female.

MANNY (N) A negress who cares for a child.

MAN AND WIFE (N) A pocket knife.

MAN BOX (N) A coffin.

MAN CATCHER (N) An employment agent; a foreman who hires men.

MAN FAKER (N) A counterfeiter.

MAN GRABBER (N) An employment agent; a foreman who hires men.

MAN HUNTER (N) A detective; a runner for an employment agent.

MAN KILLER (N) A prison where the prisoners are treated brutally.

MAN OF WAR (N) An armored car.

MAN OIL (N) The impregnating fluid of a male.

MAN TRAP (N) A whore house; a house of prostitution.

MANACLED (Adj) Married.

MANARVEL (V) To steal.

MAP (N) The face; the cheek.

MARBLE ORCHARD (N) The cemetery.

MARBLE CITY (N) A cemetery.

MARGIN MAN (N) A dealer or runner who makes trip with drugs on short margin.

MARI (N) Marihuana.

MARIA (N) A police car in which prisoners are transported.

MARK (N-V) A victim or intended victim of a pickpocket; an easy person to victimize; a dupe; a victim; to select a victim.

MARK A CONNECTION (V) To take note of a drug peddler so one may in the future resort to him for drugs.

MARKED (Adj-V) Wanted by the police; to mistrust; to have suspicion of.

MARKED MAN (N) One who has committed a crime and is wanted as a criminal; one marked to be killed.

MARKED PAPER (N) A deck of playing cards marked for dishonest purposes.

MARKS (N) Credits given a prisoner for good behavior; the system of registering a prisoner; coppers.

MARRIAGE CHEATER (N) A man who invades another's marital rights.

MARRIED (Adj) Handcuffed together.

MARRIED EGGS (N) Two fried eggs.

MARRY (V) To enter homosexual relations.

MARY (N) Morphine.

MARY ANN (N) A knockout blow.

MARY WERNER (N) Marihuana; marihuana cigarettes.

MASHER (N) A loafer who annoys women by his attention; one who tries to force his acquaintance on a woman.

MASKED (Adj) Assaulted; fascinated.

MASON (N) A homosexual type who takes the active part.

MATCH (N) A prison fare.

MATCH-TRICK (N) A method of torture by burning bare feet with matches.

MATTRESS (N) The face.

MAULER (N) A boxer.

MAVERICK (N) An orphan child.

MAWK (N) A dirty prostitute or whore.

MAYO (N) Morphine; cocaine; heroin.

MAZUMA (N) Money.
MEAL TICKET (N) A person who will buy one a meal or provide one's living; one who furnishes a meal to a beggar; furnishing one with support; a husband.
MEASURE (N-V) A sentence to hang; to assault; to strike; to stare.
MEAT (N) A corpse.
MEAT BURNER (N) A poor cook; a poor prison cook.
MEAT CART (N) A hearse.
MEAT HOOKS (N) The hands; the fists.
MEAT HOUND (N) A sodomite; a male homosexual; a lascivious person.
MEAT PACKER (N) An undertaker.
MEAT WAGON (N) An ambulance; a hearse.
MECHANIC (N) The pickpocket who actually takes the purse; the one who does the actual work of opening a safe.
MEDICAL WORKER (N) A patent medicine seller.
MEDICINE (N) An addict term for narcotics.
MEDICINE MAN (N) A physician; a doctor.
MEDICO (N) A physician; a doctor.
MEET (N) A criminal hangout; a rendezvous for thieves.
MEG (N) A penny.
MEGG (N) Marihuana; marihuana cigarettes.
MELL MOLL (N) A woman cook.
MELT THE SEAL (V) Divorce.
MENDER (N) A criminal lawyer; a claim agent.
MERRY-GO-ROUND (N) A gambling wheel; a false trial; unable to think properly.
MESHUGA (Adj) Crazy; foolish.
MESS BOILER (N) A cook; a kitchen worker.
MESS MOLL (N) A female cook.
MESS OF FISH (N) Plenty of money; wealth.
MICHAEL FINN (N) A knockout drop; something to induce sleep.
MICHIGAN ROLL (N) A roll of counterfeit bills rolled on the outside with a genuine bill.

MICK (N) An Irishman.

MICKY (N) An Irishman.

MICKEY FINN (N) A knockout blow; a knockout drop; a knockout powder to induce sleep; a drink that has been drugged.

MIDDIE (V) To be in a compromising position; to be left holding the bag.

MIDDLE PIECE (N) Pickpocket term for a vest.

MIDNIGHT OIL (N) Opium.

MIGGLES (N) Marihuana cigarettes.

MIKE (N) An Irishman.

MILK (V) To extort; to have money extorted; to steal or intercept a telegraph message.

MILK BOTTLES (N) The female breasts.

MILK ROPE (N) A string of pearls.

MINCE PIES (N) The eyes.

MINCING MACHINE (N) A machine gun.

MINISTER'S FACE (N) A boiled pig's head.

MISBEHAVE (N) A shave.

MISERY (N) Prison coffee; inferior coffee; menstrual period of a female.

MISS (N) A miscarriage.

MISS EMMA (N) Morphine.

MISSION STIFF (N-V) A religious tramp who takes advantage of mission comforts; a hobo; to become changed in character.

MISSION SQUAWKER (N) A mission preacher.

MISSIONARY (N) A pander; one who ministers to the desires of a woman who panders; a procurer.

MISSISSIPPI MARBLES (N) Dice.

MITT (N-V) A hand; to shake hands with; to pay an obligation.

MITT CAMP (N) A fortune teller's establishment.

MITT GLOM (V) To welcome; to shake hand.

MITT JOINT (N) A fortune teller's establishment.

MITT ME (V) Shake my hand.

MITTS (N) One who has lost one or both hands.

MIXED ALE OVATION (N) A cheap politician using bad grammar in addressing a multitude.

MIXED ALE PHILOSOPHER (N) A drunkard who knows it all.

MIXER (N) A fight; a pretended fight to delay the police while the thief escapes.

MIXUP (N) A fight; a fracas.

MIZZEN (N) A top story burglar.

MIZZEN MAST WORKER (N) A burglar who works top story.

MOAN AND WAIL (N) A jail.

MOB (N-V) A gang of pickpockets consisting of more than four members; a band of criminals; to commit some crime.

MOB GEE (N) A gangster.

MOB HEAD (N) A gang leader.

MOB MARKER (N) The one of the mob who lines up places to be taken.

MOB MOLL (N) A female gangster.

MOB UP WITH (V) To become a member of the same gang.

MOBSMAN (N) A pickpocket.

MOBBED (Adj) Assaulted by a member of a gang of people.

MOBBERY (N) Robbery committed by a mob.

MOJO (N) Morphine.

MOLL (N) A woman; the female companion of a gangster; a woman of the underworld.

MOLL BUZZ (N-V) A female pickpocket; to pick a woman's purse; to snatch a purse (By a female pickpocket).

MOLL BUZZER (N) A thief who steals only from women; a pickpocket who works on women; a female purse snatcher; a tramp who begs from women.

MOLL GUN (N) A female pickpocket.

MOLL PEN (N) A jail for women.

MOLL WHIZZ (N) A female pickpocket.

MOLL WIZ (N) A female pickpocket.

MOLL WORKER (N) A pickpocket who robs women; a pickpocket who snatches women's purses.

MOLLIE (N) A prostitute; a whore; a woman of easy morals; a disreputable girl.

MOLLY (N) A prostitute; a whore; a woman of easy morals; a disreputable girl; a male homosexual.
MOLTEN GLASS (N) Stolen diamonds.
MOLTEN MAMA (N) A passionate young woman.
MONA (N) An air raid alarm.
MONDAY MAN (N) A thief who steals clothes from a clothesline.
MONDAY WORKER (N) A thief who steals from clotheslines.
MONEY JOINT (N) A good place to commit a crime.
MONICA (N) A person's name.
MONIKER (N) A person's name.
MONITOR (N) The lookout on a railway caboose.
MONKEY HOUSE (N) A brothel; a house of prostitution.
MOLLESHER (N) The sweetheart of a criminal.
MOLLISHER (N) The sweetheart of a criminal.
MONK (N) The judge of a supreme court.
MONKEY (N) A policeman; a Federal Officer; a tramp; a victim of a dupe; one working in a bookmaking place; a woman's genitals.
MONKEY CAKE (N) The visitor's room of a jail.
MONKEY MEAT (N) Canned meat.
MONKEY MONEY (N) Counterfeit coins; tokens.
MONKEY ON A HOUSE (N) A mortgage.
MONKEY SUIT (N) A uniform; a dress suit; a strait jacket.
MOOCH (N-V) Victim or intended victim of a pickpocket; a gift to a beggar; to beg; to pilfer.
MOOCHER (N) A beggar; a sponger.
MOOCHERY (N) A petty theft.
MOOCHING MOLL (N) A woman beggar.
MOO-JUICE (N) Milk.
MOONLIGHT (V) To commit a crime at night.
MOONLIGHTER (N) A midnight prowler.
MOONSHINE (N) Illicit liquor or goods, made or sold.
MOONSHINER (N) An illicit whiskey distiller who pays no government taxes.
MORMON DINNER (N) A dinner mainly of potatoes.
MOP (N) A dunce; a dummy.

MOP MARY (N)   A scrub woman.
MOP UP (V)   To give a severe beating to.
MOPER (N)   A low class tramp.
MOPHY (N)   Forbidden articles smuggled to a prisoner.
MORGUE (N)   The library in a newspaper plant.
MORGUE AGE (N)   A corpse.
MORMON CURRENCY (N)   Carrots.
MOSES (N)   A man who, for a price, swears that he seduced a girl who was betrayed by another.
MOSEY (V)   To move slowly.
MOSQUITOES (N)   Cocaine.
MOSS (N)   Hair.
MOTHER AND DAUGHTER (N)   Water.
MOTOR COP (N)   A motorcycle officer.
MOUCH (N)   A gift given a beggar.
MOUNDER (N)   A beggar.
MOUNT SHASTA (V)   To be addicted to narcotics.
MOUNTED TOPPINGS (N)   Frosted cake.
MOUNTIE (N)   A mounted policeman; a policeman who rides a horse.
MOUSE (N)   A coward; a weakling; a woman; a girl.
MOUSER (N)   A detective; a sodomite.
MOUTH HABIT (N)   Taking narcotics orally.
MOUTHPIECE (N)   An attorney; a criminal lawyer; a go between who adjusts differences with the law.
MOUTHPRINTS (N)   Incriminating speech.
MOWING MACHINE (N)   A machine gun.
MR. BADGER (N)   The man who pretends to be the outraged husband in a badger game.
MRS. BADGER (N)   A woman blackmailer who plays the badger game.
MR. WHISKERS (N)   A Federal enforcement officer; the Federal Government.
MRS. WARREN'S PROFESSION (N)   Prostitution.
MUCK (N)   Coffee.
MUCK STICK (N)   A shovel.
MUSCLE (N-V) One who intrudes or infringes on another's profits or territory; to force one's way in for

a cut on the profits of a venture; to interfere in another's racket; to take a share by force.

MUD (N) Gum opium; coffee; chocolate pudding.

MUD KICKER (N) A woman who lures and blackmails men; a prostitute or whore who robs her patron; a woman who victimizes men.

MUDDER (N) A horse that runs well on muddy tracks.

MUDHOOKS (N) Feet.

MUDLARK (N) A low bred person; a street urchin.

MUFF (N) A woman or girl; a woman's genitals; the female pudendum.

MUFF DIVER (N) A sodomite.

MUFF DIVING (N) Sexual variants.

MUG (N-V) The face; the mouth; a photograph in police records; an officer; a plain clothes man; a desperado; to strangle.

MUG MAN (N) A photographer; one who takes pictures for a rogues gallery.

MUG ROOM (N) A room in which prisoners are photographed.

MUGGED (Adj) Photographed.

MUGGER (N) One who takes photographs.

MUGGINA (N) Where young mobsters seize the victim from behind, while others accost him in front, most of the victims being old women.

MUGGINS (N) A tramp word for food.

MUGGLEHEAD (N) A marihuana smoker.

MUGGLER (N) False or worthless merchandise.

MUGGLES (N) Marihuana.

MUGSMAN (N) A rogue's gallery photographer; one who takes pictures.

MUGSNAPPER (N) A rogue's gallery photographer; one who takes pictures.

MULE (N) One who sells narcotics for regular peddlers; a go between; corn whiskey; alcohol.

MULLIGAN (N) A tramp term for stew.

MULLIGAN JOINT (N) A restaurant.

MULLIGAN MIXER (N) A cook; a kitchen worker.

MUM (V) To be silent.

MUM'S THE WORD   (N-V)   Keep your mouth shut; to be silent.

MURK   (N)   Coffee.

MURPHY   (N)   Potatoes; an Irishman.

MUSCLE   (V)   To rob by force; to employ violence or coercion.

MUSCLE MAN   (N)   A gangster or racketeer who attempts to force himself into another's business for profit; an employer of violence.

MUSCLE MOLL   (N)   A masculine woman.

MUSCLE WORK   (N)   Violence; physical coercion.

MUSCLER   (N)   One who infringes on other's profits or territory; an intruder.

MUSH   (N-V)   The face; the mouth; an umbrella mender; to walk.

MUSH FAKE   (V)   To mend umbrella.

MUSH FAKER   (N)   A structural iron worker; an umbrella mender.

MUSHROOM   (N)   An umbrella mender by mush fakers.

MUSH TALK   (N)   Flattery talk; a talk to win over; a beggar's talk of woe; a confidence talk.

MUSH WORKER   (N)   A woman who works on men's sympathy in order to be able to swindle them; a beggar who works upon the emotions of his victims; a prostitute or whore who robs her patrons; a woman who lures and blackmails men.

MUSIC   (V)   To be acquitted.

MUSS   (N-V)   Trouble; to fight.

MUSSED UP   (Adj)   Beaten up.

MUSSER   (N)   A fighter; a bully; one who picks fights.

MUSTARD   (N)   A Chinese; cement.

MUSTARD PACKER   (N)   A hod carrier.

MUSTARD SHINE   (N)   Mustard applied to shoes by a fugitive to throw dogs off the scent.

MUTT   (N)   A fool; a person lacking in common sense; a simpleton.

MUTTED UP   (N)   Guarded by a dog.

MYSTERY   (N)   Hash; meat loaf.

McCOY   (N)   Real bourbon whiskey; genuine liquor;

excellent; genuine; a drug addict term for chemically pure narcotics.

McGIMPER (N) A man who lives on the earning of a prostitute or whore.

N

NAB (V) To seize; to arrest; to steal.

NABBED (Adj) Arrested.

NABBER (N) A policeman.

NAIL (N-V) A hypodermic syringe; a narcotic injection; to arrest.

NAIL A RATTLER (N) Steal a train ride.

NAIL ON THE FLY (V) To board a moving train.

NAILED (Adj) Caught; trapped; arrested; arrested in the act of picking a pocket.

NANCE (N) An effeminate person; a sissy.

NANCE WALK (N) A person who walks like a woman.

NANCY (N) An effeminate person.

NANNY (N) A fall guy.

NARCOTIC BULL (N) A Federal narcotic agent.

NARCOTIC COPPER (N) A Narcotic officer.

NARK (N) An informer.

NASTY MAN (N) The one of a gang of thieves who seizes and throttles the victim.

NATURAL (N) A sentence of seven years imprisonment.

NAVY HORSEMAN (N) One who loots ships in the day time.

NEAR-SIGHTED SHACK (N) A brakeman who allows hoboes to ride his train.

NECK CROCKER (N) A hang man.

NECKLACE (N) The hangman's noose.

NECKWEED (N) The hangman's noose.

NECKING (N) Hanging; a petting party; an association of the sexes where the exchange of caresses is chief amusement.

NECKTIE (N) The hangman's noose.

NECKTIE PARTY (N) A lynching; a hanging.

NED (N) A ten dollar gold piece.

NEDDY (N) A sling shot.

NEEDLE V) To make near beer intoxicating by injecting ether or alcohol; to add drug to a soft drink; a hypodermic syringe; a narcotic injection.

NEEDLE-FIEND (N) A hypodermic user of narcotics.

NEEDLE HABIT (N) The habit of taking narcotic hypodermically.

NEEDLE-SHY (N) Addicts who become sickish of stomach on inserting the needle into oneself.

NEEDLE YEN (N) The habit of taking narcotics hypodermically.

NEPTUNE'S DAUGHTER (N) Water.

NERVER (N) A fellow who gets by without paying at places of amusement or other places.

NERVOUS FINGER (N) One inclined to thievery; one given to petty theft.

NEST (N) A park bench.

NEW FISH (N) Arrival of a new prisoner.

NEW JUICE (N) A new prisoner.

NEWSPAPER (N) A month's sentence.

NIAGARA PINEAPPLE (N) A tear gas bomb.

NIBBLER (N) A beggar standing in front of a bakery or restaurant and while begging gnaws at a crust of bread.

NICK (N-V) A stolen object; to make a touch; to take away from.

NICKEL AND DIME (V) To beg on the streets.

NICKEL NOTE (N) A five dollar bill.

NIESTER MARK (N) A luggage thief's victim.

NIFTY (Adj) Too familiar; insolent; cocky.

NIG (V) To back out; to renege.

NIGGER GIN (N) Synthetic gin.

NIGHT CAP (N) A special watchman.

NIGHTHAWK (N) A railway detective posing as a tramp; a night watchman; a night street walker; a night prowler.

NIGHT MAN (N) A night prowler.

NIGHT OWL (N) A night pleasure seeker.

NIGGER HEAVEN (N) The roof on a car; the upper balcony in a legitimate theatre.
NIGGER ROLL (N) A roll of dollar bills.
NIGGER STEAK (N) Liver.
NIGGER TIP (N) To give lightly.
NIGGER WENCH (N) A negro prostitute or whore; a colored woman servant.
NINNIES (N) The female breasts.
NIP (N-V) A drink; to steal; to cut a diamond out of a pin with a specially made shears by a pickpocket; to unlock a door with snippers.
NIP DOUGH (N) The profits of a shortchange artist.
NIPPED (Adj) Arrested.
NIPPER (N) A tool used by burglars for turning a key from the opposite side to which it is inserted; a tool used by pickpockets to clip off jewelry.
NIPPERS (N) Handcuffs; bracelets; irons; a pickpocket shears for cutting stickpins.
NIP UP (V) To raise the amount of a check.
NITRO (N) Nitroglycerine.
NOBLE (N) A man who serves as a guard for strikebreakers; a guard for strikebreakers.
NO CAN TELL (N) A silencer; a gun with a silencer.
NO CHICKEN (N) An old woman.
NO MAN'S LAND (N) A ladies' rest room.
NOCKS (N) Narcotics.
NOGGIN (N) The head.
NOISE (N) The charge of explosive in safe blowing; heroin.
NON-SKID (N) Rough toilet paper.
NOSE (N) One who spies upon criminals for the police; a detective; a police spy.
NOSE BAG (N) A meal; a meal given a beggar; a handkerchief.
NOSE CANDY (N) Cocaine.
NOSE OF WAX (N) A weakling; a coward.
NOSE POWDER (N) Cocaine; heroin; morphine.
NOTCH GIRL (N) A prostitute; a whore.
NOTCH HOUSE (N) A whore house; a house of prostitution.

NOTCH MOLL (N) A female inmate of a house of ill repute; a female inmate of a house of prostitution or brothel.

NOTCHES ON GUN (N) A notch cut on the handle of a gun indicating the number of men killed with the gun.

NOTE COUNTERFEITER (N) One who makes paper money.

NOTE LAYER (N) A shortchange swindler.

NO TELL (N) A gun with a silencer; a silencer.

NOTION COUNTER (N) A fence; a place where stolen goods are sold.

NOT HAVE THE PRICE OF A PARK BENCH (V) To be poor.

NOT MY FUNERAL (N) None of my business or affair.

NUCK (N) A thief.

NUCKS (N) Brass knuckles.

NUMBER UP (Adj) Marked for death.

NUT (N) A demented person; a debt; the cost; the head; the cost of an operation; a reward for an arrest; a combination lock of a safe or vault.

NUT COLLEGE (N) The hospital for the criminally insane.

NUT STAKE (V) To finance.

NUT SQUEALER (N) Men working the shell game.

NUTS (N) The male testicles.

NUTS AND BOLTS (N) Insane; crazy.

NUTTY (N) Insane; crazy.

NUX (N) Tea.

O

O (N) Opium.

OAK TOWEL (N) A wooden club; a policeman's billy.

OAK TOWEL RUBDOWN (N) A clubbing.

OAKUS (N) A wallet.

OAT-BIN (N) The female pudendum.

OCEAN WAVE (N) A shave.

ODAY (N) Money.

ODD FELLOW (N) Three doughnuts and coffee.
ODDS AND ENDS (N) Scrap meat begged from a butcher by beggars.
OFAY (N) A white person.
OFFICE (N) Signal; a warning.
OFFICE MAN (N) A detective; a headquarter's detective.
OFFICE SIGNAL (N) Give him the office; give him the signal.
OFFICERETTE (N) A policewoman.
OFFISTICATE (V) To steal.
OH MY (N) Near beer.
OIL (N) Nitroglycerine.
OILED (Adj) Intoxicated.
OINTMENT (N) Money.
OKUS (N) Term used by pickpocket for wallet.
OLAF (N) A Swede.
OLD BAT (N) An old woman.
OLD BATTLE AX (N) A woman who makes life miserable for her husband by quarreling with him.
OLD BIRD (N) An old man.
OLD BUZZARD (N) An old country man.
OLD CODGER (N) A man.
OLD EGG (N) An old person.
OLD GIRL (N) A wife; an old woman.
OLD HEAD (N) A veteran convict.
OLD JOE (N) Syphilis.
OLD LADIES HOME (N) A house of prostitution in which disorderly conduct is tolerated.
OLD LADY WHITE (N) Cocaine; heroin; morphine.
OLD MAID (N) A spinster.
OLD MAN (N) The warden of a prison; main squeeze; a boss.
OLD PATROL (N) An old prostitute or whore.
OLD PULL (N) A doctor; a physician.
OLD RIP (N) A worn out prostitute or whore.
OLD SMOKY (N) The electric chair; electrocution.
OLD TIMER (N) An old person; a person who has lived in one locality for years.
OLD WOMAN (N) A fussy old man; a wife.

ON A SHORT (Adj) A street car; a pickpocket who operates on a street car.

ON A SLEIGH RIDE (Adj) Under the influence of cocaine.

ON END (Adj) Nervous.

ON GOW (Adj) Used by the Roumanian Gypsies when they are broke and their men folks order them to steal anything.

ON PAGE EIGHT (Adj) Blacklisted.

ON PROPS (Adj) On crutches.

ON SHORT DOUGH (Adj) Hungry, dirty and without money.

ON THE BEACH (Adj) Hungry, dirty and without money.

ON THE BEND (Adj) Engaged in some kind of crime; obtaining drugs through a runner.

ON THE BLINK (Adj) Broke; without any money.

ON THE BLUE (Adj) Unlucky.

ON THE BOOST (Adj) Shoplifting.

ON THE BUM (Adj) Tramping; wandering about without money.

ON THE BUST (Adj) Engaged in burglary.

ON THE CROOK (Adj) Engaged in crime.

ON THE CUFF (Adj) On credit; charged.

ON THE CUSHION (Adj) Well supplied with money.

ON THE DIP (Adj) Working at picking pockets.

ON THE DODGE (Adj) Hiding; avoiding in an evasive or skulking way.

ON THE DRAG (Adj) Tramping; wandering about from place to place.

ON THE ELEVATION (Adj) Engaged in robbery.

ON THE ERIE (Excl.) Shut up; keep quiet; a stool pigeon; some one is listening.

ON THE GRAVEY TRAIN (Adj) Well supplied with money.

ON THE GRIFT (Adj) Engaged in crime.

ON THE GUN (Adj) A busy pickpocket; one engaged in theft.

ON THE HEAVY (Adj) Engaged in robbing banks.

ON THE HEEL   (Adj)   Engaged in crime.
ON THE HOG   (Adj)   Without funds; broke; no good.
ON THE HOOK   (Adj)   Engaged in theft.
ON THE HOT BLOCKS   (Adj)   Stealing watches.
ON THE HOT BOILER   (Adj)   Stealing automobiles.
ON THE HOT SHORTS   (Adj)   Stealing automobiles.
ON THE IN   (Adj)   Having inside information.
ON THE JUG   (Adj)   Engaged in robbing banks.
ON THE LAM   (Adj)   Fleeing from the law; in flight.
ON THE LEVEL   (Adj)   Frankly; honest; fair.
ON THE LIFT   (Adj)   Engaged in shoplifting or theft.
ON THE MAKE   (Adj)   Exerting oneself to gain money
   or the attention of the opposite sex; open to a proposal;
   a female looking for a male companion.
ON THE MOPE   (Adj)   Tramping; wandering from
   place to place.
ON THE MUSCLE   (Adj)   Angry; quarrelsome; in-
   truding in a rival's territory.
ON THE NEEDLE   (N-V)   The act of injecting nar-
   cotic; to inject narcotic.
ON THE NOSE   (Adj)   A case exactly in point.
ON THE NUT   (Adj)   Living on money set aside for
   expenses; being nearly broke.
ON THE OUTS   (Adj)   Estranged.
ON THE PETER   (Adj)   Engaged in safe cracking.
ON THE POCKET PROWL   (Adj)   Working at pick-
   ing pockets.
ON THE PRIVATES   (Adj)   Engaged in robbing priv-
   ate residences.
ON THE PROWL   (Adj)   Engaged in burglary.
ON THE RATS   (Adj)   Engaged in robbing freight
   cars.
ON THE ROAD   (Adj)   Engaged in highway robbery.
ON THE ROCKS   (Adj)   Ruined; penniless; hungry
   and without any money; a marriage union broken.
ON THE SEND   (Adj)   Prospective victim who is sent
   for his money; one who acts as go-between, between the
   addict and the peddler, for a price.
ON THE SEVEN UP   (Adj)   Burglarizing stores of
   merchandise.

ON THE SHELF (Adj) Retired.

ON THE SHORTS (Adj) Picking pockets on the street car.

ON THE SINGLE O (Adj) A pickpocket working without a confederate.

ON THE SKIN (Adj) Engaged in stealing furs.

ON THE SNEAK (Adj) Engaged in sneak thievery.

ON THE SPOT (Adj) Doomed for assassination or vengeance; marked for death; selected for killing; in a predicament.

ON THE SQUARE (Adj) Honest; fair.

ON THE STUFF (Adj) Using of narcotics.

ON THE TURF (Adj) A night walker; indigent; needy; hungry and without money.

ON THE UP AND UP (Adj) Honest; straight; on the level.

ON THE UPPERS (Adj) Hungry and without money.

ON THE WIRE (Adj) Working at picking pockets.

ON THE WIZ (Adj) Working at picking pockets.

ON THE WORM (Adj) Engaged in stealing silk goods.

ONE ARM BANDIT (N) A slot machine.

ONE EYED MONSTER (N) A motorcycle policeman.

ONE FOOT IN THE GRAVE (N) Dying.

ONE GEE (N) One thousand dollars.

ONE-HORSE-TOWN (N) A small country town.

ONE SPOT (N) A sentence of one year in prison; a dollar bill.

ONE SPOT SLEEP (N) A one year sentence.

ONE WAY EGG (N) An honest person.

ONE WAY GUY (N) An honest person.

ONE WAY RIDE (N) A killing; a murder.

ONE WAY TICKET (N) A killing; a murder.

ONES AND TWOS (N) Shoes.

ONE'S NUMBER IS UP (Adj) Marked for death; marked to be killed.

ONION (N) The head: the face; a large pearl; a watch; a tear gas bomb.

OOCHRE (N) Money.

OOMPH GIRL (N) A passionate young woman.

OP (N) A telegraph operator.
OPEN WORK (N) Safecracking.
OPENER (N) A key; a jimmy used by safe crackers in opening safes.
ORANGE BOWL (N) A large half orange shell used as a shade on an opium lamp.
ORANGE POP MAN (N) A sufferer from venereal disease.
OREGON BOOT (N-V) Leg irons; to act like ball and chain.
ORGAN GRINDER (N) A machine gun.
OSCAR (N) A pistol; a revolver.
OSCAR HOCKS (N) Socks.
O'SHAUGNESSY PARDON (N) A death sentence.
OUT (N) An excuse; an alibi; a plea to avoid sentence; an escape; a means of escape.
OUT AFTER THE LONG GREEN (Adj) After the money.
OUT OF THE GUN (Adj) Stealing.
OUT OF TOWN (Adj) Imprisoned; not in accord with the code.
OUT OF THE SPUD (N) A green goods man.
OUTFIT OF DIGGERS (N) A pickpocket gang.
OUTSIDE MAN (N) A criminal lookout.
OUT-SIDER (N) A tool for turning a key from the opposite side to which it is inserted; one who is not an inmate.
OUTSIDE THE WALL (Adj) Outside of prison walls.
OVERBOARD (Adj) Dead.
OVERCOAT (N) Coffin.
OVERLOADING (N) Putting too heavy a charge of explosive in a safe.
OVERNIGHT BAG (N) A prostitute; a whore.
OVERNIGHT JOB (N) A car stolen the night before.
OVER THE HUMP (N) Drugged from using narcotics.
OVER THE RIVER (N-V) Sentence to prison; to escape.
OVER THERE (N) The death house.
OWL (N) A night street walker; a night theft.

OWL-HEAD ROD   (N)   A heavy revolver with a short barrel.

OWLS HEAD   (N)   A heavy revolver with a short barrel.

A-W-O-L   (N)   An escape.

OWNER'S JOB   (N)   A crime committed with the consent of the victim.

OXYGEN TANKS   (N)   Lungs.

OYSTER   (N)   One who advances money; a backer.

OYSTER FRUIT   (N)   Pearls.

P

P.A.   (N)   Prosecuting attorney.

PACK A HEAT   (V)   To carry a revolver or pistol.

PACK A JURY   (V)   To make up a jury in order to obtain a favorable verdict.

PACK OF ROCKS   (N)   A package of marihuana cigarettes.

PACK RAT   (N)   A prowler.

PACK THE BANNER   (V)   To walk the streets all night.

PAD   (N-V)   Highway robbery; to conceal loot on the person; a bed.

PAD MONEY   (N)   Money used for lodging; the admission charge to an opium den.

PAD THE HOOF   (V)   Take to the road.

PADDY   (N)   An Irishman; a padlock.

PADDY WAGON   (N)   A patrol wagon; a police patrol car.

PAID IN GOLD   (Adj)   Arrested after making a narcotic sale to a Federal Agent.

PAIN IN THE NECK   (N)   A vexatious person.

PAINT   (N)   Catsup.

PAINTED LADY   (N)   A prostitute; a whore.

PAIR OF BOX CARS   (N)   A pair of sixes in gambling.

PAIR OF SNAKE EYES   (N)   A pair of aces in gambling.

PALACE SLEEPER   (N)   A box car; living quarters

at a road camp.

PALE FACE   (N)   A white person.

PALE SAULT   (N)   A white woman.

PALLBEARER   (N)   A waiter's assistant.

PALM   (V)   To steal.

PALM OIL   (N)   A tip.

PAN   (N-V)   The face; an officer's badge; opium; the external parts of a female's sexual organs; the female pudendum; to belittle; to knock or vilify.

PANHANDLE   (N-V)   Begging; to beg on the street; to accost pedestrians and beg.

PANHANDLER   (N)   A beggar who begs on the street; a petty beggar.

PANHANDLER'S HEAVEN·   (N)   Boston, Mass.

PANEL HOUSE   (N)   A house of prostitution in which patrons are robbed.

PANEL JOINT   (N)   A house of prostitution in which patrons are robbed.

PANEL THIEF   (N)   One who operates in a panel house.

PANEL WORKER   (N)   A thief who uses a woman as decoy; a whore or prostitute who robs persons after enticing them into a room.

PANIC   (N)   Scarcity of drugs, usually caused by the arrest of a big peddler.

PANIC MAN   (N)   An addict desperate for narcotics.

PANSY   (N)   An effeminate man; a male homosexual.

PANSY BALL   (N)   A male homosexual dance.

PANSYLAND   (N)   The gathering place of male homosexuals.

PANTS RABBITS   (N)   Fleas; mites; lice.

PANTYWAIST   (N)   An effeminate man; a weakling.

PAP   (N)   A whore monger.

PAPER   (N)   Term used by pickpockets for newspaper or money; a small amount of narcotic done up in paper; bad checks; a railroad ticket.

PAPER HANGER   (N)   A forger; a passer of counterfeit money; a passer of bad checks.

PAPOOSE   (N)   A baby.

PARASITE   (N)   A member of the idle rich.

PARK (V) To leave for a considerable length of time.

PARK A HEAT (V) To put away a gun; to disarm.

PARK FLOPPER (N) One who sleeps on benches in parks.

PARK THE ARTILLERY (V) To disarm; to put away for safe keeping guns that are being carried.

PARLOR (N) A caboose; an establishment under criminal suspicion.

PARLOR JUMPING (N) House breaking.

PAROLED (Adj) Released from prison but not pardoned.

PART-TIME MAMA (N) A sweetheart or wife who goes out with other men.

PASHY PETTER (N) A passionate young woman.

PASS IN ONE'S CHECKS (V) To die.

PASS OUT (V) To die; to become thoroughly drunk.

PASS THE BUCK (V) To accuse another.

PASSAGE (N) The urethra; the urinary passage; the rectal passage.

PASSED THE BAR (Adj) No longer single.

PASSENGER STIFF (N) A tramp who rides passenger trains.

PASSION FLOWER (N) A passionate young woman.

PASTY (Adj) All right.

PASTY FACE (N) A drug addict.

PAT (N) An Irishman.

PAT POKE (N) A pickpocket's term for a wallet carried in the hip-pocket.

PATCHER (N) A claim agent.

PATRIOT (N) A romantic person.

PATSY (Adj) All right; O.K.; a victim; a dupe.

PAUL REVERE (N) A mounted policeman.

PAUP (N) A pauper.

PAVEMENT POUNDER (N) A prostitute; a whore; a policeman.

PAVVY (N) A peddler who sells merchandise which has been smuggled into the country duty free.

PAW (N-V) The hand; to belittle; to criticize.

PAY OFF (N) Confidence game using either racing or

stock market; a bribe; protection money; an equal division; a gift to a beggar; a stolen object; the cashier of a gang.

PAY-OFF GAME (N) A swindle in which sucker is told he has won but in which he must show certain amount of money before being paid off, then is robbed.

PAY-OFF MAN (N) A collector of protection money; the cashier of a mob; a policeman who collects protection money; a go between who adjusts differences with the law.

PAY STATION (N) A social welfare agency.

PEA (N) A French Canadian.

PEACH (N-V) A good looker; to inform against another; to betray another; to squeal; to blow.

PEANUT (N) A person of small stature or importance; small money; a petty theft; small stolen articles.

PEARL DIVER (N) A dishwasher; a sodomite.

PEARLDIVING (N) Dishwashing; sexual variance.

PEAS (N) Bullets; cartridges.

PEAT (N) A safe within a safe; a steel compartment within a safe.

PEAT MAN (N) A safe cracker.

PECK (N) A white person.

PECKER (N) The male pudendum.

PEDDLE RUBBER (V) To obtain money by means of worthless or forged negotiable paper.

PEDDLER (N) A prisoner who sells other prisoners' property; a pimp; a procurer; a slow freight train.

PEDIGREED CROOK (N) One with a police record.

PEE-EYED (N-Adj) A pimp; a procurer; intoxicated.

PEEKER (N) A detective; a plain cloth officer.

PEELER (N) A policeman; a cop. (Irish slang.)

PEEP (V) To talk.

PEEPING TOM (N) A window peeper.

PEET (N) Nitroglycerine; opiate; a safe.

PEEWEE (N) A small child; a peddler with a good sales talk.

PEG (N-V) One with a wooden leg; to recognize; to make.

PEG A JOINT   (V)   To place pegs in the jam of a door
   to determine if it has been opened; to keep watch on a
   certain place.
PEG HOUSE   (N)   A male homosexual gathering place;
   a brothel.
PEGGY   (N)   One with a wooden leg.
PELICAN   (N)   An old woman.
PEN   (N)   A prisoner; a penitentiary; a forger.
PEN AND INK   (N)   Stink.
PENCIL   (N)   A revolver or pistol.
PENITENTIARY SHOT   (N)   A drug injection made
   with a pin and using a medicine dropper.
PENMAN   (N)   An inmate informer.
PEN NAME   (N)   A prisoner's number.
PEN YEN   (N)   Opium.
PENNSYLVANIA FEATHERS   (N)   Coke   or   hard
   coal.
PENNY WEIGHT   (N)   A jewel robbery.
PENNY WEIGHTER   (N)   Person   who   substitutes
   paste or imitation diamonds; jewelry thieves.
PEONY WATER   (N)   A thin soup or soap.
PEPPER POT   (N)   A revolver or pistol.
PER   (N)   A prescription.
PERCENTAGE BULL   (N)   A   policeman   who   will
   accept a bribe.
PERJURE   (V)   To lie under oath; to go to the bat for.
PERSUADER   (N)   A policeman's billie; a burglar's
   jimmy; an employer of violence; weapons.
PETE   (N)   Nitroglycerine.
PETE BLOWER   (N)   A safe cracker.
PETER   (N)   safe;   drugs;   nitroglycerine;   opiate;
   knockout drops; a suit case; male pudendum.
PETER CLAIMING   (N)   Safe cracking.
PETERMAN   (N)   A safe cracker.
PETER MOB   (N)   A gang of safe crackers.
PETER OUT   (V)   To give out; to become exhausted.
PETER THROWER   (N)   A thief who uses knockout
   drops to steal from his victim.
PETER WORKER   (N)   A safe cracker.
PETTICOAT   (N)   A woman or girl.

PEW (N) The electric chair.

PITTSBURG FEATHERS (N) Coke or hard coal.

PHILADELPHIA LAWYER (N) A very shrewd lawyer.

PHONEY (N-Adj) An imposter; counterfeit; false;
imitation jewelry; worthless merchandise.

PHONEY COME-ON (N) A false enticement.

PHONEY CRIP (N) A beggar who pretends to be
crippled.

PHONEY DOUGH (N) Counterfeit coins.

PHONEY MONICA (N) A fake name.

PHONEY PLASTER (N) Counterfeit paper money.

PHONEY RAP (N-V) A false accusation; to lodge
false information against one.

PHONEY SOUPER (N) An imitation watch.

PHONEY SPARK (N) A paste diamond.

PHONEY TIP (N) False information.

PIANO (N) A convict's work bench.

PICK (N-V) A pickpocket; to steal.

PICK A BERRY (V) To steal from the clothesline.

PICK A GUMP (V) To steal a chicken.

PICK A LOCK (V) To perform an abortion.

PICK AND SHOVEL STIFF (N) A convict worker on
the rock pile.

PICKANINNY (N) A young child; a negro child.

PICK HER CHERRY (V) To take her virginity.

PICK MAN (N) One of gang of automobile thieves;
the one who locates cars to be stolen; a locater for
thieves.

PICKINGS (N) A stolen object.

PICKLE (V) To embalm.

PICK-UP (N) An arrest followed by no charges of a
crime; apprehension by the police; narcotic exhilaration.

PICTURE FRAME (N) The gallows.

PIDDLE (N) A hospital.

PIE BOOK (N) A book of meal tickets.

PIE CARD (N) One who furnishes meal to a beggar;
a meal ticket; one who advances money; a backer.

PIE-CARD MISSION (N) A mission that issues free meal tickets.

PIE-EYED (Adj) Intoxicated.

PIE IN THE SKY (N) A reward in heaven after you die.

PIE WAGON (N) A patrol wagon; a police patrol car.

PIECE (N) One ounce of narcotic; a share; sexual desire.

PIECE OF EVE'S FLESH (N) A woman; a girl.

PIECE OF TAIL (N) A woman; a girl; sexual intercourse.

PIECE OF WHITE MEAT (N) A woman or girl of the white race.

PIG (N) A person of unclean habits; a stool pigeon; one who eats too much; a squealer; a traitor; a leather wallet; a low dirty prostitute or whore; a locomotive; a dollar.

PIG IN THE MUD (N) An omelette of bacon.

PIG IRON (N) A hardware store.

PIGTAIL (N) A Chinaman.

PIG'S VEST WITH BUTTONS (N) Fat salt pork or bacon.

PIGEON (N) A stool pigeon; an informer; a victim; a dupe; a girl who accompanies smugglers to divert suspicion; an innocent person indicted for another.

PIGEON HOLES (N) The stocks.

PIGEON JOINT (N) A hardware store that sells burglar's tools.

PIGEON PLUCKER (N) A swindler.

PIGGING (N) Deserting.

PIKE THE EYE (V) To look at.

PIKER (N) A quitter; a coward; a hobo; a cheap skate; a petty crook; one who backs down on a bet.

PILL (N) A portion of opium rolled and prepared for cooking and smoking; a cigarette.

PILL COOKER (N) An opium addict.

PILL DISPENSER (N) A doctor or physician.

PILL DOCTOR (N) An inferior doctor.

PILL JOINT (N) A poolroom.

PILLINGS (N) A street beggar.

PILLOW (N) Knockout drops; opiate.

PILOT (N) A beggar who accompanies a blind beggar.

PIMP (N) A male supported by a prostitute or whore.

PIMP STICK (N) A cigarette.

PIMPLE (N) A pimp; a procurer.

PIN-SHOT (N) An injection of narcotic made by simply using a pin to make a large enough wound so the end of dropper may be inserted and injection made.

PINCH (N-V) A theft; stolen object; to arrest.

PINCH BACK (N) A prison uniform.

PINCH OFF (V) To steal.

PINCH OUT (N) Oil swindler's term for cutting down the flow of oil from a well.

PINCH PENNY (N) A Scotchman.

PINCHED (Adj) Arrested.

PINCHERS (N) Shoes.

PINEAPPLE (N) A bomb; a tear gas bomb.

PINEAPPLE GROWER (N) A bomb maker.

PINE OVERCOAT (N) A coffin.

PING SHOT (N) An injection of narcotic made by using a pin and a medicine dropper.

PING IN WING (N) An injection of narcotic.

PING-PONG (N) One who curry's mules.

PIN HEAD (N) A drug addict; a clerk; a fool.

PINK (N) Pinkerton detective.

PINK EYE (N) A Pinkerton detective.

PINKIE (N) Pinkerton detective.

PIN-YEN (N) Opium.

PIN-YEN TOY (N) A small tin box used for prepared opium.

PIPE (N-V) Something easy; a person under the influence of intoxicants; the urethra; to look.

PIPE-DOWN (N-V) Keeping quiet; to cease talking.

PIPE DREAM (N) The dream of an opium smoker.

PIPE FIEND (N) An opium addict.

PIPE OFF (V) To make clever remarks; to do much talking.

PIPE THE BULL (V) To spy for the police.

PIPE THE STEM (V) To beg on the streets.

PIPED (Adj) Under the influence of narcotics; intoxicated.

PIPEY (Adj) Under the influence of opium.

PIRATE (N-V) A pimp who steals another's mistress; to steal.

PISS AND PUNK (N) Prison fare of bread and water.

PISS CAN (N) A toilet; a privy; a rest room.

PISSHOUSE (N) A police station; a toilet; a privy; a rest room.

PIT (N) Pickpocket's term for the inside pockets of a coat or vest.

PIT POKE (N) Pickpocket's term for the inside pocket in which the wallet is carried.

PITCH (V) To peddle or smuggle narcotics.

PLACE (N) Horse coming second in race.

PLAINER (N) A street beggar.

PLANK DOWN (V) To spy; to contribute.

PLANT (N-V) A cash for loot; a hiding place of a criminal; a place located for crime; a place where synthetic liquor is made; a detective or spy hired to watch workers; a place where opium is cooked; a frame up; a confidence game; to produce fraudulent evidence; to an overindulgence in narcotics.

PLANT A TOWN (V) To survey a town and establish connections for a swindle game or other crimes.

PLANT RACKET (N) Swindling game.

PLANTED (Adj) Hid; buried; saved.

PLANTING (N) A funeral.

PLASTER (N) A dollar bill.

PLASTERED (Adj) Intoxicated; drunk.

PLATE (N) A badge.

PLATE OF MYSTERY (N) Hash.

PLATES (N) The feet.

PLATTERS OF MEAT (N) The feet.

PLAY (V) To scheme; to rob; to gamble.

PLAY DUMB (N-V) A refusal; to confess.

PLAY FOR A SUCKER (V) To cheat; to swindle; to take a person's money and give him little or nothing.

PLAY-GIRL (N) A female of easy morals; a lively passionate woman.

PLAY NOSE CHECKERS (N) To look through the bars of a prison.

PLAY POSSUM (V) To act dumb; to hide.

PLAY THE GRIND ORGAN (V) To shoot a machine gun.

PLAYING AROUND (N) When an addict has been off the drug and begins to use a little now and then.

PLAYING THE NOD (V) To doze or go to sleep from an overindulgence in narcotics.

PLAYTHING (N) A woman or young girl who is a companion to any male; one that is easily made.

PLEASURE-SMOKER (N) One who smokes the opium pipe now and then but is not addicted; an irregular smoker of opium.

PLEASURE USER (N) One who uses narcotics now and then for pleasure only and is not addicted.

PLUCK (V) The plunder; to fleece.

PLUG (N-V) A fellow; a desperado or thug; a horse; to shoot; to kill.

PLUGGER (N) One who encourages others to enter a game of chance; an energetic worker; a gun-man.

PLUGGING PARTY (N) A gun battle.

PLUSH (N-V) Money; to be in good circumstances.

PLUTE (N) A member of the idle rich.

POACH (V) To steal.

POCKET-PROWL (N) Pocket picking by a pickpocket.

POCKET-PROWLER (N) A pickpocket.

POCKET TWISTER (N) A young woman who accepts a male's attention only for the sake of his gifts.

POCO (N) An old clothesman.

POGE (N) A pocket book.

POGEY (N) A prison hospital; a poorhouse; a county jail.

POGGIE (N) A jail.

POINT SHOT (N) An injection of narcotic made with the use of a pin and medicine dropper.

POISON (N) A doctor who will not sell narcotics to an addict; a tobacco train.

POISON JOINT (N) A drug store; pharmacy.

POKE (N) A wallet; a pocket-book; a purse; (Terms used by pickpockets.) ; a jab.

POKE-A-MOKE (N) A policy game; a swindling game in which a swindler finds a purse or let's the victim find it and return it to the owner, the owner being a confederate, will then give them a good tip on an investment as a reward.

POKE COPPER (N) A purse snatcher.

POKE OF LEATHER (N) A pocket book.

POKE OUT (N) A meal given to a beggar.

POKE-SACK (N) A pocket.

POKER FACE (N) A face which shows no evidence of changing emotions or thoughts.

POKEY STIFF (N) A house to house beggar.

POLICE DICK (N) A plain clothesman.

POLICE MOLL (N) A policewoman.

POLICE STORM (N) The third degree.

POLICE UP (V) To assault.

POLISH OFF (V) To kill.

POLITICAL PAUPER (N) One holding office under a political government.

POLY (N) A prison clerk.

PONCE (N) A lover of a prostitute or whore.

POOL (N) An aggregated stake to which each player has contributed.

PLOUGH JOCKEY (N) A farmer.

PLOW THE DEEP (V) To sleep.

POP (N) An injection of narcotic by hypodermic needle; a pistol or revolver.

POP SHOP (N) A place where stolen goods are disposed of by criminals.

POPPY (N) Opium.

POPPY ALLEY (N) An opium district.

POPPY HEAD (N) An opium addict.

POPPY TRAIN (N) Opium.

PORCH (N) A prison yard.

PORCH CLIMBER (N) A second story burglar; a house prowler who enters through an upstairs window.

PORCH CLIMBING (N) Entering through an upstairs window for the purpose of committing burglary.

PORK (N) A Jew; a corpse.

PORK BARREL (N) A graft fund; the spoils of office.

PORK CHOPS (N) Food, a term used by tramps.

PORK DUMP (N) Clinton Prison, New York.

PORK PACKER (N) A person with a morbid fondness for dead bodies.

PORKER (N) A Jew.

POSSESH (N) A boy catamite who travels with an older tramp.

POSSUM BELLY (V) To lie flat on one's stomach; to ride on the deck of a train car; to ride on the deck of the tool box under a car.

POST BILLS (V) To pass counterfeit money.

POT GANG (N) A gang of tramps who eat together while at a jungle.

POT OF HONEY (N) Wealth; a large amount of money.

POT RASSLER (N) A cook; a dish washer.

POT WATCHER (N) A street beggar.

POTEEN (N) Irish whiskey.

POTIGUAYA (N) Crude marihuana.

POULTICE (N) A money belt worn next to the body; bread and jam or gravy.

PULTRY (N) A female; a woman.

POUND THE AIR (V) To sleep.

POUND THE BELL (V) To sleep.

POUND THE EAR (V) To sleep.

POUND THE HIGHWAY (V) To take to the road.

POUND THE PAVEMENT (V) To walk the streets.

POUND THE TRACKS (V) To walk along the railroad track.

POUR (V) To shoot.

POW (N) A pistol or revolver.

POWDER (V) To depart; to escape; to flee; to run away.

POWDER HAND (N) The person who handles dynamite on a construction gang.

POWDER MONKEY (N) The one who handles dynamite on a construction gang.

POWDER PUFF (N) A silly girl; an effeminate man.

POWER (N) A charge of explosive in a safe blowing.

POX (N) A ration of opium prepared for smoking.

PRAT (N) The searching and robbing of a person; the rectum or posterior; pickpocket term for hip pocket.

PRAT BOYS (N) Members of a pickpocket gang who gently bumps against victims about to be taken by a pickpocket, done to distract victim's attention.

PRAT DIGGER (N) A pickpocket.

PRAT FRISK (N) A pickpocket stealing a purse from victim's hip pocket.

PRAT-KICK (N) A hip-pocket.

PRAT MAN (N) One who searches a person; a pickpocket.

PRAT POKE (N) A pocket book.

PRATT (N) The rectum; the posterior.

PRATT DIGGING (N) The stealing, by a pickpocket, from the hip pocket.

PRATT LEATHER (N) A pocket book kept in the hip pocket.

PRATT POKE (N) A pocket book kept in the hip pocket.

PRESHEN (N) A boy tramp, a catamite, who travels with an older tramp.

PRESS BRICK (V) To wander about town.

PRETTY ANKLE (N) An attractive young woman.

PRETTY BOY (N) An employer of violence.

PRETZEL BENDER (N) A player of the French horn.

PRICK (N) A hard taskmaster; the male pudendum.

PRICKLEY (N) Air getting into the vein while a drug addict is injecting a shot.

PRIDE AND JOY (N) A boy.

PRIG (V) To pilfer; to practice petty theft; to steal.

PRIGGISH (V) To steal; to practice thievery.

PRIGGISM (N) Habit of stealing; addiction to theft.

PRIMED TO THE EARS (N) Drugged.

PRINTS (N) Fingerprints.

PRISON CRAZY (Adj) Having the mind affected by serving a long prison sentence.

PRISON JUNKER (N) A prisoner who uses drugs.

PRIVATE JOB (N) The burglary of a private residence.

PRIVATE OFFICE (N) A toilet; a privy; a rest room.

PRIVATE PROWL (N) The burglary of a private residence.

PRIVATE PROWLER (N) A residence burglar.

PRO (N) A prosecuting attorney; a liquor enforcement agent.

PROG (N) A meal given a beggar.

PROHI (N) A Federal liquor enforcement agent.

PROMENADE (N) A prisoner removed to the death house.

PROMOT (V) To patronize an illicit affair.

PROMOTE (V) To steal; to plan a theft; to inform against a person.

PROMOTION (N) A theft.

PRONE THE BODY (V) To sleep.

PROOF CRIB (N) A safe that is burglar proof.

PROP (N) A stickpin; crutches; a stolen diamond stickpin.

PROP GETTER (N) A pickpocket who steals stickpins.

PROP GETTERS (N) Pickpockets who make a specialty of lifting stickpins.

PROP MAN (N) A pickpocket who steals stickpins.

PROP WIRES (N) Pickpockets who steal stickpins.

PROTECTION (N) Money extorted by racketeers as insurance against threatened violence; forgiveness of an offense, extended to crooks by dishonest officials.

PROWL (N-V) A sneak theft; to make an investigation prior to committing the crime.

PROWL A HOUSE (V) To make an investigation of a residence prior to burglarizing same.

PROWL A POCKET (V) To work at picking pockets.

PROWL A PRIVATE (V) To burglarize a private residence.

PROWL CAR (N) A police radio car.

PROWL THE JOINT (V) To search the place.

PROWLER (N) A sneak thief; a burglar; one who searches steadily.

PRUSSIAN (N) A tramp who has a boy to beg for him; a tramp accompanied by a young man.

PSALM SINGER (N) A prison trusty; an informer.

PSYCHOLOGICAL MOMENT (N) The right time to accomplish a thing.

PUBLIC ENEMY (N) A criminal.

PUBLIC ENEMY NUMBER ONE (N) The most vicious criminal operating at any given time.

PUFF (N-V) Explosive powder; a charge of explosive in safe blowing; to blow a safe; to land.

PUFF BOX (N) A machine gun.

PUFFER (N) One who speaks well of another.

PUFFING (N) Smoking opium.

PULL (V) To arrest; to steal.

PULL A BEEF (V) To commit an error.

PULL A BONNER (V) To make a mistake.

PULL A BRODIE (V) To fail.

PULL A FAST ONE (V) To cheat; to swindle; to play a clever trick.

PULL A JOB (V) To commit a crime.

PULL A TRICK (V) To commit a criminal offense.

PULL IN YOUR EARS (V) To be quiet.

PULL THE PIN (V) To leave one place for another; to go.

PULL THE STAKE (V) To withdraw a bet.

PULL THE SUBON (V) To tell a hard luck story.

PULLER (N) A smuggler of liquor; a tool for pulling the combination from a safe; a pickpocket.

PULLET (N) A young adolescent girl.

PUMPS (N) The female breasts.

PUNCH (V) To force open; to crack a safe.

PUNCH THE WIND (V) To ride on the outside of a train.

PUNCHER (N) A safe cracker.

PUNK (N) A young man who acts as the apprentice and opens buildings so safe man may enter; a boy tramp who travels with an older tramp; a catamite; a pervert.

PUNK AND GUT (N) Bread and sausage.

PUNK AND PLASTER (N) Bread and butter.

PUNK KID (N) A boy who begs and panhandles for beggars; a catamite; a young child.

PUNKIN YELLOW (N) A mulatto.

PUPPIES (N) The feet.

PUPPY (N) A newly painted stolen car.

PUPS (N) The feet.

PUSH (N-V) Associated; a crowd; a gang of tramps; to peddle or smuggle narcotics; to pass counterfeit money.

PUSH 'EM UP (N) A robber's command to stick up your hands.

PUSH-EM UP STICK (N) A revolver or pistol.

PUSH ON (N) A passionate female; lust; passion.

PUSH OVER (N) A young woman of loose morals; an easy job; an easy victim; a weakling; a coward; an easy case.

PUSH UP (N) Robbery at the point of a gun.

PUSH UP THE DAISIES (V) To be buried; to be dead.

PUSHER (N) A gang leader; a foreman; a prostitute; a whore; a narcotic peddler.

PUSHER-OUT (N) One who dispenses drugs.

PUSS (N) The face; milk; a female's genitals.

PUSSY (N) An effeminate boy; the female's genitals; a female pudendum; a young girl or woman.

PUSSY BUMPER (N) A sodomite.

PUSSY BUMPING (N) Sexual variance.

PUSSY FOOTERS (N) Gumshoes worn by burglars.

PUT AWAY (N-V) Imprisoned; to imprison in a penitentiary.

PUT HIS BACK UP (N) A pickpocket's accomplice who distracts a victim by placing him in a good position for the pickpocket.

PUT IN A STATE OF SUSPENSE (V) To hang.

PUT IN THE CAN (V-Adj) To imprison; placed in prison.

PUT IN THE FEELERS (V) To cross-examine a prisoner.

PUT IN THE MIDDLE (V) To be placed in an untenable or dangerous position.

PUT IT ON THE CUFF   (V)   To buy on credit.

PUT MACK ON IT   (V)   To blow a safe.

PUT ON ICE   (Adj-V)   Imprisoned; to place in prison; to kill; to murder.

PUT ON THE GRILL   (V)   Give the third degree; cross examine a prisoner.

PUT ON THE PRESSURE   (V)   To cross examine; to give the third degree.

PUT ON THE SPOT   (N-V)   A prison discipline compelling a prisoner to stand in one spot for a long time; to assassinate; to mark for assassination; to mark for killing.

PUT ON THE VARNISH GOPHER   (V)   To seek to gain favor by flattery.

PUT OVER A JOB   (V)   To victimize.

PUT OVER A RACKET   (V)   To victimize; to be made a victim by deception.

PUT OVER A SCORE   (V)   To victimize; to dupe; to cheat.

PUT THE ARMS ON   (V)   To commit robbery by the use of the strangle hold.

PUT THE BLAST ON   (V)   To shoot.

PUT THE BEE ON   (V)   To swindle; to cheat; to defraud.

PUT THE CHOKE ON   (V)   To commit a robbery by the use of the strangle hold.

PUT THE CLAMPS ON   (V)   To suppress crime in a community.

PUT THE CLOWN TO BED   (V)   To make sure an officer is home before committing a crime in his territory.

PUT THE CLUB ON   (V)   To beat with a club.

PUT THE CROSS ON   (V)   To mark for death; to place on the spot.

PUT THE DUKES DOWN   (V)   To pick pockets.

PUT THE FINGER ON   (V)   To betray to the police; to identify; to point out; to accuse another; to mark for death.

PUT THE GUN ON   (V)   To rob at the point of a gun.

PUT THE SCREWS (V) To employ physical violence or coercion; to give the third degree.

PUT THE STING ON (V) To swindle; to cheat; to defraud.

PUT THE SQUEEZE ON (V) To extort by intimidation.

PUT THE TOUCH ON (V) To rob a person; to be a victim of a pickpocket.

PUT THE WORKS ON (V) To employ violence.

PUTT-PUTT (N) An outboard motor used in liquor running.

PUT-UP JOB (N) A conspiracy; a plot.

Q

QUACK (N) A patent medicine seller.

QUAIL (N) An unmarried woman; an old maid; a spinster; a woman or young girl.

QUALITY GENTLEMAN (N) A gentleman by birth and education.

QUALITY WORKER (N) A peddler who sells articles made of wire.

QUARRY CURE (V) To kick the drug habit cold turkey in jail or prison.

QUARTER PIECE (N) A fourth of an ounce of narcotic.

QUEEN (N) A charming young woman; an effeminate man; everybody's sweetheart.

QUEENIE (N) A male homosexual; a woman or girl.

QUEER (N) Counterfeit money; insane; false; a petty crook; a homosexual criminal.

QUEER A FLAT (V) To swindle; to cheat; to defraud.

QUEER IN THE HEAD (Adj) Insane; crazy.

QUEER JACK (N) Counterfeit money.

QUEER QUEEN (N) A masculine woman.

QUEER SHOVER (N) One who passes counterfeit money or bad checks.

QUEERED (Adj) Disappointed.

QUEERVERT (N) A homosexual.

QUILL   (N)   A steam locomotive whistle. (Term used by hobos) ; genuine whiskey.
QUIN   (N)   Genuine whiskey.
QUINEA FOOTBALL   (N)   A tear gas bomb.
QUIRT   (N)   A small child; a small person.

R

RABBIT   (N)   A coward; a fugitive.
RABBIT FOOT   (N)   An escaped prisoner; a prisoner not to be trusted.
RABBIT HEART   (N)   One of a cowardly nature.
RACKET   (N)   A criminal scheme for obtaining money; any questionable business or undertaking; a criminal vocation or enterprise; an illegitimate business.
RACKET BOY   (N)   A petty crook.
RACKET LANE   (N)   The underworld outside of prison walls.
RACKET MAN   (N)   A petty crook.
RACKET MOLL   (N)   A woman criminal.
RACKET PUSHER   (N)   A gangster leader.
RACKET WORK   (N)   A criminal enterprise.
RACKETEER   (N-V)   One who obtains money by criminal means; one who profits by a racket; a petty crook; person who earns his living in an illegitimate way; to commit a crime.
RACKETRESS   (N)   A woman criminal who profits by a racket.
RAFFLES   (N)   A burglar.
RAFTER CREEPER   (N)   A skylight burglar.
RAG   (N)   Money; a woman or girl.
RAG AFLAG   (N)   Paper money.
RAG AND BONE   (N)   A woman or girl.
RAG DOLL   (N)   An untidy or slovenly woman.
RAG HEAD   (N)   A Hindu.
RAIL   (N)   A railroad watchman or detective.
RAILROAD   (V)   To be sent to prison after a hasty and apparently inadequate trial; to sentence or convict unjustly.

RAIN CHECK (N) The change of a death penalty to a life sentence; the change of a penalty or punishment to a lesser one; a polite way of turning down an invitation; a special check issued to ticket holder.

RAISE (V) To steal.

RAISE UP (N) Robbery at the point of a gun.

RAKE-OFF (N-V) A dishonest profit; bribe money; a gift to a beggar; to receive extortion money; to practice petty theft.

RALL (N) Any wasting disease.

RAMBLER WOLF (N) A tramp who rides passenger trains.

RAMMER (N) The arms.

RAMROD (N) The male pudendum.

RAMRODS THE OUTFIT (N) The leader of a criminal gang.

RANGE LINE (N) A kitchen job.

RANGER (N) A prowler.

RANK (Adj-V) Rotten; vile; no good; to blunder; to spoil; to hinder an unsuccessful crime; to fizzle; to inform on a pal.

RANK A JOB (V) To make a failure or blunder on a job; commit an unsuccessful crime.

RANK CAT (N) A low dirty tramp.

RANKED (Adj) Gone away.

RANSOMAN (N) The go between or the handler of the money in a kidnapping.

RAP (N-V) A prison term; a punishment; a criminal charge; a warrant of arrest; a jail sentence; a court trial; a betrayal; an accusation; to prosecute.

RAP FOR THE HOT SQUAT (N) A sentence to be electrocuted.

RAPE HOUND (V) To receive a sentence for raping.

RAPPER (N) A prosecutor; a complainant; a judge; a witness.

RARE (N) Inhalation of cocaine or heroin.

RARE DISH (N) An attractive young woman; a virtuous woman.

RASPBERRY (N-V) A heart; to ridicule or send away; to flaunt.

RASPBERRY TART (N) The heart.

RASTUS (N) A male negro.

RAT (N-V) A traitor; one who informs the police; a stool pigeon; a squealer; prisoner who steals from another; a thief; one who turns states evidence; a freight train; a box car; a private detective or spy hired to watch workers; to rob a corpse; to work as a strike breaker.

RAT AND MOUSE (N) A house.

RAT CAPER (N) A swindling; a petty trick.

RAT-CRUSH (N-V) A freight car burglary; to rob a box car.

RAT CRUSHER (N) One who burglarizes freight cars.

RAT HOLE (N) An informer's hangout; a basement relief station.

RATION (N) The addict's regular dose; (the size depends on how long he has been using it).

RATS AND MICE (N) Dice.

RATS IN THE ATTIC (Adj) Insane; crazy.

RAT'S NEST (N) A group of informers; a hangout of informers.

RATTLE (V) To blackmail.

RATTLEBONES (N) A skinny person.

RATTLESNAKE (N) A machine gun; a machine gun in action.

RATTLE THE CUP (V) To turn informer.

RATTLE UP (V) To burglarize a freight car while it is moving.

RATTLER (N) A car; a freight car; a locomotive; a stool pigeon informer.

RAVEN BEAUTY (N) A beautiful negress.

RAW HIDE (N) A hard worker; a severe task master.

READER (N) A prescription; a warrant for arrest; a wanted man; a circular; a pocket book.

READERS (N) Playing cards marked on the back.

REAL GREEN (N) Wealth; a large amount of money; being well supplied with money.

REAL McCOY (N) The real thing; a clever crook.

REALIZE (V) To obtain money by begging.

REAM (V) To commit sodomy.

REAMER (N) A sodomite; a male pudendum; the penis.

REBECCA (N) A Jewess.

RECEIVING SET (N) The female pudendum.

RECLAIM (V) To marry a divorced person.

RECORD (N) Police history.

RED (N) A Russian; gold; a penny.

RED BALL (N) A fast freight train.

RED COMB (N) Lust; passion.

RED CROSS (N) Morphine.

RED EYE (Adj) Catsup; intoxicated.

RED EYES (N) Fried eggs.

RED OUT (N) Red sausage.

RED HERRING (V) To mislead.

RED HOT (N) A passionate woman; a wanted criminal; a petty crook.

RED HOT MAMA (N) A passionate young woman.

RED HOT WIPER (N) An assassin; a killer.

RED INK (N) Cheap wine.

RED LEAD (N) Catsup.

RED LIGHT (N-V) A whore house; a house of prostitution; to kill.

RED LIGHT SISTER (N) A whore; a prostitute.

RED LIGHTER (N) A whore; a prostitute.

RED NECK (N) A union man; a criminal who carrys a union card for a stall.

RED SHIRT (N) A prisoner who is incorrigible.

RED SLANG (N) A gold watch chain.

RED TAPE (N) The tongue.

RED TICKET (N) A permit to visit a prisoner.

RED TOY (N) A gold watch.

REEF (N-V) The lifting of a purse by a pickpocket; pocket picking by a pickpocket; to steal and make a false replacement.

REEF A BREECH (V) To lift a purse (A pickpocket term).

REEF A KICK (V) To pick a pocket by gently pulling out the lining (a pickpocket term).

REEF A LEATHER (V) To pick a pocket of a purse; to pick a purse by gently pulling out the lining.

REEF A TICKER   (V)   To pick a pocket of a watch.
REEFED   (Adj)   After a pickpocket has accomplished his lift he uses this slang.
REEFER   (N)   Marihuana cigarette; a refrigerator car; a pickpocket.
REEFING MAN   (N)   A marihuana smoker.
REF   (N)   A reformatory.
REGISTER   (N)   An addict practice of permitting the blood to appear in the medicine or eye dropper before making the injection, to be sure that the needle is in the vein.
REGULAR   (N)   A habitual criminal; a criminal who is frequently imprisoned; an equal division.
REINDEERS   (N)   The ears.
REINDEER DUST   (N)   Cocaine; heroin; morphine.
RELIEF STATION   (N)   A toilet; a privy; a rest room.
RELIEVERS   (N)   Shoes.
RELOAD   (V)   To victimize a person for the second time.
RELOADING   (V)   To victimize a person for the second time on worthless stocks.
REMITTANCE STIFF   (N)   A tramp whose family does not want him to return home and sends him money at intervals.
REP   (N)   Reputation.
REPAIR SHOP   (N)   A hospital.
REPEATER   (N)   A criminal who is frequently imprisoned.
REPEATERS   (N)   Beans.
REST CAMP   (N)   A cemetery.
REST HOME   (N)   A prison where the prisoner's work is easy.
REST HOUSE   (N)   A prison where the prisoner's work is easy.
REST POWDER   (N)   Snuff.
RETAKE   (N)   Term used by thieves who by impersonating officers, after taking a victim's money, go back for more.
REVENUE   (N)   A revenue officer.

REVENUER (N) A revenue officer.

R.F.D. DOPEHEAD (N) A drug addict who travels about in the country or small towns to obtain his supply from doctors.

RHINO (N) Money; cash.

RIB (N-V) A bed; a woman or girl; to influence; to goad; to kid; to beguile.

RIB ROAST (N) A young child; an infant.

RIB STICKERS (N) Beans.

RIB UP (V) To accuse falsely; to sentence or convict unjustly; to give false evidence with the intention of convicting falsely.

RICKETTY (N) Sticks of wood; ticks.

RIDE (N-V) A District Attorney; to sentence or convict unjustly; to accuse falsely; to take a victim to a remote spot for the purpose of killing him.

RIDE THE BELLY (V) To ride the draw bars of a freight train.

RIDE THE CUSHIONS (V) To have plenty of money; to ride in a passenger coach.

RIDE THE DECK (V) To commit sodomy.

RIDE THE GRAVY TRAIN (V) To have plenty of money; to be wealthy.

RIDE THE PLUSH (V) To have plenty of money; to ride in a passenger coach.

RIDE UNDER COVER (V) To ride inside a passenger coach.

RIDING A WAVE (Adj) Drugged by the use of narcotics.

RIDGE (N) A gold coin of any denomination.

RIDING ON THE CUSHIONS (N) Being well supplied with money; in good circumstances.

RIG (N) A suit; the layout of a crime.

RIGHT (N) A person to be trusted; having a good reputation with the gang; a friend.

RIGHT BRITCH (N) A term used by pickpockets for the right front trouser pocket.

RIGHT COP (N) A policeman who will accept a bribe.

RIGHT CROAKER (N) A doctor who sells narcotics illegally.

RIGHT D.A. (N) A District Attorney in sympathy with the underworld.
RIGHT FALL (N) Legitimate arrest.
RIGHT GUY (N) A friend; a person to be trusted.
RIGHT LIP (N) A lawyer who is in sympathy with the underworld.
RIGHT ON THE BALL (Adj) Done correctly.
RIGHT PRATT (N) A term used by pickpockets for the right rear trouser pocket.
RIGHTY (N) A person who has lost a right arm or leg; a duplicate key; a disguise.
RIM (V) To cheat; to swindle; to defraud.
RING FINGER (N) A blast used in the combination of a safe.
RING TAIL (N) An ill natured person; an ill natured tramp.
RING TAIL WIFE (N) A catamite; a boy kept for unnatural purpose by a tramp.
RING TAIL BELL (N-V) Two persons of equal passion; to win the case; to be acquitted.
RING UP (V) To alter stolen goods' appearance; to disguise.
RINGER (N-V) A duplicate; of the same kind; a substitute; a bell; to look alike.
RINGER EYE (N) A visible burglar alarm; a door bell.
RINSINGS (N) The residue taken from cloth through which drugs have been strained.
RIP (V) To steal with impunity.
RIPPER (N) A vicious attacker of women; tool used by burglars in opening windows, doors and safes.
RISER (N) An artificial sore.
RIVER HOUSE (N) Ohio State penitentiary.
RIVER RAT (N) A thief who steals on the river front.
RIVETER (N) A machine gun; one who handles a machine gun.
ROACH (N) Marihuana cigarettes; a marihuana smoker.
ROAD AGENT (N) A highway robber.

ROAD BO (N) A tramp; a tramp who does not vol-
untarily work.
ROAD HOG (N) A tramp who travels a great deal;
a customer who does not tip.
ROAD KID (N) A boy tramp companion of an older
tramp; a catamite.
ROAD MALE (N) A female tramp.
ROAD SISTER (N) A female tramp.
ROAD STAKE (N) A tramp's money saving for travel.
ROAD STIFF (N) A tramp; a hobo; a tramp who does
not voluntarily work.
ROAD WISE (Adj) Experienced in tramp life.
ROAR (N-V) An alarm given after a crime is com-
mitted; to complain.
ROAST (V) To be electrocuted.
ROASTING (N) The third degree.
ROBBER STICK (N) A stick carried by a foreman.
ROB THE MAIL (V) To eat choice bits.
ROCK (N) A black jack weighted with lead; a dollar.
ROCKS (N) Diamonds; gems.
ROCKS AND BOULDERS (N) The shoulder.
ROCK CANDY (N) Diamonds; gems.
ROCK PILE (N) Where prisoners break rocks; a jail
sentence.
ROCK PULLER (N) A gem smuggler.
ROCK WORKER (N) A cheap jewelry peddler.
ROCKETS (N) Marihuana cigarettes.
ROD (N) A gun; a weapon.
ROD MAN (N) A tramp who rides the rods of a freight
train.
ROD OUT (N) A death by shooting.
ROD ROUTE (N) A death by shooting.
ROD UP (N-V) Armed; to arm one's self with a gun.
RODS (N) The under bracing of a freight train.
RODSMAN (N) A tramp who rides the rods of a freight
train.
ROLL (N-V) A bundle of money; personal wealth;
to steal from one who is asleep or drunk.
ROLL A FLOP (V) To steal from a sleeping person.

ROLL A LUSH (V) To steal from an intoxicated person.

ROLL A PILL (V) To prepare opium for smoking.

ROLL OVER (N) The night before being released from prison.

ROLL THE BOY (V) To smoke opium.

ROLLER (N) A prostitute or whore who robs her patrons; one who steals from sleeping or intoxicated persons.

ROLLER-SKATER (N) A young girl who walks home from an automobile petting party.

ROLLING STUFF (V) To be transporting narcotics.

ROLLING THE LOG (N) The act of smoking opium.

ROOFER (N) A tramp who rides the roof of trains.

ROOKIE (N) A new policeman; a prison guard.

ROOM (N) A prison cell.

ROOSTER BRAND (N) A cheap grade of bootleg opium which is refined from residue.

ROOSTER CHASER (N) A lascivious man.

ROOT (N) A pickpocket who causes a crash to take place in a crowd or jostles his victim in order to pick his pocket.

ROOT WITH THE OLIVER (V) To commit a crime while the moon is not shining.

ROPE (N-V) Death by hanging; a hangman's noose; a necklace; to frame.

ROSCO (N) A revolver or pistol.

ROSCOES (N) Automatic pistols.

ROSIE LEE (N) Tea.

ROTARY (N) A circular group of prison cells.

ROUGH EM (N) A pickpocket who causes a crush to take place in a crowd or jostles his victim in order to pick his pocket.

ROUGH NECK (N) A bully; a fighter; a rough fighter; an honest laborer.

ROUMANIAN BOX TRICK (N) A swindle game in which victim places money in a money making machine and loses it.

ROUND HEAD (N) A Swede.

ROUND HEELS (N) A detective; plain clothes officers.

ROUND HOUSE   (N)   A ladies' rest room.

ROUNDER   (N)   A person of sporting tendencies; an habitual criminal; one who is in prison frequently.

ROUNDING   (N)   Betraying.

ROUNDING TO   (N)   Coming to ones senses.

ROUNDUP   (N)   A wholesale arrest.

ROUST   (V)   To put out; to jostle; to steal from an intoxicated person.

ROUSTABOUT   (N)   A person out of employment; one whose means of livelihood is questionable.

ROUTE   (N)   Suicide.

ROWDY   (N)   One who causes a crush in a crowd; one who jostles a victim so his pocket may be picked.

ROWDY-DOWDY   (N)   The act of causing a crush in a crowd.

RUB DOWN   (V)   To be given the third degree.

RUB OUT   (V)   To kill.

RUBBER   (N-Adj)   A paid assassin; a killer; forged.

RUBBER BUM   (N)   One who travels in a cheap automobile, usually with a family.

RUBBER CHECK   (N)   A forged check; a no good check.

RUBBER EAR   (N)   One who has a tendency to listen in on other people's conversation.

RUBBER GLUE   (N)   A detective; a plain clothes officer.

RUBBER HEEL   (N)   A detective; a plain clothes officer .

RUBBER HEELS   (N)   Hash; meat loaf.

RUBBER MAN   (N)   A toy balloon vender.

RUBBER NECK   (N)   A worthless check; an inquisitive person; a gawky person.

RUBBER SOCK   (N)   A timid person.

RUBBER TIRED GOODS   (N)   Horn-rimmed glasses.

RUBBER TRAMP   (N)   A tramp who travels in a cheap automobile, usually with a family.

RUBE   (N)   A hoosier; a farmer; an employee of a circus; an easy person; a stranger in town.

RUBY NOSE   (N)   The nose.

RUM AROUND (N-V) Deceit; to give wrong information; to double cross.

RUM BEAK (N) A judge open to bribery.

RUM DUM (N) A shiftless, no account, drunken person; intoxicated.

RUM RING (N) A liquor gang.

RUM RUNNING (N) Illicit liquor transporting.

RUMBLE (N-V) Term used by pickpockets when victim feels his purse being taken; to spoil or hinder; to recognize.

RUMBLED (Adj) Detected when trying to pick a pocket.

RUMMY (N) A picker of grapes; a wine worker.

RUN A TEMPERATURE (V) To be in a passionate condition.

RUN GOODS (N) Smuggled goods.

RUN IN (V) To be arrested.

RUN OUT (V) To escape.

RUN THE ROADS DOWN (V) To plan the escape from the scene of a crime which is to take place.

RUN THE RULE OVER (V) To search a person.

RUNG UP (N) Altered in appearance.

RUNNER (N) A pimp; a procurer; a messenger; one who carries messages in prison; a smuggler of liquor.

RUNNING JEANS (N) Bibbed overalls.

RUNT (N) A very small person.

RUSSIAN BOOTS (N) Leg irons.

RUSSIAN ROULETTE (N) Placing a cartridge in the cylinder of a revolver, spinning the cylinder and then placing the muzzle of the gun against the temple and pulling the trigger.

RUST EATER (N) A track layer; a structural iron worker.

RUST IN (V) To settle down and remain in one place.

RUSTLER (N) A cattle thief; a pimp or procurer.

S

S.A. (N) A State Attorney.

SACK (N) The scrotum; the pouch which contains the testicles.

SACK OF DUST (N) A sack of smoking tobacco.

SADDLE AND BRIDLE (N) An opium smoker; an opium outfit.

SADDLE BLANKETS (N) Pan cakes.

SAD PAN (N) A face with a suffering look.

SAFETY FIRST (N) A welfare worker.

SAFETY PIN (N) Bail; a bondsman.

SAGE BRUSH SAVAGE (N) A cattle ranch worker.

SAIL (V) To consent to sell an addict narcotics.

SAILS (N) The ears.

SAILING (N) Listening.

SAILOR'S BAIT (N) A prostitute; a whore; a woman; a girl.

SAILOR'S DELIGHT (N) A prostitute; a whore; a woman of easy morals.

SALESLADY (N) A prostitute; a whore.

SALESMAN (N) A homosexual who looks for patrons; a pimp; a procurer.

SALLY (N) A Salvation Army girl.

SALT CREEK (N) A jail; an electrocution; the electric chair.

SALT DOWN (V) To be imprisoned.

SALT WATER (N-V) Urine; to urinate.

SALTING (N) Putting gold in a mine.

SALVAGE (V) To steal.

SALVATION RANCHER (N) A prison chaplain.

SALVE (N-V) Apple butter; getting on the right side of an arresting officer; to bribe an officer with money; to bribe an officer with soft words.

SAM (N) A machine gun.

SAM LO (N) Cheap bootleg opium refined from residue; third run opium.

SAM LOW (N) Cheap bootleg opium refined from residue; third run opium.

SAND (N) Sugar.

SAND BAG (N) A bag or tube filled with sand and used as a black jack.

SAND HOG (N) A worker in underground tunnel or caisson.

SANDWICH MAN (N)   A person who carries advertising board on his back; a walking advertisement.

SAP (N)   A victim; a rubber hose used in administering the third degree; a black jack; a wooden club; a policeman's billy.

SAP SUCKER (N)   An extortionist.

SAP UPON (V)   To beat; to hit; to slug; to club.

SAPLING (N)   A wooden club; a policeman's billy.

SAPS (N)   Crutches.

SARDINE (N)   A dirty and filthy prostitute or whore.

SATCHELS (N)   A person with extra large feet.

SAUERKRAUT (N)   A German.

SAVAGE (N)   A policeman over-anxious to make arrests.

SAVAGES (N)   A tramp working crew.

SAVER (N)   A pardon; a release from prison.

SAWBONES (N)   A surgeon.

SAW BUCK (N)   Ten-dollars; a five year sentence; five five-dollar bills.

SAWDUST (N)   Dynamite.

SAW-LOG (N)   A toothpick.

SAWED OFF (N)   A shot gun with the barrel sawed off; a shot gun with a short barrel.

SAWYER (N)   A shot gun with the barrel sawed off; shot gun with a short barrel.

SAXOPHONE (N)   An opium pipe.

SCAB (N-V)   A strikebreaker; an article sold for less than the price presented by a trade union; to act as a strikebreaker; to work as a strikebreaker.

SCAB HERDER (N)   A strikebreaker's guard.

SCALY (N)   A person of unclean habits.

SCALY BUM (N)   A dirty tramp; a tramp infected with lice; a lousy person.

SCARE (N)   The extortion racket.

SCARED-CAT (N)   A coward.

SCARLET SISTER (N)   A prostitute; a whore.

SCAT (N)   The drug addict's name for heroin.

SCATTER (N)   A resort; a blind pig; a machine gun.

SCATTER-GUN (N)   A shot gun.

SCENERY BUM (N) A tramp with an appreciation for nature.

SCENERY GRABBER (N) A tramp who exposes himself in order to watch passing scenery, when stealing a ride.

SCHACKESTER (N) An extortionist.

SCHACKLES (N) Soup.

SCHLOCK (N) False or worthless merchandise; narcotics; junk.

SCHNORRER (N) A Jewish beggar who begs at the doors of synagogues or Jewish places.

SCHOOLMATE (N) A fellow prisoner or convict.

SCOOTER (N) A legless beggar who goes about on a board mounted on rollers.

SCISSOR-BILL (N) A farmer; a victim; a dupe; a stool pigeon; an informer; an outsider.

SCOFF (N-V) A voracious eater; to eat a lot.

SCOFF JACK (N) Food money.

SCOFF LAW (N) Scornful law; a no good law; a useless law; one who manifests contempt by derisive acts or language toward the law.

SCOFFING (N) Taking the drug orally.

SCOFFINGS (N) Food.

SCOPP (N-V) Large plunder; a wholesale arrest; to get the first news.

SCOTT (V) To run; to flee.

SCORE (N) A successful crime; a stolen object.

SCORE DOUGH (N) Money with which to buy narcotics.

SCORING (N) Buying narcotics.

SCOTLAND YARD (N) The London, England, police headquarters.

SCOTTISH MAIDEN (N) The guillotine.

SCRAM (V) To leave in a hurry; to get away; to move.

SCRAM AND HOLLAR (N) A dollar.

SCRAMBLED YEGG (N) An insane yegg.

SCRAP (V) To fight.

SCRAPE OFF THE PAVEMENT (V) To shave.

SCRAPER (N) A barber.

SCRATCH (N) A forger; a forged check; a barber.

SCRATCH HOUSE (N) A vermin infested jail; a cheap lodging house; a barber shop.

SCRATCH MAN (N) A forger; a floater of bad commercial paper or check.

SCRATCHER (N) An engraver of counterfeit money plates; a forger.

SCREEVER (N) A beggar who lays a written appeal on the sidewalk or begs by letter.

SCREW (N-V) A guard in a prison; a turnkey in a prison; a key; a prostitute; a whore; to defraud; to cheat; to swindle; to have sexual relation.

SCREWBALL (N) An insane person; a crazy person; one with poor mentality.

SCREWMAN (N) A burglar who uses keys; a turnkey in a jail.

SCREWS (N) Force.

SCREWY (Adj) Criminally insane; crazy.

SCREWY SCRIPT (N) Counterfeit coins.

SCRIBE (N) An engraver of counterfeit money plates.

SCRIP (N) A dollar.

SCRIPT (N) A prescription.

SCROUNGE (V) To engage in sneak thievery.

SCRUB (N-V) A low bred person; to plunder; to flee.

SCRUB GANG (N) The sanitary squad of a prison.

SIDEWALK SUSIE (N) A prostitute; a whore.

SEA DUST (N) Salt.

SEA RAT (N) A pirate.

SEA STIFF (N) A sailor who has turned to be a tramp; a tramp who beats his way on ships.

SEAM SHOOTER (N) A safe burglar who loads his nitroglycerin in the cracks of the safe.

SEAM SQUIRRELS (N) Fleas; mites; lice.

SECRET WORKS (N) The genitals.

SECOND ON THE SNIPE (N) The second user of the butt of a cigarette.

SECOND STORY WORK (N) An upstairs burglary.

SECOND STORY WORKER (N) A burglar who burglarizes through upstairs windows.

SEDOCTOR (N) A doctor seducer.

SEEDS (N) The testicles.

SEEING STEVE (N) Bull horrors; a cocaine user.

SELL A PUP (V) To swindle; to cheat; to defraud.

SELL ONE'S BACON (V) To engage in prostitution.

SELL ONE'S FLESH (V) To engage in prostitution.

SELL ONE'S HIP (V) To engage in prostitution.

SELL OUT (N-V) The act of being shot to death; to betray; to double cross; to be killed rather than surrender.

SEND (V) To send someone out to buy narcotic from a peddler so as to avoid risk of arrest.

SEND ACROSS (V) To send to prison.

SEND TO COLLEGE (V) To send to prison.

SEND TO SIBERIA (V) To send to prison.

SEND UP THE RIVER (V) To send to prison.

SERIOUS MONEY (N) A large amount of money; wealth.

SERVICE STATION (N) A whore house; a brothel.

SET DOWN (N) A square meal; a free meal; a meal at a table.

SET IN (V) To be protected; to be protected against interference by the law.

SET OUT (N) A meal given to a beggar.

SET OVER (V) To kill.

SET UP (N-V) A prearranged crime; a meal at a table; a sentence of one day; an easy case; a fixed jury; a pickpocket accomplice's placing a victim in a good position to have his pockets picked; to become pregnant.

SETTLE IN STIR (V) To sentence a pickpocket operator in court.

SETTLE WRONG (N) An unjust sentence or conviction.

SETTLED (Adj) Sentenced to the penitentiary; in prison; a prison sentence.

SEVEN UP (N) A general store; the robbery of a store.

SEVEN-UP HUSTLER (N) A person who robs stores.

SEVEN-UP HUSTLING (N) Robbing general stores.

SEW UP (V) To produce overwhelming evidence; to produce convincing evidence for conviction.

SEWAGE (N) Dung.

SEWER   (N)   The vein into which a drug addict makes his injection.

SEWER HOG   (N)   A ditch digger.

SEWER COVER   (N)   An officer's badge.

SEXTORTION   (N)   Sex extortion.

SHACK   (N)   A brakeman on a train; a small old building; a mine guard.

SHACK FEVER   (N)   Weariness.

SHACKLES   (N)   Cheese.

SHADE   (N)   A burglar's mask; a pickpocket confederate.

SHADOW   (V)   To follow; to keep track of.

SHADOW BOX   (N)   The room in which prisoners are lined up for inspection or identification.

SHADOW DICK   (N)   A detective who does shadow work.

SHADY LADY   (N)   A negress prostitute or whore; a dirty woman.

SHAG   (N-Adj-V)   Hurry; hustle; worthless; a brakeman; a police chase; to follow.

SHAGGER   (N)   A detective who shadows.

SHAKE ART   (N)   Extortion.

SHAKE ARTIST   (N)   An extortionist.

SHAKE-DOWN   (N-V)   Extortion of protection money; to pay for protection against one's will.

SHAKE-DOWN WORKER   (N)   An extortionist.

SHAKE JOINT   (N)   A detective agency.

SHAKE ONE DOWN   (N)   To rob a person; to search a prisoner.

SHAKE THE DEW OFF THE LILY   (V)   To urinate.

SHAKE THE LILY   (V)   To urinate.

SHAKE UP   (N)   A campaign by law enforcement to break up crime conditions.

SHAM-DUCK   (N)   A warning that a policeman is approaching.

SHAMING PUSHER   (N)   A prize fighter.

SHAMROCK   (N)   An Irishman.

SHAMUS   (N)   A policeman; a spy; an informer; a stool pigeon; a private detective.

SHANGHAI (V) To kidnap a person and force him to serve as a sailor.

SHANTY (N) The caboose of a train.

SHAPED (Adj) Loaded dice.

SHAPELY LIMB OF THE LAW (N) A policewoman.

SHARK (N) A money lender; an employment agent; an unscrupulous criminal; a lawyer.

SHARK HUNTER (N) One who is on the lookout for drunken persons to be robbed.

SHARP SHOOTER (N-V) A crooked gambler; a swindler; a clever crook; to investigate prior to committing a burglary.

SHARPS (N) Needles.

SHAVE (V) To plunder; to fleece.

SHAVE TAILS (N) A long or short cigarette stub.

SHAVER (N) A young child.

SHEBEEN (N) A small shanty in which whiskey is sold.

SHEEP HERDER (N) An epithet implying sexual aberration.

SHE-FLUNKEY (N) A lady's maid.

SHE SAILS (N) A woman of easy morals.

SHEENY (N) A mean person; a Hebrew; a Jew; a stingy person.

SHEEPSKIN (N) A pardon or discharge certificate from prison.

SHEET PASSER (N) One who passes forged checks.

SHEET SLINGER (N) A chamber-maid.

SHEETS (N) Cigarette paper; newspapers used by tramps as a bedding.

SHELL VAULT (N) A vault with a thin door.

SHELL GAME (N) A sleight of hand trick in which the victim tries to determine under which shell a small article is placed.

SHERIFFETTE (N) A woman deputy sheriff.

SHERIFF'S BALL (N) An execution.

SHERLOCK (N) An amateur detective.

SHERRY FLIP (N) The lips.

SHIEVE (N) A knife.

SHILL   (N)   Taxi cab driver steering players to a gambling game.

SHILLABAR   (N)   A decoy; an accomplice of a gambler or other cheat.

SHINDIG   (N)   Any kind of entertainment.

SHINE   (N)   A negro.

SHINER   (N)   A ring with a mirror in it to reflect faces of cards in gambling; a smoked lamp; a flash light; a discolored eye; a lantern; a black eye.

SHINING MARK   (N)   A mean person; a suspicious person.

SHIVE   (N)   A safe cracker's term for a knife; a knife.

SHIVE UP   (V)   To stab.

SHIVY   (N)   A knife.

SHOCK   (N)   A burglar proof safe.

SHOE-LEATHER EXPRESS   (N)   Walking; tramping on foot.

SHOE STRING   (N)   A bluff.

SHOFUL   (N)   The Dutch term for bad money.

SHONEEN   (N)   An Irish disturbance.

SHONNACKER   (N)   A Jew; a pawnbroker; a receiver of stolen goods.

SHONNIKER   (N)   A Jew; a pawnbroker; a receiver of stolen goods.

SHOOFLY   (V)   To go around a town where tramps are not welcomed.

SHOOT   (N-V)   An injection of narcotic; to blow a safe.

SHOOT A BOX   (V)   To blow a safe.

SHOOT A PETER   (V)   To blow a safe.

SHOOT ONE'S WAD   (V)   To copulate; to have sexual intercourse.

SHOOT THE BULL   (V)   To be talkative.

SHOOT THE CURVE   (V)   To purchase narcotics from a peddler.

SHOOT THE LEMON   (V)   To be talkative.

SHOOT UP   (N)   A raid in which there is gun play; a gun battle.

SHOOTER   (N)   A safe cracker.

SHOOTING A JUG   (N)   Blowing a safe.

SHOP (N-V) A shoplifting job; a fence; a place where stolen goods are sold; to stool on one; to shoplift; to arrest.

SHOP BOOSTER (N) A shoplifter who operates under the protection of an overcoat.

SHOPLIFTER (N) A person who steals from stores.

SHORT (N) An automobile; a street car.

SHORT-ARM (N) A railroad employee who appropriates railroad fares.

SHORT-ARM PRACTICE (N) Sexual intercourse; copulation.

SHORT-ARM TAIL (N) The male pudendum; the penis.

SHORT BIT (N) Ten dollars.

SHORTCHANGER (N) One who shortchanges.

SHORT CHANGE ARTIST (N) One who shortchanges.

SHORTCAKE (N) The profits of a shortchange artist.

SHORT CONNER (N) A person who sells false securities.

SHORT CUT (N) Tobacco.

SHORT END (N) The smaller end of a deal.

SHORT FAKER (N) One who works long enough to get some money and then live a life of leisure.

SHORT GO (N) A weak injection of narcotic.

SHORT HUSTLER (N) A pickpocket who operates on street cars.

SHORT JOB (N) An automobile theft.

SHORT PIECE (N) Less than an ounce of narcotic.

SHORT STAKE MAN (N) A person who works long enough to get a grubstake and then lay off for a period of leisure.

SHORT STORY (N) A bad check.

SHORT STORY WRITER (N) A forger; a maker of bad checks.

SHORT TIMER (N) A prisoner who has a short time to serve.

SHORTY (N) Strong inferior liquor.

SHO-SHO (N) A machine gun.

SHOT (N) A colored pickpocket; a narcotic injection; a charge of explosive in a safe blowing.

SHOT GUN MARRIAGE (N) An enforced marriage brought on by the parents of the girl.

SHOT IN THE ARM (N) A hypodermic injection of narcotic; a narcotic injection.

SHOT OF DOPE (N) A narcotic injection.

SHOT UP (N) Drugged from the use of narcotics.

SHOULDER TAPPER (N) A policeman.

SHOVE (N) A gang of tramps; a peddler of narcotics.

SHOVE ACROSS (V) To kill.

SHOVE THE QUEER (V) To pass counterfeit money.

SHOVEL AND BROOM (N) A room.

SHOVEL BUM (N) A pick and shovel laborer.

SHOVER (N) A party receiving counterfeit coins, from a bodle carrier, so he may cash it; one who passes counterfeit money; a gang; a narcotic peddler.

SHOVING THE QUEER (N) Passing counterfeit money.

SHOW (N) Third place in a horse race.

SHOW CASE (N) A hearse.

SHOW FOR MONEY (N) A square deal; an honest deal.

SHOW UP (N) The lining up of prisoners for identification by victims; a room in which prisoners are inspected.

SHOW WINDOW (N) The window in a crib from which a prostitute or whore solicits.

SHROUD (N) A suit of clothes.

SHRUBBERY (N) Salad greens; sauerkraut; whiskers.

SHUCK THE ICE (V) To take off the diamonds from stolen jewelry.

SHUT EYE (V) To sleep.

SHUT HEAD (N) Giving no information; not talking.

SHUT YOUR TYPEWRITER (N) Stop your conversation; stop talking.

SHYSTER (N) A dishonest lawyer; a very bad lawyer; no good; an unscrupulous criminal lawyer.

SHYSTER LIP (N) An unscrupulous lawyer.

SIBERIA (N) Sing Sing Penitentiary, New York.

SICK   (N)   Withdrawal from narcotics.
SICK HOUSE   (N)   A hospital.
SICKEY ACKEY   (N)   A psychiatrist.
SIDE DISH   (N)   A mistress.
SIDE-DOOR PULLMAN   (N)   A box car.
SIDE KICK   (N)   A close friend; a buddy.
SIDE TRACK   (N-V)   An alias; to leave without any
   formality.
SIDETRACKED   (N)   Arrested; left without any excuse.
SIDE-WALK SNAIL   (N)   A policeman.
SIGN   (N)   A signal used by card bunco men.
SIGHS AND TEARS   (N)   The cars.
SIGNIFIES   (N)   Fingerprints.
SILENT EYE   (N)   A detective; a spy who watches
   workers.
SILK STOCKING BULL   (N)   A policeman working a
   wealthy district.
SILKEN   (N)   Wine.
SILKEN WRAPPER   (N)   A toilet; a privy; a rest
   room.
SILVER   (N-V)   A chip off the old block; a frosted
   cake; to give a penny with the appearance of a dime.
SILVER DOLLAR ROUTE   (N)   A railroad where the
   crew charges tramps a dollar to ride.
SIMOLEON   (N)   A dollar.
SIMPLE SIMON   (N)   A diamond in a stick pin.
SIMPLETON   (N)   A prisoner who is insane from con-
   finement.
SIN BUSTER   (N)   A preacher.
SIN HOUND   (N)   A prison chaplain.
SIN SISTER   A whore; a prostitute.
SIN SPOT   (N)   A whore house; a brothel.
SING   (V)   To make a confession to the police; to turn
   state's evidence.
SINGING SCHOOL   (N)   A third degree; the rooms at
   police headquarters in which confessions are obtained.
SINGLE O   (N)   A tramp who travels alone.
SINGLE SAWBUCK   (N)   A ten dollar bill.
SINKER   (N)   A judge; a doughnut.
SINKERS AND SUDS   (N)   Doughnuts and coffee.

SISS   (N)   A woman; a girl.

SISSY   (N)   A weakling; a coward.

SISTER-IN-LAW   (N)   One of two women working for a pimp or procurer; a criminal's female confederate other than his wife or sweetheart.

SISTER OF MERCY   (N)   A prostitute; a whore.

SIT IN THE RIGHT   (V)   To have political protection.

SIT ON THE LID   (V)   To have crime conditions under control.

SITTER   (N)   A prostitute who accompanies her pimp while soliciting trade; a drug addict at spirit medium.

SIWASH OUTFIT   (N)   An inferior working crew.

SIX-BITS   (N)   A gangster's term for seventy-five dollar bills.

SIX GUN   (N)   A revolver or pistol.

SIXER   (N)   A six month sentence; a six shooter pistol or revolver.

SIXTY-NINE   (N)   Sexual variants.

SIXTY NINER   (N)   A sodomite.

SIXTY THREE   (N)   Sexual variants.

SIZZER   (N)   A cook; a kitchen worker; a stove.

SKAMAS   (N)   Smoking opium.

SKATE ON THE UPPERS   (V)   To be poor.

SKATER   (N)   A legless cripple who goes about on a board mounted on rollers.

SKATING ON THE UPPERS   (N-V)   Walking   on shoes with poor soles; to be hungry and dirty.

SKEE   (N)   Opium.

SKELETON   (N)   A burglary where a skeleton key has to be used in making an entrance.

SKELETON SCREW   (N)   A skeleton key.

SKIBBY   (N)   An oriental.

SKIBOO   (N)   A gun man; a gun fight.

SKID GREASE   (N)   Butter.

SKID ROW   (N)   A tenderloin district; a section of the city in which the underworld hangs out.

SKI JUMPER   (N)   A Norwegian.

SKILLY   (N)   Gravy.

SKIN   (N)   A shirt; a pocket book; a dollar bill; an onion; a fur.
SKIN FLINT   (N)   A Scotchman.
SKIN GAME   (N)   A dishonest trick.
SKIN GLOMMER   (N)   A purse snatcher.
SKIN SHOT   (N)   An injection, by a drug addict, in the skin instead of the vein.
SKIN WORK   (N)   The theft of furs.
SKIN WORKER   (N)   A fur thief.
SKINNED   (Adj)   Having the head shaved convict style.
SKINNER   (N)   A diamond.
SKINNING A LEATHER   (N)   The stealing of a purse by a pickpocket.
SKINNING A RATTLER   (N)   The robbery of hoboes by the crew of a freight train.
SKINNY   (N)   A ten-cent piece.
SKINNY WORKER   (N)   A sneak thief.
SKINS   (N)   Paper money.
SKIP BAIL   (V)   To flee the country while on bond.
SKIPPER   (N)   A police captain; a fugitive; the captain of a boat.
SKIPPY   (N)   A police captain.
SKIRT   (N)   A woman; a girl.
SKIRTDOWN   (N)   A man.
SKIRT MAN   (N)   A pimp; a procurer.
SKIVIES   (N)   Underwear.
SKULL   (N)   A ticket.
SKULL BUSTER   (N)   A policeman; a plain clothes officer.
SKULL-DRAG   (V)   To beg for a drink of liquor from a drinking establishment.
SKUNK   (N)   A mean person; a tightwad; a stool pigeon; an informer; a negro.
SKY   (N)   A guard or watchman; a thin soup; a pocket.
SKY-BLUE   (N)   Vegetable soup; a thin soup.
SKY KICK   (N)   The inside pocket of a vest or coat.
SKY LINE   (N)   Something that is given free; something that is on the establishment.
SKY PILOT   (N)   A minister of the gospel; a preacher.
SKY ROCKET   (N)   The inside pocket of a vest or coat.

SKY THE LIMIT   (N)   Betting where there is no limit.

SLAB   (N)   A tray; a slice of anything; an undertaker's table; a dissecting table.

SLAG   (N)   A watch chain.

SLAM OFF   (V)   To die; to kill.

SLANG   (N)   A watch chain.

SLAP A SHIVE   (V)   To cut with a knife; to stab with a knife.

SLATE WRITER   (N)   A spirit medium who pretends to receive messages by writing on a slate.

SLATS   (N)   A skinny person; the ribs.

SLAVE   (N)   A worker; a clerical worker.

SLAVE MARKET   (N)   The section of a city where employment agencies are found; the section of a city patronized by prostitutes; an employment agency.

SLAVEY   (N)   A servant.

SLEEP   (N)   A one year prison sentence.

SLEEPER   (N)   A night watchman.

SLEEPING BILL   (N)   A wooden club; a policeman's billy.

SLEEPING TIME   (N)   A short prison sentence.

SLEEPY HOLLOW   (N)   Trenton prison, New Jersey.

SLEIGH RIDE   (N)   A spree after using narcotics; a narcotic user; a cocaine addict.

SLEUTH FOOT   (N)   A detective; a plain clothes officer.

SLEUTH HOUND   (N)   A detective; a plain clothes officer.

SLEUFOOT   (N)   A person performing the work of a detective; one who collects protection money; a detective; a plain clothes officer.

SLICER   (N)   A knife.

SLICK   (N)   Silk.

SLICK ACE   (N)   A slick or extra slick card in a crooked deck of cards.

SLICK SKIRT   (N)   An attractive and well dressed young woman.

SLICKER   (N)   A clever crook; a newly painted stolen automobile.

SLIDES   (N)   Shoes.

SLIM (N) A police spy.

SLIM PICKING (N) An unsatisfactory begging adventure.

SLING (V) To talk.

SLING THE BULL (V) To tell clever lies; to tell untrue stories.

SLING THE LINGO (V) To be able to converse in slang well.

SLIP THE CANNED HEAT (V) To use a bomb.

SLIP A PINEAPPLE (V) To use a bomb.

SLIP A TORPEDO (V) To use a bomb.

SLIP THE HEAT (V) To commence shooting; to put under pressure.

SLIP THE IN (V) To give confidential information to an officer.

SLIP THE JACKET (V) To accuse another of a crime.

SLIP THE LUMP (V) To kill.

SLIP THE WORKS (V) To be given a death sentence.

SLIPPERY TIT (N) A cheap restaurant.

SLOB (N) A dirty person; a hoggish person; a person easy to impose upon.

SLOBBING (N) Love making; kissing.

SLACK-PULLER (N) A woman or girl of easy morals.

SLOP (N) Beer not fit to drink; food not fit to eat.

SLOP-HOUSE (N) A cheap restaurant.

SLOP-UP (V) To get intoxicated.

SLOPE (V) To run away; to leave abruptly; to escape.

SLOPMAN (N) A plain clothes officer.

SLOT (N) The female pudendum; a woman's genitals.

SLOUGH (N-V) A house; to assault.

SLOUGH PROWLER (N) A burglar.

SLOUGH WORK (N) Housebreaking; a burglar; a burglar who ransacks houses.

SLOUGHED (N) Drunk.

SLOW GRIFFER (N) A burglar who enters houses in the daytime.

SLUG (N-V) A dollar; a shot of whiskey; a bullet; to fight; to hit; to shoot.

SLUG DUCKER (N) A petty crook.

SLUG OF MUD (N) A cup of coffee.

SLUG STICK (N) A policeman's billy.

SLUGGER (N) One who uses a wooden club or billy in a fight; a prize-fighter.

SLUM (N) Articles obtained in a safe burglary and returned to the person who gave him the information as a reward; cheap or false jewelry; a prison fare.

SLUM CHOW (N) Food.

SLUM GULLION (N) A stew.

SLUM JOINT (N) A jewelry store.

SLUMBER PARTY (N) Morphine.

SLUNG SHOT (N) A flexible handle used as a weapon from which a solid is thrown.

SLUSH (N) Counterfeit coins.

SLUSH FUND (N) A fund kept for bribery purpose.

SLUSH UP (V) To get drunk; to drink.

SLUSHED (Adj) Drunk.

SMACK (N) A coin matching racket; narcotics.

SMALL PIECE OF WHITE MEAT (N) An adolescent girl.

SMALL TOWN CHISELER (N) A petty thief.

SMART FELLOW (N) A thief who makes good hauls and escapes arrest.

SMASH (V) To crack a safe.

SMEAK (N) Narcotics.

SMEAKER (N) A drug addict.

SMEAR (N) An ink eradicator used by forgers; a case that has no merits.

SMELLER (N) The nose; a detective.

SMOKE (N-V) A negro; to shoot; cheap liquor.

SMOKE HOUSE (N) A toilet; a privy; a rest room.

SMOKE IRON (N) A pistol; a revolver; firearms.

SMOKE OUT (V) To chase out; to shoot until defeated.

SMOKE POLE (N) A revolver; a pistol; firearms.

SMOKE STACK (N) A pipe.

SMOKE WAGON (N) A revolver; a pistol; firearms.

SMOKED HERRING (N) A French gendarme.

SMOKED LAMP (N) A discolored eye; a shiner.

SMOKER (N) A revolver; a pistol; firearms.

SMOKING IRON (N) A revolver; a pistol; firearms.

SMOKING ROD (N) A revolver; a pistol; firearms.
SMOKY (N) A revolver; a pistol; firearms.
SMOKY SEAT (N) The electric chair.
SMUT HOUND (N) A reformer.
SMUTCH (N) An escape that is not observed.
SNACKS (N) An equal division of loot.
SNAG (V) To steal; to commit sodomy.
SNAKE (N-V) A stool pigeon; an informer; a petty crook; a pickpocket; to tamper with a lock so that it can be opened when desired; to tamper with the combination of a safe lock.
SNAKY (V) To be nervous.
SNAPPER RIG (N) A second-hand suit of cloth.
SNAPS (N) Handcuffs.
SNARE (V) To steal; to secure a catamite.
SNARK (N) An informer; a stool pigeon.
SNATCH (N-V) A kidnapper; the female pudendum; the female genitals; to kidnap.
SNATCH A LETTER (N) The stealing of a purse by a pickpocket.
SNATCHMAN (N) A kidnapper.
SNATCH MOB (N) A gang of pickpockets.
SNATCHER (N) A kidnapper; a shoplifter who operates under the protection of an overcoat.
SNATCHING (N) Kidnapping.
SNEAK (N-V) A sneak thief; to escape.
SNEAK GATE (N) A steel gate within a vault.
SNEAK JOINT (N) An establishment under criminal suspicion.
SNEAKER (N) A motor-boat used in smuggling.
SNEAKERS (N) Rubber sole shoes worn by burglars.
SNEAKS (N) Shoes with rubber soles worn by burglars.
SNEEDER (N) A detective; a plain clothes officer.
SNEEZE (N-V) The taking of the drug cure by an addict; to kidnap; to apprehend the operator of a pickpocket.
SNEEZE WAGON (N) An automobile.
SNEEZER (N) A police station; a kidnapper.
SNIDE (N) A cheap person; a mean person; a short change artist; something not genuine.

SNIFFER   (N)   A cocaine addict.

SNIP SHOOTER   (N)   A tramp who secures cigar or cigarette butts from the street gutter.

SNIPE   (N-V)   A cigarette or cigar butt; a railway section house; a very small person; to steal.

SNIPE KING   (N)   A railway section foreman.

SNIPER   (N)   A pickpocket.

SNIPS   (N)   Scissors.

SNITCH   (N-V)   A thief; an informer; an informer who supplies a lawyer with clients; to pilfer; to steal; to practice petty theft.

SNITCHEL   (V)   To strike.

SNITCHER   (N)   A stool pigeon; an informer.

SNITCKERS   (N)   Handcuffs.

SNOOPER   (N)   A detective; a plain clothes officer.

SNOOPER HOUND   (N)   A detective; a plain clothes officer.

SNOOZER   (N)   A hotel thief.

SNORT   (N)   The inhalation of cocaine or heroin.

SNOTS   (N)   Oysters.

SNOUT   (N)   Pipe or cigarette tobacco.

SNOW   (N)   Sugar; cocaine; heroin; morphine.

SNOW BALL   (N)   Cocaine; heroin; morphine; a very light negro.

SNOW-BALL EATER   (N)   A tramp who stays put during the winter months.

SNOWBANK   (N)   An establishment where cocaine is obtained.

SNOW BIRD   (N)   A user of cocaine; a tramp who goes south for the winter; an addict.

SNOW-CAINE   (N)   Cocaine.

SNOW DODGER   (N)   A tramp who goes south for the winter.

SNOW-FLIER   (N)   A tramp who goes south for the winter.

SNOWED   (Adj)   Under the influence of cocaine.

SNOWY   (N)   Linen.

SNOZZLE   (N)   A Jew.

SNUFF-DIVER   (N)   A pervert narcotic addict.

SNOT RAG   (N)   A handkerchief.

SOAK (N-V) A drunken person; to assault; to serve a long term in prison.

SOAKE EYES (N) Tapioca pudding.

SOAKER (N) One who assaults.

SOAKING (N) Placing in pawn; assaulting.

SOAP RACKET (N) The practice of eating soap, by a prisoner, in order to become sick.

SOAPING (N) Soaping the cracks of a safe before blowing it open.

SOB SISTER (N) A beggar who works upon the emotions of his victims; an interceder for prisoners while in prison.

SOB TALK (N) A sorrowful talk; a beggar's tale of his trouble.

SOBBIE (N) A beggar who grieves.

SOCK (N) One's personal wealth.

SOD (N) A sodomite.

SODDEN BUM (N) A drunkard tramp.

SOFT (N) One easily victimized; a good sales talk peddler.

SOFT BELLY (N) A wooden freight car; the underside of a box car.

SOFT DOUGH (N) Money easily acquired.

SOFT HEEL (N) An informer for the police; a detective.

SOFT JOB (N) A woman of easy morals.

SOFT PETE (N) The rectum; the posteriors.

SOFT PETER (N) A fireproof safe.

SOFT SHOE (V) To go about quietly; to sneak about.

SOFT-SONG MAN (N) A confidence worker.

SOFT TIME (N) An easy jail sentence.

SOFT TOUCH (N) An easy victim; a victim who gives no resistance.

SOILED DOVE (N) A young prostitute; a young whore.

SOL (V) To be placed in solitary confinement.

SOLITAIRE (N) Suicide.

SOLO DIP (N) A pickpocket who works without a confederate.

SON-OF-A-GUN (N) A boy born at sea.

SON OF ISRAEL   (N)   A Jew.

SONG AND DANCE   (N)   A beggar's tale of grief; a good talk to win over; a confidence talk.

SONG MAN   (N)   One with a good sales talk.

SON-LO   (N)   A cheap grade of opium refined from the residue.

SONNY   (N)   A young boy.

SOPPINGS   (N)   Gravy.

SORORITY GIRL   (N)   A female prisoner.

SORORITY HOUSE   (N)   A jail for women.

SORORITY SISTER   (N)   A fellow female inmate in the same jail.

SORROWFUL TALES   (N)   Confined in jail.

SO-SO   (Adj)   Fairly well; goodby.

SOUND   (N)   A pickpocket feeling a victim's clothes.

SOUND A MAN   (V)   To try to locate the purse of an intended victim by a pickpocket.

SOUND HIM OUT   (V)   To question him.

SOUP   (N)   Nitroglycerine; an old expression for nitroglycerine, now known as grease.

SOUP AND PETER MAN   (N)   A safe cracker who uses nitroglycerine in blowing open a safe.

SOUP AND PETER WORK   (N)   Using nitroglycerine in a safe cracking.

SOUP TWISTER   (N)   A watch twister; a watchmaker patronized by criminals.

SOUPER   (N)   A French Canadian; a watch; an insincere convert; one who works the churches to advance himself.

SOUR DOUGH   (N)   Counterfeit money.

SOUR NOTE   (N)   A bad check.

SOUR PAPER   (N)   Bad checks; counterfeit bills.

SOUTH GATE DISCHARGE   (N)   Death of a prisoner while in jail.

SOUVENIR   (V)   To steal.

SOW BELLY   (N)   Fat salt pork; fat bacon.

SPACE   (N)   A one year sentence; a one year measure of time to serve in prison.

SPADE   (N)   A very dark negro.

SPAGHETTE   (N)   An Italian.

SPANISH GUITAR (N) A cigar.
SPANISH LETTER (N) A letter sent out from Spain
to swindle people out of money; a well known fraud.
SPANISH WINDLASS (N) A strait jacket.
SPARE RIB (N) A married man's mistress.
SPARK PROP (N) A diamond stick pin.
SPARK STONE (N) A diamond.
SPARKER (N) A diamond.
SPARKLER (N) A diamond.
SPARROW (N) A young girl who flits from lover to
lover.
SPARROW COP (N) A park policeman.
SPEAK EASY (N) A gun with a silencer; a silencer;
a joint; a kitchen; an illegal bar room.
SPEAR (V) To arrest; to steal.
SPEAR BISCUITS (V) To obtain food from garbage
cans.
SPECK BUM (N) A low class tramp.
SPECKS (N) Pepper.
SPEED BALL (N) A mixture of mixed cocaine and
morphine, usually used by negroes; a mixture of mor-
phine and heroin and cocaine; an injection of a mixture
of morphine, heroin or cocaine.
SPEED COP (N) A motorcycle officer.
SPEED WAGON (N) A police patrol car.
SPEEDY SISTER (N) A prostitute; a whore; a woman
of easy morals.
SPELLBINDER (N) A political stump speaker.
SPICK (N) A foreigner; a Mexican or Cuban.
SPICY DISH (N) A passionate young woman.
SPIDER (N) A tall lanky person; a stripped car.
SPIEL (N-V) A talk to win over; a beggar's tale of
woe; a confidence talk; to talk.
SPIELER (N) A ballyhoo man; any peddler of articles.
SPIELING (N) Talking; waltzing; giving information
out.
SPIFFS (N) Extra money.
SPIG (N) A Mexican; a Cuban; a foreigner.
SPIGGOTY (N) An Italian; a Portuguese.
SPIKE (N) Narcotic; drugs; a hypodermic needle

or syringe; an injection of narcotic; an Italian; a foreigner.

SPILL   (N-V)   A terminus and transfer station of a railroad; to tell all; to give voice; to talk.

SPILL ONE'S GUTS   (V)   To confess all; to turn informer; to turn state's evidence.

SPILL RED INK   (V)   To bleed.

SPINACH   (N)   Whiskers.

SPINDLE   (N)   The bar to which the combination of a safe is attached.

SPINE STRETCHING   (N)   Hanging.

SPITFIRE   (N)   A shrewish woman.

SPIT LEAD   (N)   A gun fire; discharging a gun.

SPIT UP   (V)   To confess; to tell all.

SPLICED   (Adj)   Married.

SPLINTER BELLY   (N)   A rough carpenter.

SPLIT   (N)   A female; a woman; the division of loot; a share in the loot; a cut.

SPLIT FINGER   (N)   A clerical worker; a prison clerk.

SPLIT OUT   (N)   A mob breaking up and going in different places.

SPLIT TAIL   (N)   A woman; a young girl.

SPLIT THE BLANKET   (V)   To divorce.

SPLIT THE TAKE   (V)   To give a share.

SPLITS   (N)   An equal division.

SPLITTING OUT   (N)   A pickpocket's separating from his victim in case of trouble.

SPOILED WATER   (N)   A soft drink.

SPONGE   (N)   A crook who lives on another; a liquor enforcement officer.

SPONGE HEAD   (N)   One without common sense.

SPONGING   (V)   To live on another; to get whatever one can for nothing.

SPOOK   (N)   A detective; a spy; a spirit.

SPOOL   (N)   A roll of bedding.

SPOON   (N)   A receptacle in which narcotics are cooked.

SPORTING HOUSE   (N)   A whore house; a brothel.

SPORTING WOMAN   (N)   A whore; a prostitute.

SPOT   (N-V)   A sentence of one year in jail; a flash-

light; a victim; to examine a place for future criminal
operation; to point out; to investigate prior to the
crime; to select a victim.

SPOT A LAY   (V)   To prepare a place for future crime.

SPOT DUTY   (N)   Guard duty; a lookout for criminal
operation.

SPOTTED   (Adj)   Wanted by the police.

SPOTTER   (N-V)   A detective; a lookout for criminals;
an advance man for criminals; a reconnoiter for thieves;
a gang of automobile thieves; the one who locates the
cars to be stolen; a fluent talker; a loud mouthed person;
to place.

SPOTTING   (N)   Guard duty; a lookout for criminal
operation.

SPREAD   (N)   Smoke opium.

SPREAD THE JOINT   (V)   To get an opium outfit
ready for use.

SPREAD TRICK   (N)   A gambling trick by which an
accomplice gives a pal a good hand while spreading
the cards on the table.

SPREADER   (N)   A device for spreading prison bars.

SPRING   (V)   To obtain one's release from prison,
usually on bail; to liberate from custody; to secure a
prisoner's release on bail.

SPRING A LEAK   (V)   To turn informer; to urinate.

SPRING MAN   (V)   To bail out a prisoner who is under
arrest.

SPRING CHICKEN   (N)   An adolescent girl.

SPRINGER   (N)   A bail bondman.

SPRINGS   (Adj)   Laced up in a strait jacket.

SPRINKLE THE FLOWERS   (V)   To distribute bribes.

SPROUT   (N)   A young girl.

SPRUNG   (Adj)   Discharged from prison.

SPUDS WITH THE BARKS ON   (N)   Unpeeled potatoes.

S.Q.   San Quentin Penitentiary, California.

SQUAB   (N)   A young girl.

SQUAD WAGON   (N)   A police squad car.

SQUARE   (N)   A non-addict; one who is not a drug
addict.

SQUARE A BEEF   (V)   To settle or satisfy a complaint.
SQUARE A RAP   (V)   To bribe the authorities to drop a charge.
SQUARE A SUCKER   (V)   To reimburse a victim to avoid prosecution.
SQUARE COP   (N)   An officer who gives one a square deal.
SQUARE HEAD   (N)   A Swede.
SQUARE IT   (V)   To give up grafting.
SQUARE-JOHN   (N)   A non-addict; one who is not a drug addict.
SQUARE ONESELF   (V)   To recompense; to settle an account.
SQUARE THE JUDGE   (V)   To bribe the Judge.
SQUARE THE SUCKER   (V)   To give back what was stolen; to pay the sucker back to prevent prosecution; to buy off a victim.
SQUARING IT   (N)   Reforming; repairing a loss.
SQUAW   (N)   A woman; a girl.
SQUAWK   (N-V)   A complaint; to make a confession implicating others.
SQUAWK WOMAN   (N)   A female accomplice who diverts the victims.
SQUEAKY SHOES   (N)   An employee who spys on the job to detect dishonesty.
SQUEAL   (V)   To talk; to betray; to turn state's evidence.
SQUEAL AND ARTILLERY   (N)   Pork and beans.
SQUEALER   (N-V)   An informer; a stool pigeon; a rat; a welcher; to double cross.
SQUEEZE   (N)   Extortion money; a share of a graft; silk.
SQUEEZER   (N)   The hangman's noose.
SQUIB   (N)   A fuse.
SQUIRE OF DAMES   (N)   Pimp; procurer.
SQUIRREL CAGE   (N)   The hospital for the criminally insane.
SQUIRREL RANCH   (N)   The hospital for the criminally insane.
SQUIRT   (N)   A young child.

SQUIRT GUN   (N)   A revolver or pistol of no value.

S.S.   (N)   A skin injection by an addict.

STABLE   (N)   A group of prostitutes under one manager; a brothel.

STABLE BOSS   (N)   A brothel manager.

STABLE DOG   (N)   A caretaker of a brothel.

STACH   (N-V)   A hiding place; to conceal.

STACK OF BONES   (N)   A skinny person; a dish consisting mainly of boiled spare ribs.

STAFF OF IGNORANCE   (N)   A hickory club carried by train crews.

STAG   (N)   An employee who spies on a job to detect dishonesty.

STAKE   (N)   Money; assistance.

STAKE HOUND   (N)   One who works long enough to get some money and then live a life of leisure.

STAKE MAN   (N)   One who advances money for a project; a backer.

STAKE OUT   (N-V)   Lying in wait for someone; to lie in wait for a criminal; to prevent the escape of a criminal.

STAKE TO A MEAL   (V)   To give one the price for a meal.

STAKING   (V)   To assist; to give; to loan.

STAKY   (N)   One who works long enough to get some money and then live a life of leisure.

STALL   (N-V)   Man or woman confederate to a pickpocket, who distract victim's attention while pickpocket operates: to put off.

STALLING FOR THE DIP   (N)   A confederate engaging victim so that pickpocket successfully operates.

STAND IN   (V)   To have an equal division; to have a share coming.

STAND ON A CORNER   (V)   To be disappointed.

STAND PAT   (V)   To be firm; to refuse to change.

STAND STILL   (N-V)   A refusal to confess; to withhold information.

STAND THE GAFF   (V)   To undergo a dungeon confinement, a water cure, or a sweat; to suffer punishment.

STAND UP (N-V) A cross examination of prisoners; to place in line for identification.

STAR BOARDER (N) A boarder or lodger who is in good financial standing with the landlady and has all the privileges of a husband.

STAR CHIEF (N) A cook; a kitchen worker.

STAR LODGER (N) A boarder or lodger who is in good financial standing with the landlady and has all the privileges of a husband.

STAR PITCH (V) To sleep in the open.

START TO SING (V) To commence confessing; beginning to tell all.

STASH (N-V) A hiding place for loot; to conceal equipment for narcotics.

STATE (N) Tobacco furnished to prisoners.

STATE COLLEGE (N) A state penitentiary.

STATE HOUSE (N) A rest room; a toilet; a privy.

STATE PEN (N) A state penitentiary.

STATUE (N) A penitentiary guard.

STEAL (N) A stolen object.

STEAM-UP MAN (N) One who arouses others to commit a crime.

STEAMED GRUB (N) Prison food.

STEEL (N-V) A cold prison bath; a knife; to stab.

STEEL AND CONCRETE CURE (V) To kick the narcotic habit cold turkey in jail or prison.

STEER (V) To mislead by false information; to pilot; to reform.

STEER CUT (N) The share given to a steerman.

STEER JOINT (N) A brothel which employs procurers.

STEERER (N) One who supplies a lawyer with clients; one who directs victims into a bunco game; a pilot for a band of thieves; a procurer.

STEIN (N) An opium pipe.

STEM (N-V) The main street of a town; a drill used in the blowing of safes; the bar to which the combination of a safe is attached; an opium pipe; to beg.

STEM HITTER (N) A street beggar.

STEM IN (V) To drill a hole into the combination of a safe.

STEM SIREN (N) A prostitute; a whore.

STEMMER (N) A tramp who begs on a public thoroughfare.

STENED (N) Drugged from the use of narcotics.

STENOGRAPHER (N) A machine gunman.

STEPMOTHER (N) A mother given to stepping out on her husband.

STEPPING (N) A machine gun.

STEPPING HIGH (N) Drugged from the use of narcotics.

STETSON (N) A low class tramp.

STEVE HART (V) To start.

STEW (N-V) Nitroglycerine; drunk; to die in the electric chair.

STEW BUILDER (N) A cook; a kitchen worker.

STEW BUM (N) A cook; a cook for a gang of tramps; a drunken tramp.

STEW-VIC (N) An arrest for drunkenness.

STEW WITH A CRUST (N) A meat pie.

STEW WITH THE LID ON (N) A meat pie.

STEWED (Adj) Drunk.

STHREEL (N) A slouchy woman.

STICK (N) Marihuana cigarettes; crutch; a burglar's jimmy; a match; a wooden club; a policeman's billy; a prison meal; a home made opium pipe; not to part company.

STICK AND SLUG (V) To keep together and fight; to stay with the gang and fight; to remain and fight.

STICK TO ONE'S FINGER (N) One given to petty theft.

STICK UP (N) A robbery; a robbery at the point of a gun.

STICK UP SUCKERS (N) Pickpockets.

STICK WAGON (N) A revolver or pistol.

STICKS (N) Any rural district; a small town or village; one with a wooden leg; a hobo camp.

STICKER (N) A knife; a judge; a stickpin; a postage stamp; a postoffice; a safe cracker.

STICKERS   (N)   Postage stamps; prisoner friends.
STICKY FINGERS   (N-V)   One given to petty theft; to steal.
STIFF   (N)   A corpse; a hobo; a customer who does not tip.
STIFF BED   (N)   A dissecting table.
STIFF JOINT   (N)   A hospital where students practice on cadavers; a morgue.
STIFF PRICK   (N)   A rigid warden; a hard taskmaster.
STIFF RACKET   (N)   Death.
STIFF RAP   (N)   A long sentence.
STIFF TICKET   (N)   A certificate; a severe sentence.
STIFF WAGON   (N)   A hearse; a dead wagon.
STIFF WORKER   (N)   An undertaker.
STIFFY   (N)   A paralytic; one who feigns paralysis.
STILTS   (N)   Crutches; the legs.
STING   (V)   To cheat; to report a prisoner for breach of prison rules; a theft; a pocketbook.
STINGER   (N)   A judge; a fast freight train; an exhibit of suspects for the purpose of identification by victims; violation of prison rules.
STINKER   (N)   A stink bomb.
STINKIN   (N)   Full of narcotics.
STINKO   (N)   No good; scornful; untrustworthy.
STIR   (N)   Time spent in the penitentiary; a prison; a penitentiary.
STIR AGENT   (N)   A lawyer who solicits business around a prison.
STIR BIRD   (N)   A prisoner; a convict.
STIR BUG   (Adj)   Crazy or demented as a result of being kept in prison confinement; one who is insane from prison confinement.
STIR CRASH   (N)   An escape from prison.
STIR CRAZY   (Adj)   One whose mind is affected from serving a long prison sentence.
STIR FEVER   (N)   Typhus fever.
STIR SCREWY   (Adj)   Mentally deranged after a long stay in the penitentiary.
STOMACH BURGLAR   (N)   A poor cook; an unworthy prison cook.

STOMACH ROBBER (N) A poor cook; an unworthy prison cook.

STOMP (N) Shoes.

STOMPING (N) When rural gang members, seize the hands and feet of their victims, while another member jumps up and down on the victim's stomach.

STONE (N) A diamond; testicle.

STONE BAG (N) Sing Sing Penitentiary, New York.

STONE DUMP (N) A prison; a penitentiary.

STONE GETTER (N) A thief who steals diamonds or precious stone stick pins; a jewel thief.

STINE JUG (N) A police barracks in England; Sing Sing Penitentiary, New York.

STONE MANSION (N) A jail.

STONE TAIL ELEVATION (N) Following a person who has plenty of jewelry for the purpose of robbery.

STONE WORK (N) A jewel theft.

STOOD OUT (Adj) Place in line for the purpose of identification by victims; held out of prison line for punishment; infracting a prison rule.

STOOGE (N) A novice.

STOOL (V) To betray.

STOOL MARK (N) A brand made by a cut on the face of a stool pigeon by a gang of criminals.

STOOL PIGEON (N) One who betrays a fellow crook; a thief in the pay of the police as an informer.

STOOLIE (N) An informer; a stool pigeon.

STOP OVER (V) To serve a short sentence; to be given a short sentence.

STOP TICKET (N) A warrant placed as a hold against a convict waiting release.

STORK DOCTOR (N) An obstetrician.

STORK MAD (N) One passionately inclined; lust.

STORM (N) A wife.

STOWAWAY (N) A heeler who is placed on a padded pay roll; one who hides in a boat.

STRADDLER (N) A motorist who straddles the white line and delays traffic.

STRAGGLER (N) A tramp who tramps from place to place and does not voluntarily work.

STRAIGHT (N) Legal; right.

STRAIGHT CRIP (N) A beggar whose deformity is not faked.

STRANGER (N) A stolen automobile disposed of in another locality.

STRAP (N) A black jack; a leather weighted with shot or lead.

STRAW BAIL (N) Worthless bail.

STRAW BOND (N) A bond given by one who offers a worthless bail.

STRAW JAY (N) A small bank.

STRAW MAN (N) A shyster lawyer; a person who hangs around court rooms.

STRAW WITNESS (N) A perjured witness; a witness who is paid to make a false oath.

STREET OF SIN (N) A street which is occupied by prostitutes.

STREET SISTER (N) A prostitute; a whore.

STREET WALKER (N) A prostitute; a woman who solicits trade on the street and takes her make to her room.

STRETCHER (N) A year; a judge; a prisoner; a sodomite.

STRETCHERS (N) Shoe laces.

STRETCHING MATCH (N) A lynching.

STRETCHING YARD (N) The gallows.

STRIDES (N) Trousers; wearing a coat and hat.

STRIFE (N) A wife.

STRIKER (N) A match lighter; the rough side of a match box.

STRING (N-V) The fuse used by a safe cracker in blowing a safe; to steal.

STRING OF FLATS (N) Pancakes.

STRING UP (V) To handcuff a prisoner to the cell bars; to hang.

STRINGERS (N) A shackle.

STRIP (V) To rip away the outer case of a safe.

STRIPPER (N) A pickpocket; an automobile parts thief; extra wide cards in a deck which enable a dishonest gambler to strip out cards he needs.

STRONG (N-Adj) A criminal; having much money.
STRONG ARM (V) To rob by force; to assault; to employ violence.
STRONG ARM MAN (N) A person using violence; a highway man; a slugger.
STRONG ARM SQUAD (N) A guard.
STRONG ARM STUFF (N) Using violence.
STRONG ARM WORK (N) Where violence is used.
STRONG METHODS (N) Use of violence.
STRONG STUFF (N) A very passionate young woman.
STUCK (Adj) Losing; fascinated.
STUDENT (N) An educated political heeler living off a padded city pay-roll; an individual who has difficulty establishing the drug habit.
STUFF (N) Narcotics; stolen object; something of value.
STUFFER (N) A sodomite.
STUNG (Adj) Fleeced; arrested; swindled; deceived by a woman.
SUB (N) A machine gun.
SUBMARINES (N) Doughnuts.
SUBURB (N) A hobo's camp.
SUCK DRY (V) To fleece one of everything he has.
SUCK IN (N) A swindler.
SUCK IN YOUR GUTS (V) To be quiet; to stop talking.
SUCK THE BAMBOO (V) To smoke an opium pipe.
SUCKER (N) Victim or intended victim of a pickpocket; one who is easily swindled; an easy mark; a new prisoner; a cheat; an innocent person sentenced for another's stead; a sodomite; a confidence game; a witness.
SUCKER BAIT (N) A decoy to entice a victim; an artifice to lure a victim.
SUCKER CLIPPER (N) A swindler.
SUCKER MEAT (N) A victim; a dupe; one easily swindled.
SUCKER TRAP (N) A fraudulent trick; a fraudulent device.
SUDS (N) Beer.

SUEY BOWEL (N) A Chinese opium den.
SUEY-POW (N) Narcotic extracted from a syringe used in cleaning and cooling an opium pipe.
SUGAR (N) Money; cocaine; heroin; morphine; a woman or girl.
SUGAR AND HONEY (N) Money.
SUGAR FACTORY (N) The liver.
SUGAR SUCKER (N) A wealthy victim.
SUICIDE KID (N) A motorist who makes a left hand turn from a right hand lane.
SUMMER BOARDER (N) A fellow who makes love to girls; a fellow who sits in hammocks and makes himself generally foolish and silly.
SUN DODGER (N) A night pleasure seeker.
SUNNY SIDE UP (N) Two eggs fried on one side only.
SUNRISE (V) To hold a tramp over night in jail and order him to leave town in the morning.
SUNSHINE (N) Gold; a young bright girl.
SUPER (N) A watch.
SUPER TWISTER (N) A pickpocket who steals watches.
SUPPER PROWLER (N) A burglar who enters a house while the occupants are eating.
SURE THING GAMBLER (N) A character who bets with suckers at race tracks and steals when he is broke.
SWAG (N-V) Stolen property; loot; a bundle; a pocketbook; plunder other than cash; to arrest.
SWAGMAN (N) A receiver of stolen goods.
SWAMPER (N) A janitor who scrubs floors.
SWAP (N) A stolen object.
SWAPER (N) A janitor who scrubs floors.
SWATCH (N) A sample of stolen articles offered the fence by a thief.
SWEAT (N-V) Extortion by intimidation; to administer the third degree; to brow beat a prisoner; to torture; to cross examine.
SWEAT BACK (N) A dandy; a lady's man.
SWEAT BOARD (N) A hand and shovel concrete mixture.
SWEAT BOX (N-V) The third degree; cross examin-

ation of a prisoner; to brow beat a prisoner in order to make him divulge information in his possession.

SWEAT CURE (N) The abstinence narcotic cure; the third degree given a prisoner.

SWEAT IT OUT (V) To take the drug cure.

SWEAT PADS (N) Pancakes.

SWEAT ROOM (N) A jail or hospital room where a drug addict is confined without access to narcotics.

SWEAT SHOP (N) A work house.

SWEATING A GUY (N) Forcing him to confess; giving him the third degree.

SWEATER (N) A strait jacket.

SWEETHEART (N) A stolen automobile in good condition.

SWEET HOMO (N) A male homosexual.

SWEET LINE (N) A confidence talk; a beggar's tale of woe; a good talk to win over.

SWEETMAN (N) A pimp; a procurer.

SWEET MARGUERITE (N) A cigarette.

SWEET MEAT (N) A young girl; a young woman.

SWEET PATOOTIE (N) A young girl or woman.

SWEET PEA (N) An easy victim; an easy job; a good place to commit a crime.

SWEET STUFF (N) Cocaine; heroin; morphine.

SWEET TAKE BUNDLE (N) A large plunder.

SWEET YOUNG THING (N) An adolescent girl.

SWELL BOOSTER (N) A successful female shoplifter; a clever shoplifter; an expert woman thief.

SWELL FRONT (N) One with a nice appearance.

SWELL MOB (N) A gang of pickpockets with good financial backing and able to hire the best legal talent; a prosperous gang of pickpockets; a gang of imposing thieves.

SWELL MOBSMAN (N) A swell dressed pickpocket.

SWELL MOUTHPIECE (N) A first-class lawyer.

SWELL ROCKS (N) Perfect diamonds.

SWELL SHAPE (N) A very attractive woman or girl.

SWIG (N) A drink of liquor.

SWILL (N) Poor prison food.

SWINDLE SHEET (N) A bill of no account.

SWINDLER   (N)   One who steals by fraud and device.
SWING   (V)   To hang.
SWINGER   (N)   The name given by pickpockets to a woman's purse with a handle.
SWIPE   (N-V)   A theft; to steal; to assault.
SWITCH   (V)   To turn informer.
SWITCH PULLER   (N)   An electrocutioner.
SWITCHING   (N)   Transferring; passing from one to another.
SYMPATHY STICKS   (N)   A beggar's crutches.

T

TAB   (V)   To keep in touch with.
TABS   (N)   Keeping in touch.
TABLE OF HORROR   (N)   A dissecting table.
TACKLE   (N)   A watch chain.
TAD   (N)   An Irishman.
TADPOLE   (N)   A French child.
TAGGED   (Adj)   Arrested.
TAIL   (N-V)   A detective who follows a person in order to spy upon him; a reward attached to a police bulletin; copulation; the female pudendum; to follow.
TAILMAN   (N)   A detective who shadows.
TAIL OF A READER   (N)   A reward attached to police bulletin.
TAIL PEDDLER   (N)   A prostitute; a whore.
TAILER   (N)   A detective who shadows.
TAILETTE   (N)   A female detective.
TAIT   (N)   A prostitute; a whore.
TAKE   (N)   A stolen object; a share.
TAKE A FALL   (V)   To be arrested.
TAKE A GANDER   (V)   To look at.
TAKE A GANDER AT   (N-V)   Take a look; to glance at.
TAKE A POWDER   (V)   To run away; to make one's escape; to escape.
TAKE A ROPE   (V)   To hang oneself.
TAKE A SCRAM   (V)   To beat it.
TAKE A SLEIGH RIDE   (V)   To inhale cocaine.

TAKE A VACATION (V) To serve a jail sentence.
TAKE A WALKOUT POWDER (V) To go on strike.
TAKE CHECKERS (V) To be taken for a ride.
TAKE DOWN THE PIKE (V) To take a person where he may be made the victim of a criminal act.
TAKE FOR A RIDE (V) To kidnap and kill; to take for a killing.
TAKE GAME (N) A swindling trick; a confidence game.
TAKE IT ON THE LAM (V) To escape.
TAKE IT ON THE NUT (V) To lose.
TAKE IT OUT IN TRADE (N) Copulate.
TAKE JOINT (N) A gyp cabaret; a crooked gambling house.
TAKE ONE FOR HIS ROLL (V) To take all the money a person has.
TAKE OVER (V) To rob at the point of a gun.
TAKE STRIPES (V) To be imprisoned in a penitentiary.
TAKE THE BOIL OUT (V) To take the drug cure.
TAKE THE NEEDLE (V) To take an injection of narcotics.
TAKE THE RAP (V) To be punished; to suffer punishment.
TAKE THE RAP FOR (V) To suffer punishment for a crime committed by another; to stand trial for a crime committed by another.
TAKE THE RODS (V) To ride the draw rods of a freight car.
TAKE UP (N-V) Arrest; to leave the scene of a crime.
TALENT (N) A clever crook.
TALK (N-V) Lies; to squeal.
TALL ENGLISH (N) The words used by an educated person.
TALL SISTER (N) A female stool pigeon; a female informer.
TALL TALK (N) False conversation; lies.
TALLOWPOT (N) A locomotive engineer or fireman.
TAMP (N) Make a safe ready for blowing.
TAMP UP (V) To assault.

TANK (N) An armored car; a heavy drinker; drunk.

TANK TOWN (N) A small town; a town where trains take water.

TANK UP (V) To get drunk.

TAP (V) To hit on the head; to open.

TAP A SOFT PLUG (V) To drill through a hole plugged with a softer metal in a safe door.

TAP A TILL (V) To steal from a cash register.

TAP THE CLARET (V) To cause one to bleed.

TAPE (N) The tongue.

TAPER OFF (V) To cure an addict by a gradual reduction of the portion of narcotic.

TAR (N) Opium.

TARGET (N) A lookout for a criminal gang.

TART (N) A young girl.

TA-TA (N) A machine gun; machine gun fire.

TATOO (V) To riddle with bullets.

TATTER (N) A night watchman.

TATTOO ARTIST (N) One who handles the machine gun.

TATTOO NEEDLE (N) A machine gun.

TAXI (N) A five to fifteen year sentence.

TAXI STEERER (N) A taxicab driver who acts as a guide or takes customers to a brothel or house of prostitution.

TAV (N) Gum opium.

TCHI (V) To roll a pill of opium and prepare it for smoking.

TEA (N) Marihuana.

TEA HOUND (N) A marihuana smoker.

TEAKETTLE (N) A locomotive.

TEAR BABY (N) A beggar who works upon the emotions of his victims.

TEAR OFF A PIECE (N-V) Copulate; to have sexual relations.

TEARS (N) Pearls.

TEASER (N) A cigarette stub; a girl who never quite goes the limit.

TECK (N) An employee who spies on a job to detect dishonesty.

TEED UP (Adj) Full of narcotics; intoxicated.
TEENY WEENY (N) Very small; a small child.
TELEPHONE NUMBER (N) A large number.
TELL IT TO THE JUDGE (V) To go to court.
TELL THE BAD NEWS (N) Informing one of a death.
TEMPLE (N) A rest room; a toilet; a privy.
TEN SPACER (N) A ten year prison sentence.
TEN SPOT (N-V) A ten year prison sentence; a ten dollar bill; to rob a person.
TEN YARDS (N) One thousand dollars.
TENDERLOIN MADAM (N) A prostitute; a whore; a brothel hostess.
TENT (N) A suit; a prison informer.
TEO (N) A marihuana smoker.
TERMAGANT (N) A female scold; a common railer and brawler.
TERRIER (N) An Irishman; a railway section hand.
TESTICLES (N) Oysters.
TEXAS TEA (N) Marihuana.
THE ARM (N) A stickup by the application of the strangle hold.
THE BIG BREAK (N) A parole.
THE BIG CAGE (N) The penitentiary.
THE BIG DITCH (N) The penitentiary.
THE BIG HOUSE (N) The penitentiary.
THE BOYS (N) Members of a criminal gang.
THE BRICKS (N) Freedom from prison.
THE BUFF (N) Bare skin.
THE BUSINESS (N) Third degree; copulation; hypodermic syringe used by an addict; cross examination.
THE CHEAT (N) The gallows.
THE CLAMP (N) Overpowering a gang of criminals; subduing.
THE COLD TURKEY CURE (N) The drug cure.
THE CREEP (N) A sneak theft.
THE CUSHIONS (N) A passenger train; comfort.
THE DOUBLE ACT (N) Marriage.
THE DEVIL AND ALL (N) The entire gang; everyone.

THE DEVIL'S BONES (N) Dice.

THE ELECTRIC CURE (N) Electrocution;   electric chair.

THE EYE (N) Warning.

THE FAIR (N) A woman or girl.

THE FUZZ (N) The third degree.

THE COAT GAME (N) Theft.

THE GREAT DIVIDE (N) A divorce.

THE GRILL (N) A third degree; a cross examination.

THE HEAT (V) To shoot; to put the pressure on; the electric chair.

THE HEAVY (N) A bank robbery.

THE HIPE (N) Short change.

THE HYPE (N) Short change.

THE HOT SEAT (N) The electric chair; electrocution.

THE JUMP (N) Marriage.

THE KLINK (N) Prison.

THE LID (N) Clamp down on criminal activities.

THE LITTLE MAN IN THE BOAT (N) The clitoris of a female pudendum.

THE LINE (N) The underworld outside of prison walls.

THE MAN HIGHER UP (N) The leader of a criminal gang whose identity is not known to the gang.

THE NOOSE (N) Marriage; a sentence of hanging; hanging.

THE OLD MAN (N) The principal keeper of a jail; a warden of a penitentiary.

THE ONE-TWO (N) A flight; an escape.

THE PANEL GAME (N) Operation of a thief in a panel house where men are lured by prostitutes and robbed.

THE PRESSURE (N) The third degree; cross examination.

THE PIPE (N) Smoking opium.

THE PLUSH (N) A passenger train; comfort.

THE POSSUM TRICK (N) One feigning injury or illness so he may be able to rob the one who comes to his aid.

THE PRICE   (N)   The price of a meal given a beggar.

THE RAW   (N)   The bare skin.

THE REAL McCOY   (N)   The real thing; real money; nitroglycerine.

THE ROD ROUTE   (N)   Travel via the underbracing of a train.

THE ROPE   (N)   Hanging.

THE RUSH ACT   (N)   Fast working by a pickpocket in a crowd.

THE SCREW   (N)   The third degree; cross examination.

THE SNATCH RACKET   (N)   A kidnapping.

THE SNEEZE   (N)   One who kidnaps; graft.

THE STREETS   (N)   Freedom from prison; a prostitute; a whore.

THE STRONG-ARM ACT   (N)   Use of physical force in a stickup.

THE STRONGER SEX   (N)   The male; man.

THE SQUEEZE   (N)   The third degree; extortion money.

THE TAKE RACKET   (N)   Stealing.

THE TRADE   (N)   A prostitute; a whore.

THE VELVET   (N)   Comfort or luxury.

THE WARDEN'S OFFICE   (N)   A prison toilet.

THE WEAKER SEX   (N)   The female; woman.

THE WEEDS   (N)   A hobo camp.

THE WHOLE LAYOUT   (N)   The entire group or gang; everyone.

THE WHOLE SHEBANG   (N)   The entire group or mob; everyone.

THE WHOLE SMEAR   (N)   The entire group or mob; everyone.

THE WORK   (N)   The equipment used by a drug addict.

THE WORKS   (N)   A death sentence; the third degree; a killing or murder; the hypodermic syringe used by a drug addict; a severe treatment given a prisoner to secure a confession.

THESE AND THOSE   (N)   A suit of clothes; the toes.

THICK AND DENSE   (N)   Expenses.

THICK AND THIN   (N)   The chin.

THIN-HIPS   (N)   An old time opium smoker who has smoked so long that his hips are of unequal size.

THIMBLE   (N)   A watch.

TIMBLE RIGGER   (N)   A swindler who uses the shell game racket; a swindler who fleeces one at the shell game.

THIRD DEGREE   (N-V)   Brow beating a prisoner; to give a prisoner a severe treatment to extort a confession.

THIRD RAIL   (N)   A pickpocket who operates on passenger trains; a luggage thief; an official who is incorruptible.

THIRTEEN AND A WASHOUT   (N)   The death house.

THOUSAND MILER   (N)   A starched dark shirt.

THRASH OUT GREASE   (V)   To extract nitroglycerine from dynamite.

THRASH OUT OIL   (V)   To extract nitroglycerine from dynamite.

THRASH OUT STEW   (V)   To extract nitroglycerine from dynamtie.

THREE-DAY HABIT   (N)   One who smokes the opium pipe now and then but is not addicted.

THRILL DAME   (N)   A prostitute; a whore.

THRONE   (N)   A toilet; a privy.

THRONE ROOM   (N)   A rest room; a toilet; a privy.

THROW A BRODIE   (V)   To make a failure of a criminal act.

THROW A SCARE INTO   (V)   To intimidate.

THROW A HUMP   (N)   A pickpocket accomplice who distracts a victim so he may be placed in a good position for the pickpocket.

THROW DOWN   (V-N)   To betray; leave behind; desert.

THROW OUT   (N)   A beggar who throws joint out at will to work sympathy.

THROW SLUGS   (V-N)   To stage a gunfight; gunfire.

THROW THE BOOK   (V)   To be given a life sentence.

THROW THE GUTS   (V)   To confess; to tell all; to give in; to be very talkative; to turn informer.

THROW THE MITTS (V) To pick pockets.

THROW UP THE SPONGE (V) To acknowledge defeat.

THUG (N) A criminal; a violator of the law.

THUGDOM (N) The underworld outside of prison.

THUMB CUFFS (N) A small pair of cuffs placed on the thumb of each hand.

THUMB SCREWS (N) An instrument of torture placed on the thumb and tightened.

TICKER (N) A watch; the heart.

TICKET (N) A pardon or discharge certificate; a warrant of arrest; a jail sentence; a report for violation of prison rules; a board used by tramps in riding the rods of a freight train.

TICKET LEAVE (N) A release from prison.

TICKET PLASTERER (N) A motorcycle officer.

TICKETS (N) The underbracing of a freight car.

TICKLE (V) To work the combination of a safe.

TICKLE THE PALM (V) To tip.

TIDDLYWINK (N) A drink of liquor.

TIE THE KNOT (V) To marry.

TIE UP (N) Marriage.

TIER (N) A row of cells.

TIGER (N) A criminal lookout; a lascivious man.

TIGHT LIP (N) Not talkative.

TIGHT WAD (N) A Scotchman.

TIGRESS (N) A shrewish woman.

TILL TAPPER (N) One who steals from cash registers or drawers.

TILL TAPPING (N) Theft from cash registers.

TIMBER (N) Lead pencils; a policeman's billy.

TIMBERS (N) A beggar who peddles pencils; a beggar with a wooden leg.

TIMBLE (N) A watch.

TIME (N) A jail sentence.

TIMER (N) A prisoner who has been convicted twice.

TIN (N) A can of opium; an officer's badge.

TIN AND TAP (N) A cap.

TIN CAN (N) A safe easy to open.

TIN CAN COP (N) A special officer.

TIN EAR   (V-N)   To listen; to eavesdrop; an ear dropper.

TIN HORN   (N)   A cheap gambler; a petty crook.

TIN HORN GAMBLER   (N)   A petty gambler.

TIN HORN SPORT   (N)   A cheap gambler.

TIN THRONE   (N)   The chamber pot in a prison cell.

TINPOT LAWYER   (N)   A second rate lawyer.

TINSTER   (N)   A private detective.

TINKER   (N)   A novice burglar.

TIP   (N-V)   A safety zone, or a train entrance, or a place where people congregate, selected by pickpockets to operate in; a gift; advance knowledge; a criminal lookout; to give confidential information.

TIP OFF   (N-V)   Secret information given in advance; confidential information; a betrayal; a warning; to accuse another.

TIP OFF THE BUG   (V)   To disconnect a burglar alarm.

TIP OVER   (N)   A raid made on a blind pig without a warrant; a theft.

TIP OVER A JUG   (V)   To rob a bank.

TIP THE FLIPPER   (V)   To give a welcome hand shake.

TIPPER   (N)   A stool pigeon; an informer.

TIRE CLOUDER   (N)   An automobile tire thief.

TIT FOR TAT   (N)   A hat.

TITLE TAPPER   (N)   One who raises money on forged deeds; a deed forger.

TITS   (N)   The female breasts.

TOADSKIN   (N)   Paper money; bill.

TOAST   (V)   To be electrocuted.

TOASTER   (N)   One who refuses to work.

TOBY   (N-V)   Highway robbery; to commit robbery.

TOCKER   (N)   A murderer.

TODINE   (N)   Coffee.

TOG   (N)   A coat; a coat carried over the left arm by a pickpocket to cover up while lifting a purse.

TOGS   (N)   Clothing.

TOM CAT (N) An improvised hypodermic needle made from sewing machine needle in prison.

TOM FOOLERY (N) Cheap imitation jewelry.

TOMATO (N) A woman; a girl; a loose woman or girl; a female of easy morals; a stolen automobile.

TOMATO CAN (N) A policeman's badge.

TOMATO CAN VAG (N) A tramp who gets his food out of garbage cans.

TOMB (N) A bank.

TOMCAT (N) A prison sewing machine; a sewing machine needle used by drug addicts in taking a hypodermic shot.

TOMMY (N) A machine gun; a girl; a woman.

TOMMY BOY (N) A young boy.

TOMMY BUSTER (N) A woman beater; a raper of women; an abuser of women.

TOMMY GEE (N) The operator of a machine gun.

TOMMY GUN (N) A machine gun.

TOMMY MAN (N) The operator of a machine gun.

TOMMY NODDY (N) The body.

TOMRIG (N) A female of easy morals.

TON (N) A fellow; a person.

TON OF LAW (N) A large policeman.

TONGUE (N) A criminal lawyer.

TOOL (N) The member of a pickpocket mob who takes the roll; a pickpocket who has a confederate; a pickpocket who does the actual stealing.

TOOT THE DING-DONG (V) To beg from house to house.

TOOTHPICK (N) A knife; the nickname for a Bowie knife used in Arkansas.

TOOTS (N) A young girl.

TOP (V) To give a death sentence.

TOP OFF (V) To kill.

TOPER (N) A drunkard.

TOPPED (Adj) Hanged; executed.

TOPPINGS (N) Desert.

TORCH (N) A professional arsonist; a flashlight; a weapon.

TORCH A SQUIB (V) To light a fuse.

TORCH MAN (N) A safe cracker who uses an acetylene torch.

TORPEDO (N) An imported assassin; a gunman serving as a body guard to a gangster; a paid killer; a tear gas bomb.

TORTURE CHAMBER (N) A jail or hospital in which drug addict is confined without access to narcotics.

TOSS OUT (N) A narcotic addict feigning a spasm.

TO THE COUNTRY (Adv) To prison.

TOTSIE (N) A small child; a young girl.

TOUCH (N-V) A criminal enterprise; a theft; a stolen object; a pickpocket; a gift to a beggar; to secure; to steal; to secure a loan.

TOUCH ARTIST (N) A beggar.

TOUCH-OFF (N) A fire set by an incendiary.

TOUCH UP (N-V) A beggar receiving a gift; to steal.

TOUCHABLE (N) A policeman who is susceptible to a bribe.

TOUCHED (Adj) Having the pocket picked; having had sexual intercourse before marriage.

TOUCHER (N) A beggar; a robber of intoxicated persons.

TOUGH BABY (N) A woman of easy morals.

TOUGH CASE (N) A case that is difficult to convict.

TOUGH MUG (N) An ugly face; a desperado.

TOUGH STEM (N) A street on which begging is difficult.

TOUGH TIME (N) A jail sentence which is hard to do.

TOURIST (N) A tramp who goes south for the winter.

TOUT (N) One who gives information regarding races; one who gives knowledge in advance.

TOWEL (N) A policeman's billy.

TOWER HOCK (N) One who stands guard on a prison wall.

TOWN CLOWN (N) A town constable.

TOY (N) A container in which smoking opium is kept; a small tin box used for preparing opium; a watch.

TOY COPPING (V) To steal watches.

TOY GETTER (N) A watch thief.

TRACK STIFF (N) A tramp who walks railroad tracks.

TRACK THIRTEEN (N) A life sentence.

TRACKS (N) Fingerprints.

TRAILER (N) A beggar who follows the circus.

TRAIN BULL (N) A railroad detective; a railroad watchman.

TRAIN DICK (N) A railroad detective.

TRAIN FLIPPER (N) A tramp who steals train rides.

TRAIN JUMPER (N) A tramp who steals train rides.

TRAINED NURSE (N) Narcotics smuggled into prison or jail by an addict to "take care of him" while he is there.

TRAMP (N) A woman of easy morals; a prostitute; a whore.

TRAMP HERDER (N) An officer of the law.

TRAP (N-V) A hiding place; the mouth; a fine residence; to catch.

TRAP HEAP (N) A stolen automobile.

TRAP TOOL (N) A stolen automobile.

TRAPEZE ARTIST (N) A tramp who rides the rods of a freight car; a sodomite.

TRASH DYNAMITE (V) To separate nitroglycerine from the other substances.

TRAVEL ITCH (N) Wanderlust; impulse toward wandering.

TRESPASSER (N) A tramp who walks the railroad tracks.

TREY (N Three.

TRIBE (N) A gang of tramps.

TRICK (N) A crime; a pretty girl; a job; a theft; a small child.

TRICK BUZZER (N) An unauthorized badge; an imitation badge.

TRICKING BROAD (N) A prostitute; a whore.

TRICKS (N) Men brought to brothels by bell boys, or taxi drivers.

TRIGGER MAN (N) The bodyguard of a gambler; an assassin; one who does the killing for a mobster gang.

TRIGGER MOLL   (N)   A gun woman.

TRIGGER TALK   (N)   A gun battle; a discharge of firearms.

TRIM A WINDOW   (V)   To burglarize a display window.

TRIMMER   (N)   A bunko artist; a swindler.

TRIP   (N)   Arrested.

TRIP BACK   (N)   The removal to the death house.

TRIP UP THE RIVER   (N)   A penitentiary sentence.

TROLLY   (N)   A system of smuggling messages within prison.

TROLLY WIRE   (N)   A cord used to pass messages from cell to cell of a prison.

TROMBO   (N)   A tramp pugilist.

TUCK-UP   (N)   Hanging.

TUMB PUSHER   (N)   A tramp who will not voluntarily work.

TUMBLE   (V)   To get wise; to understand; to recognize; to be discovered.

TURF DOPE   (N)   Race track information.

TURKEY   (N)   The truth; a clothes bag; a fake capsule containing sugar or chalk, instead of the real narcotic.

TURKEY MERCHANT   (N)   A fence for stolen silk.

TURN   (V)   To consent selling narcotic to an addict.

TURN A TRICK   (V)   To commit a crime; to accomplish one's purpose of a prostitute.

TURN ON THE HEAT   (V)   To shoot; to discharge a gun; to put the pressure on a criminal.

TURN ON THE WEEPS   (V)   To tell a hard luck story.

TURN OVER   (N)   The night before being released from prison.

TURN THE HEAT ON   (V)   To shoot; to kill.

TURNED OUT   (Adj)   Released from prison and put on the street.

TURNER   (N)   A fugitive.

TURNIP   (N)   A gold watch.

TURRETT   (N)   A bootlegger's warehouse; a steel cage used by gambling house guards for protection.

TURRET MAN (N) A gambling house guard.

TURTLE (N) A motorist who crosses right in the middle of heavy traffic, instead of waiting for a break and when half way across stops completely, creating a traffic jam.

TURTLE DOVE (N) A pair of women's gloves; a young lover.

TUSH (N) Dangerous.

TUX (N) A strait jacket.

TUXEDO (N) A strait jacket.

TWAT (N) The female pudendum.

TWENTY DOLLAR GOLD PIECE (N) The brass part of a yale lock.

TWENTY SPACES (N) A twenty year sentence.

TWIG AND BERRIES (N) The male pudendum.

TWINE (N) Wine.

TWINS (N) The male testicles.

TWIRL (N) A skeleton key.

TWIST (N) A woman of loose morals; a girl; a pickpocket stealing a watch by breaking the chain; marihuana cigarette.

TWIST A DREAM (V) To roll a cigarette; to roll a marihuana cigarette.

TWISTER (N) A marihuana smoker; a narcotic addict feigning a spasm.

TWO BITS (N) Twenty-five dollars.

TWO LOOKING UP (N) Two eggs fried on one side only.

TWO PIPE (N) A double barrel shot gun.

TWO SPOT (N) A two dollar bill; a two year sentence.

TWO-STEP (N) Chicken.

TWO TIME LOSER (N) One who has been convicted two or more times.

TWO-WAY GUY (N) A person not to be trusted.

TWO-WAY SPLIT (N) An equal division of spoil.

TWO YEARS (N) A two dollar bill.

TYPER (N) A machine gun.

TYPEWRITER (N) A machine gun.

TYPEWRITER PARTY (N) A machine gun.

U

UGLY (N) A desperado; a mean person.

UKELELE (N) A machine gun; a short handled shovel.

UKELELE MUSIC (N) Machine gun fire.

UNBUTTON (V) To tear open; to rip the covering of a safe.

UNBUTTON A SAFE (V) To rip the plates of a safe.

UNCLE (N) A Federal narcotic agent; a fence; a receiver of stolen goods; a pawn broker; a place where stolen goods are disposed of.

UNCLE BENNY (N) The proprietor of a pawn shop.

UNDAMAGED GOODS (N) A virgin.

UNDER A FLAG (Adj) Using a false name to cover up the real one; using an alias.

UNDER COVER (Adj-N) In hiding; clandestine; an undercover operator; a detective; secret.

UNDER-COVER MAN (N) A detective; a secret agent; a male homosexual.

UNDER-GRAD (N) A prisoner; a convict.

UNDER-GROUND (V) To transact anything secretly.

UNDER-GROUND JUNGLE (N) A graveyard; a cemetery.

UNDER-GROUND RAILROAD (N) A smuggling system.

UNDER-GROUND WIRES (N) The necessary details in procuring the release of one under arrest.

UNFINISHED BUSINESS (N) A wounded rival.

UNFORTUNATE (Adj) Arrested; tried; convicted.

UNHARNESS (V) To take jewels from their mountings; to take off one's uniform.

UNSLOUGH (N-V) A pickpocket who steals a watch when victim's coat is unbuttoned; to open; to unbutton.

UNTOUCHABLE (N) An officer who cannot be bribed.

UP AGAINST THE EIGHT BALL (Adj) In a bad predicament.

UP AND UP (Adj-V) On the level; square; legitimate; to quit using narcotics.

UP SALT CREEK   (N)   In a bad predicament; sent
   to the electric chair.
UP THE CHIMNEY   (N)   A mortgage; a legal remedy.
UP THE RIVER   (Adj-N)   In a prison or penitentiary;
   dead; Sing Sing Penitentiary, New York.
UPHOLSTERED   (Adj)   Having venereal disease.
UPPER BEN   (N)   An overcoat.
UPPER BERTH   (N)   The roof of a railroad car.
UPPER-CUT   (N)   Brandy.
UPPER DECK   (N)   The roof of a railroad car.
UPPERS AND BENEATH   (N)   The teeth.
UPSTAIRS   (N)   An inside pocket of a coat or vest, term
   of pickpockets.
USELESS   (Adj)   Dead.
USER   (N)   A drug addict.

V

VAG   (N-V)   A vagrant; a beggar; one without visible
   means of support; one arrested for vagrancy; to jail for
   vagrancy.
VAGABOND   (N)   A tramp who does not like to work.
VAGGED   (Adj)   Arrested for vagrancy; committed to
   prison for vagrancy.
VALENTINE   (N)   A jail sentence of a short term; one
   year prison sentence; one skilled in opening the com-
   bination of a safe by use of fingers.
VALET   (N)   A trusty who is house orderly to a prison
   official; a prison attendant.
VALLEY OF THE DEAD   (N)   A cemetery; a grave-
   yard.
VAMP   (V)   To attract by use of sex appeal.
VAMPIRE   (N)   A seductress.
VARNISH CAR   (N)   A passenger coach.
VARNISH WAGON   (N)   A passenger coach.
VASE   (N)   Nitroglycerine.
VEIN-SHOT   (N)   An intravenous injection by a drug
   addict.
VELVET   (N-V)   Money that is easily gotten; to be well
   fixed financially.

VELVET PLUSH   (N)   Society folks.
VENTULATED   (Adj)   Shot full of holes; kill.
VERMONT CHARITY   (N)   A feeling of sorrow.
VERT   (N)   A homosexual.
VERY BEST   (N)   The chest.
VESTRY THIEF   (N)   A thief who fleeces church members; one who preys upon church goers.
VICE SISTER   (N)   A prostitute; a whore.
VILLAGE YUX   (N)   A bullet-proof vest.
VINE   (N)   A suit.
VIOLENT   (Adj)   Suffering with a bad case of syphilis.
VIOLIN   (N)   A machine gun.
VIOLIN CASE   (N)   A case in which a machine gun is carried; a machine gun case.
VIPER   (N)   A marihuana smoker.
VIPER'S WEED   (N)   Marihuana.
VIRGIN   (N)   A burglar-proof safe; a young girl who has not been ruined; a young girl who has never had sexual relation.
VITAL STATISTIC   (N)   A new born infant.
VOICE   (N)   A criminal lawyer.
V.S.   (N)   Vein shot by a drug addict.
V SPOT   (N)   A five dollar bill.

W

WAD   (N)   A package of bills; personal wealth.
WAFFLE IRON   (N)   The electric chair.
WAGE SLAVE   (N)   A worker.
WAGON   (N)   A revolver or pistol; a police car.
WAGON BUM   (N)   One who travels in a cheap automobile and usually with a family.
WAGON STIFF   (N)   A worker who travels from place to place in an automobile; a person who travels in a cheap automobile usually with a family.
WAIL   (N)   A trial.
WAKE-UP   (N)   The day of release from prison.
WALK ONTO A SPOT   (V)   To walk into a death trap.
WALK OUT POWDER   (N)   Escape.

WALK THE PAVEMENT (V) To walk the street for patrons of a prostitute.

WALK THE TIES (V) To walk along the railroad tracks.

WALK UP BACK (N) The removal to the death house.

WALKING IN THE AIR (Adj) Full of drugs; a drug addict.

WALKING TREE (N) A guard; a watchman.

WALLFLOWER (N) One who hangs about bars for free drinks; an unpopular girl at a dance.

WALL PAPER (N) Counterfeit bills.

WALL-WALL (N) Walla Walla Penitentiary, Washington.

WALLED CITY (N) Sing Sing Penitentiary, New York.

WANG (N) A talkative person.

WANY (N) A shoestring peddler.

WAR HORSE (N) An agressive woman; an old person.

WARPHAN (N) A soldier's orphan; an illegitimate child.

WARD HEELER (N) One who caters to and works for the ward boss.

WARM BABY (N) A passionate young woman.

WART (N) A small person.

WASH OUT (N-V) A life sentence in a penitentiary; to kill.

WASH UP (N) Take the drug cure.

WASHED UP (Adj) Ready to quit.

WATER CURE (N) A punishment by forcing water in large quantities into one's stomach.

WATER HAUL (N) An unproductive crime.

WATER HOLE (N) A small town.

WATER PIPE (N) The urethra.

WATER RAT (N) One who hangs along the water front; one who steals along the water front.

WATER TANK (N) The bladder; the urethra.

WEAK AND WEARY (N) A prison clerk.

WEAR A ROD (V) To carry a gun.

WEAR STRIPES (V) To serve a penitentiary sentence.

WEARY WILLIE (N) A tramp; a hobo; a tramp who is not very fond of work.

WEASEL (N) An informer; a stool pigeon; a Federal narcotic agent.

WEAZEL (N) An employee; one hired to spy on a job to detect dishonesty.

WEDDED WENCH (N) A wife.

WEDGE (N) Silver plate.

WEED (N-V) Pickpocket removing articles from a purse; tobacco; marihuana; to steal more than one's share from the loot; cheat; to give alms.

WEED A LEATHER (V) To extract the money from a stolen purse.

WEED HEAD (N) A marihuana smoker.

WEED HOUND (N) A marihuana smoker.

WEEDER (N) A person who steals in small amounts to avoid detection.

WEEDS (N) Marihuana cigarettes.

WEAK SISTER (N) A weakling; a coward.

WEEK-END HABIT (N) The use of narcotics for a day or two, a week, or irregularly without becoming an addict.

WEEPER (N) A whining beggar; a crying beggar.

WEEPING WILLOW (N) A pillow; a motorist who repeatedly blows his automobile horn.

WEEPY LINE (N) A beggar's tale of woe.

WEIGHT (N) A wooden club; a policeman's billy.

WEINIE (N) A loaf of bread.

WELCHER (N) One who takes too long, refuses or fails, to pay a gambling debt; a squealer on bets; a gambler who does not pay his losses; twisting.

WELL-HEELED (N) Well armed; well supplied with money.

WELSH (N-V) A cheap sport; a coward; to refuse to pay a debt or bet.

WENCH (N) A woman or girl; a woman of easy morals; a negress maidservant; a lively or passionate woman.

WESTERN GUY (N) An out of town thief.

WET DECK (N) A woman having sexual relation, with two or more men in succession.

WET GOODS   (N)   Stolen articles; liquors.
WHACKS   (N)   Force.
WHARF RAT   (N)   A vagabond who hangs around the water front and steals from vessels and drunken sailors; a wharf prowler.
WHAT IT TAKES HONEY   (N)   Passionate; lust.
WHEELS   (N)   The legs.
WHEELER   (N)   A motorcycle officer.
WHIP   (N)   A bail bond.
WHIP OVER   (V)   To smuggle liquor; to smuggle in.
WHIP-SAW   (Adj)   Completely routed; beaten.
WHIP-SAWED   (Adj)   Defeated at all points.
WHISKERS   (N)   The Federal Government; a Federal law enforcement agent; A Federal narcotic agent.
WHISKEY TENOR   (N)   A bad soloist; a cracked voice.
WHISTLE BAIT   (N)   Pretty girls who get advance data on dates.
WHISTLE GUY   (N)   A criminal lookout.
WHISTLE STOP   (N)   A small town.
WHISTLER   (N)   A police patrol car.
WHITE   (Adj-N)   Morphine; gin; alcohol; fair; silver; a silver watch.
WHITE ANGEL   (N)   A nurse or attendant in a hospital who smuggles narcotics to an addict.
WHITE COFFEE   (N)   Any colorless alcohol or whiskey.
WHITE COLLAR   (N)   A clerical worker.
WHITE CROSS   (N)   Cocaine; morphine; heroin.
WHITE DEATH   (N)   Cocaine; morphine; heroin.
WHITE EYE   (N-V)   A colorless whiskey; to turn state's evidence.
WHITE GUT   (N)   White sausage.
WHITE LINE   (N)   An alcohol drink.
WHITE LINER   (N)   A raw alcohol drunkard.
WHITE MOSQUITOES   (N)   Cocaine; morphine; heroin.
WHITE MULE   (N)   Raw corn whiskey; any colorless whiskey.
WHITE ONE   (N)   A silver watch.
WHITE POWDER   (N)   Cocaine; morphine; heroin.

WHITE RAB (N) A stool pigeon; an informer.

WHITE SLANG (N) A silver watch chain.

WHITE STUFF (N) Alcohol; cocaine; morphine; heroin.

WHITE TRASH (N) Poor white people.

WHITE WASH (N-V) The act of clearing a bankrupt person of debt; to exonerate one of a criminal charge; to be cleared of a charge.

WHITE WINE (N) Water.

WHIZ (N) Lookout for pickpockets.

WHIZ-BANG (N) A mixture of cocaine, heroin or morphine; an injection of a mixture of cocaine, morphine or heroin.

WHIZ COP (N) A pickpocket detective.

WHIZ COPPER (N) A pickpocket detective.

WHIZ GANG (N) A pickpocket gang or mob.

WHIZZ (N) A pickpocket at work; a pickpocket picking pockets.

WHOLE PUSH (N) The entire mob or gang.

WHOOPIE WENCH (N) A prostitute; a whore.

WHOP (N) A sentence less than thirty days and more than fifteen.

WHOREHOUND (N) One who patronizes prostitutes or whores.

WHORE HOUSE (N) A brothel; a house in which prostitutes ply their trade.

WHOREPHAN (N) A prostitute orphan.

WHORESON (N) A prostitute's son.

WIDE (N) Clear off.

WIDOW JONES (N) A rest room; a toilet; a privy.

WIFF (N) A wife.

WILD CAT (N) A dishonest schemer in oil.

WILLIE (N) A tramp; a hobo; a tramp who carries a bed roll.

WILLIE BOY (N) An effeminate man; a male having the characteristics of a woman; submerged manhood.

WILLIES (N) Nervousness; something of fear.

WILLOW (N) A wooden club; a policeman's billy.

WIND JAMMER (N) A talkative person; one who talks much of trivial things.

WIND UP   (N)   Death.

WINDOW   (N)   Eyeglasses; spectacles.

WINDOW TAPPEEY   (N)   A brothel; a house of prostitution; a whore house.

WINDOW TRIMMING   (N)   The burglary of a store window.

WINDY   (Adj)   Very talkative; loquacious.

WING   (N)   A section of a penitentiary.

WING-DING   (N)   A narcotic addict feigning a fit or spasm; a fit; berserk.

WING-DINGER   (N)   A fit; a pretended fit or spasm; a forced faint.

WING WAITER   (N)   A prison mail carrier.

WINGED   (Adj)   Shot; hit by a bullet.

WINGS   (N)   Cocaine; morphine; heroin.

WINGY   (N)   A person with one arm.

WINKED OUT   (Adj)   Dead.

WINO   (N)   A picker of grapes; a worker in wine; a drunkard from drinking wine.

WINO GOOD FOR NOTHING   (N)   A no good drunkard.

WINO STIFF   (N)   One who gets drunk from drinking wine; a grape picker.

WINTER STAKE   (N)   The money saved by a tramp for the winter.

WIPE   (N-V)   A handkerchief; a burglar's mask; to kill; to assassinate; to clear out.

WIPE OUT   (V)   To kill; to murder.

WIPE THE CLOCK   (V)   To stop suddenly.

WIPER   (N)   A killer; an assassin.

WIRE   (N)   A skilled pickpocket who actually extracts the pocketbook; a pickpocket.

WIRE MAN   (N)   The pickpocket who actually does the stealing for a gang.

WIRE TAPPER   (N)   One who pretends to tap telegraph wires to get information, for bucket shops and bunco games.

WIRED JOB   (N)   A prearranged crime.

WISE   (Adj-N)   Having an intelligent idea of what is going on; the expert pickpocket who picks the pockets.

WISE CRACK (V) To make a clever remark.

WISEMAN (N) A person with the appearance of an officer; a person who knows everything.

WISE MONEY (N) Gambling money placed on a hot tip.

WISED UP (Adj) Informed.

WITCH (N) Cocaine; morphine; heroin.

WITH THEIR EYES OPEN (N) Two eggs fried on one side only.

WIZ COPPER (N) A pickpocket detective.

WOBBLY (N) An I.W.W. known by his speech.

WOLF (N-V) An older tramp who takes a boy under his care, usually for perverted reasons; a young man who has many girl friends; to complain.

WOMAN ABOUT TOWN (N) A prostitute; a whore.

WOMAN CHASER (N) A lascivious man.

WOOD (N) A wooden club; a policeman's billy.

WOOD BUTCHER (N) A poor carpenter.

WOODEN JUDGE (N) An easy judge.

WOODEN KIMONA (N) A coffin.

WOODEN OVERCOAT (N) A coffin.

WOODEN SHOES (N) A Dutchman; the stocks.

WOODY (Adj) Insane; crazy; mad.

WOOL (N) Worthless merchandise.

WOP (N) An Italian; a sentence of less than a month.

WOP GAME (N) A swindle game worked on Italians.

WORK OVER (V) To cross examine a prisoner; to give a prisoner the third degree.

WORK PLUG (N) A hard worker.

WORK THE DRAG (V) To beg on the street.

WORK THE SHORTS (V) To pick pockets on the street car.

WORK-WISE (N) One who has considerable knowledge of work; one who is too smart to work.

WORKING (N) Stealing.

WORKING SLEEPERS (N) While woman shopper leaves purse to try on a hat or other articles, and while her attention is attracted to shopping, sleep worker operates, steal woman's purse, reefs it and discards the purse.

WORKS (N) A severe beating; a policeman; the female pudendum; the third degree; a rough treatment.

WORM (N) A woman; a girl; silk.

WORM DRAG (N) A train hauling silk goods.

WORM FOOD (N) A corpse.

WORM WORK (N) Silk theft.

WORM WORKER (N) One who steals silk goods.

WORMS IN BLOOD (N) Spaghetti with tomato sauce.

WRAPPERS (N) Cigarette paper.

WRECKED ADAM AND EVE (N) Two scrambled eggs.

WRECKED ADAM AND EVE ON A RAFT (N) Two scrambled eggs on toast.

WREN (N) A young woman or girl.

WRING ONESELF (V) To change one's clothes.

WRISTLETS (N) Handcuffs.

WRITE SCRIP (N) A prescription for narcotic supplied to an addict by a physician.

WRITE SHORT STORIES (V) To forge checks; to write bad checks.

WRITING (N) A letter or note on a paper saturated with narcotics and ironed out.

WRONG (Adj) Said of a member of a criminal gang who is too familiar with the police and is not to be trusted.

WRONG GUY (N) A member of a criminal gang who cannot be trusted.

X

X-RAY (N) A one thousand dollar bill; a District Attorney.

Y

YACK (N) A watch.

YAMP V) To steal.

YANNIGAN BAG (N) A clothes bag.

YAP (N) An easy victim; a fool; a farmer; a newcomer.

YARD (N) One hundred dollars.

YARD BULL (N) A railroad detective or watchman.

YARD DICK (N) A railroad detective.

YARD HOCK (N) A railroad yard guard.

YAWP (V) To complain.

YEAR (N) A bill.

YEGG (N) A tramp; a criminal tramp; a safe cracker; a burglar; a thief; a desperado.

YEGG JOB (N) A brutal act; a poor burglary job.

YEGGMAN (N) A safe cracker; a criminal tramp.

YELLOW (N) Gold; a watch.

YELLOW BACK (N) A coward; one who has fear.

YELLOW-BELLY (N) A coward; one who has fear; a Chinaman.

YELLOW-BLACK (N) A mulatto.

YELLOW BOY (N) A Chinaman.

YELLOW DOG (N) A coward; one who has fear.

YELLOW GOODS (N) Smuggled Chinese.

YELLOW GOODSMAN (N) A smuggler of Chinese or aliens.

YELLOW HEEL (N) A coward; one who has fear.

YELLOW LIVER (N) One who is a coward; one who has fear.

YELLOW PUNK (N) Bread and butter.

YELLOW SLANG (N) A gold watch chain.

YELLOW STREAK (N) Cowardice.

YELPER (N) A stool pigeon; a police informer.

YEN (N) A keen desire for narcotics; an intense desire for a shot of narcotic.

YEN-CHEE (N) An opium pellet after cooking; the residue left in an opium pipe after it has been smoked.

YEN CHIANG (N) An opium pipe.

YEN-HOCK (N) A dipper used in preparing opium to smoke; an instrument for cooking opium pill; a hooked needle used to hold opium pellets while cooking.

YEN HOKE (N) A hooked needle used to hold opium pellets while cooking.

YEN ON (N) Withdrawal of narcotics.

YEN POCK (N) A ration of opium prepared for cooking.

YEN POOK (N) Small cooked opium pills.

YEN SHEE (N) Name given by Chinese to the cake that forms in the bowl of the opium pipe, addicts drink it in wine; ashes of smoked opium.

YEN SHEE #1 (N) First run opium ashes.
YEN SHEE #2 (N) Second run opium ashes.
YENSHEE BABY (N) Constipation caused by smoking opium; constipation of the bowels following a period of indulgence in smoking opium.
YEN SHEE BOY (N) An opium addict.
YEN SHEE GHOW (N) The residue left in an opium pipe after smoking; an opium pellet after cooking; instrument for scraping out yen shee.
YEN SHEE GOW (N) A tool for cleaning the residue from opium pipe.
YENCHEE QUAY (N) A drug addict.
YEN SHEE SUEY (N) Opium solution.
YESSA (N) Marihuana.
YIDDISHER (N) A Jew.
YODELER (N) A Swiss.
YOUNG COLT (N) A young child.
YOUNG FRY (N) A young child.
YOUNG PIECE OF SUGAR (N) A pretty young girl.
YOUNG STER (N) A reformatory.

Z

ZAGGER (N) A cheap watch.
ZEBRA (N) A convict wearing striped clothes.
ZIB (N) An easy victim; an inexperienced person.
ZIGABOO (N) A negro.
ZIPPER (V) To shut up; to keep your mouth shut.
ZOO (N) A brothel of girls of various nationalities; a prison.
ZOOLOO (N) A negro.

WHETHER YOU

B-E-L-I-E-V-E I-T O-R N-O-T.

In 1619, a full year before the Mayflower's passengers landed on Plymouth Rock, hundreds of persons were banished from his domain by James I of England, instead of being imprisoned or hanged.

Historians' estimates run all the way from 15,000 to 100,000. No one knows how many were transported to the Colonies in America before the practice ended in 1776. It is to be remembered that by far the greater number of these convicted were guilty only of poverty.

*   *   *

The old Spanish prisoner swindle dates back to the days of pirates and the Spanish Main.

A wealthy or reasonably well-to-do person receives a letter purporting to come from a distant kinsman being held a prisoner in one of the Latin Countries. The letter asks that a certain amount of money be sent him to bribe his guard, so adding that he has a map to a fortune in buried treasure, or a fortune in money in a false bottom of a trunk being held by officials.

If the money is sent him he will quickly be free, claim the fortune and divide it with his benefactor.

With variations, this old trick is still being worked on easily duped persons.

*   *   *

Jesse James was killed by Robert and Charles Ford who were tried and found guilty of murder.

Governor Crittenden immediately pardoned them when it became known they had acted under the orders of Missouri Authorities.

*   *   *

There are no national legal holidays in the United

States. Holidays we do observe are set by customs or by proclamations or statutes of individual governments.

Sunday is a common-law holiday, though it is not called a holiday.

*   *   *

American Indians when off the reservation are subject to game laws the same as a white man. On reservations Tribal Councils determine the laws.

No white man anywhere is permitted to kill seals but Indians of the Northwest Coast in both the United States and Canada can take seals if they use canoes and spears only.

*   *   *

Ashes of burned money can be redeemed. The Treasury Department has a division which analyzes the ashes. Full value of a bill is paid if three fifths is presented, one half value for less than three fifths and more than two fifths.

The silk threads are inserted during the manufacturing of the paper.

*   *   *

Washington, D. C., has no Mayor. It has three commissioners and is governed by them and by the President and Supreme Court. Residents of the District have no voice in its government, have no representative in Congress and cannot vote in Presidential Elections.

*   *   *

A child born to an American soldier by a foreign mother in a foreign country is a citizen of the United States provided the father has resided in this country for five years after his sixteenth birthday. Overseas service in the armed forces is considered as time in residence.

*   *   *

The translation of the Japanese word JUJITSU, is a combination of the Japanese words, JU meaning to bend or yielding, JITSU meaning art, skill or knack.

*   *   *

A poisonous dose of arsenic taken internally produces no symptoms whatever for about half an hour. Burning sensations then appear in the throat, also severe stomach pains and vomiting. An antidote is washing the stomach and intestines with a mixture of water, milk, oil and lime-water.

*   *   *

The so called truth serum is scopolamine hydrobromide. This same drug with some morphine added goes by the name of twilight sleep.

"Injection of scopolamine as a lie-detector is a dangerous practice", the Medical profession warns.

"Unconstitutional" the courts have ruled.

*   *   *

In 1913 Thomas Mott Osborne, noted prison reformer, served a term as a voluntary inmate in (Copper Johns) Auburn Prison, New York, before he assumed his duties as warden of Sing Sing in 1914.

*   *   *

At the turn of the Century there were only two penal institutions for women in the United States, in Indiana and Massachusetts.

Today there are separate institutions for delinquent women in twenty-one States.

*   *   *

Identification experts have lifted fingerprints from oranges, apples, plums, bananas, and other fruits which have landed crooks behind bars.

The trick is to use carbonate-of-lead dusting powder.

*   *   *

A sample of the paint job on every make of car off the assembly lines goes to the FBI crime detection laboratory in Washington. Here the bureau has a comprehensive specimen file of factory paint on private cars and trucks of previous years.

In hit-and-run cases, especially, particles of paint left behind at the scene of the crime pay off as leads and later as evidence in court.

Arson investigators use a miracle dye, rhodokrit, to test charred timbers for the presence of kerosene, gasoline or other inflammable oils.

Dusting rhodokrit powder over the suspected area, allowing the chemical formula twelve hours to do its work, if in contact with greasy or oily residue it stains the spot red.

* * *

In China all police officials are required by law to take a course at the Central Police Academy in Chungking, an institution patterned after the FBI academy in Washington.

Under the judicial set up in China only cases involving more than one hundred dollars go to court; in lesser crimes the local police chiefs mete out justice.

* * *

The world's first prison inspector was a monk, seven hundred years ago. His report is preserved in parchment to this day: "I see a pyty ful abuse for prisoners, oh, Lord God, their lodging is too bad for hoggys, and as for their meat it is euilso enough for doggys, and yet, the Lord knoweth, thei have not enough thereof."

* * *

In olden times a cruel and unusual punishment meted out by law consisted of a surgical operation to remove the tear glands from a lawbreaker's eyes. Any person thus afflicted can no longer shed a tear or produce the necessary moisture to lubricate his eyeballs. In a short space of time the eyeballs dry up and the individual becomes blind as a bat.

* * *

Although not a bookie in one thousand realizes it, the numbers racket is at least a couple of centuries old. The bookies, in those days, were known as "Morocco Men" because they took their bets in Red Morocco leather note books instead of on slips of paper. The Morocco men kept ten per cent of their collections as a commission and like today's bookies also handled pay off.

Mouldering Court Records in Maryland show that an elm tree that was blown down crushing to death a man was duly tried and found guilty.

The fallen timber was ordered turned over to the family of the deceased to do with as they saw fit.

*   *   *

By scientific examination of the ear wax in the auditory canal it is often possible to determine the previous occupation of a homicide victim, especially in cases of mutilated corpses from which all means of indentification has been deliberately removed.

Coal miners, sawmill workers, house painters, bakers, to name but a few, carry with them through life traces of their trade in the form of dust imbedded in the wax of the inner ear.

*   *   *

Four hundred years ago black markets were plaguing the subjects of Edward VI of England just as they are the citizens of the United States.

King Edward VI passed a law, which in those times was a simple matter as no lobbyist-inspired congressman had better filibuster against a royal decree, or he might talk right out of place to a knot around his neck.

Edward's law said that food merchants could not conspire to fix prices, and workmen or labourers must not set hours, rates and job jurisdictions.

Guilty person for the first offense was fined ten pounds or given twenty days on bread and water. A second offense brought a little steeper penalty, twenty pounds to the king, or a stretch in the pillory. The third time a black market operator was caught, the king would settle for forty pounds fine. If the offender could not pay he not only had his neck in the pillory, but one of his ears was lopped off.

*   *   *

The St. Louis Police Department was the first in the United States to adopt fingerprinting. In 1904 while Scotland Yard Operators were assigned to guard the historic

British Crown jewels on display there, the new science of
dactyloscopy was put to work under their tutelage.

* * *

Curfew, is derived from an ancient custom. It comes
from the French "Couvre-feu", cover fire, the old custom
being to cover the fires before retiring at night.

* * *

During the Colonial days, children had no difficulty in
learning their ABC's.
The court for erring offenders would order the condemned branded with hot irons. A blasphemer would be
branded with the letter B, a fisticuff fighter with the letter
A, a thief with the letter T, a vagrant with the letter V,
a robber with the letter R, etc.

* * *

When a man and a woman are being executed, the rule
is for the woman to go first to spare her the suspense of
having to wait.

* * *

In one-half of the United states condemned felons are
electrocuted. Ten States hang, and eight others use the
gas chamber. In the remaining six the courts observe the
Sixth Commandment by life sentence.

* * *

Under the old Quaker law in Pennsylvania crime did
not pay. A convicted arsonist had to give double indem-
nity to the person whose property he destroyed. A burglar
breaking and entering a place got the choice of making
four-fold restitution. If restitution were not made an
extra seven years was tacked on their sentence.

* * *

Two thousand years ago the Chinese had names for the
arch and loop patterns of fingerprint.
The arches were known as LO or Snail, while the loops
were designated by KI or the Sieve. The two words together, LOKI, mean good luck.

One hundred and fifty years ago under English law embezzlement was not considered a crime. The same was true in our country in the early years.

A cashier who juggled his accounts was simply guilty of a breach of trust and a private matter between himself and his employer, and the only recourse was to fire him.

* * *

European prison keepers took great pains in concealing the identities of inmates from each other. Whenever a foreign convict took exercise or came in contact with others, he had to wear a mask or hood. The purpose was to eliminate the possibility of ex-convicts blackmailing an alumnus of the same institution who may be making every effort to outlive his past and go straight.

* * *

In the Field Museum in Chicago Records show that as early as two hundred BC fingerprints were made in China.

* * *

The oldest recorded fingerprints in America were carved on the face of a cliff in Nova Scotia.

* * *

The first fingerprint classification system was established by Sir Francis Galton. He established the fact that no two fingerprints are alike.

* * *

Mark Twain advocated fingerprinting as a measure of identification.

* * *

J. Edgar Hoover compiled the first major set of fingerprint files in the United States.

* * *

For centuries murder was not against the law in Japan, if the slayer was a member of the military caste and the victim a person of the lower classes.

Young nobles with their two handed sword swinging at their sides, with too many cups of sake, might decapitate an innocent bystander merely to test the cutting edges of their swords.

The first murder trial in North America was around Thanksgiving time, 1630. The accused was one John Billington who waylaid and shot one John Newcomin. The accused who had come over on the Mayflower ten years before, was found guilty of "willful murder by plain and notorious evidence" and was hanged.

*   *   *

The New York City Legal Aid Society is one of the World's largest law offices. Each of the twenty attorneys handles approximately 1700 cases and appears in court in 5000 cases every year.

*   *   *

In Leningrad and Moscow a drunk is still tovarisch to the local police. Instead of lodging a drunk in jail the law escorts him to the nearest Turkish bath where he is steamed into a state of sobriety, fed and bedded for the night. However, the bath proprietor either collects his charges the morning after or the drunk goes to the work house.

*   *   *

The word murder occurs only four times in the Bible.

*   *   *

The inspiration for the modern penal reform in the United States was from the following:
"I was in prison and ye came unto me"—Matthew, XXV, 36.

*   *   *

During the first war 2200 men and women parolees were inducted from New Jersey. Of these 99 per cent made good; and only 22 offenders had to be dishonorably discharged.

*   *   *

In the City of Taylorville, Ill., one is not permitted, under penalty, to "feed razor blades to hogs."

*   *   *

In Muncie, Indiana, one can be arrested and fined for carrying fishing tackle in a cemetery.

In the old days in England, under a British law, if a
man went bankrupt his tongue was split, his nose cut
off and his eyeballs ripped out of their sockets, and then
he was hanged, and his every last penny confiscated.

*   *   *

There are approximately 2700 languages in the world.

*   *   *

In Alaska the average jail sentence given one by a Federal Judge is for only six months.

*   *   *

In the Virgin Islands the average jail sentence runs for
a full year.

*   *   *

Edward I, King of England, forbade the burning of coal
in London under the penalty of death.

*   *   *

Francis I, King of France, decreed a capital punishment
to any one in the realm sporting a mustache or set of
whiskers.

*   *   *

London Bobbies, officially known as Constables, carry
no billies but a short staff or cudgel. They book offenders
on a charge sheet instead of blotters as in the United
States.

*   *   *

Before San Quentin Penitentiary streamlined its capital
punishment setup with a lethal chamber it took the hangman a full year to properly season his rope. Lengths of
three-ply, three-quarter-inch pure manila whale line were
tied to the rafters of the death house with a 200 pound
weight suspended on the other end. Each rope bore a
date tag; when a year was up it had no stretch. The name
of the one to be hanged was placed on a rope and this rope
was not to be used for any other hanging.

*   *   *

New York City has the only special court for young
girls in the country. The judges leave their robes outside,

sit at an ordinary business office desk and dispense justice without the racket of a gavel. Bobby-soxers are treated like human beings instead of hardened criminals from the time they are picked up by plain clothesmen or women, never by officers in uniforms. They do not ride in Black Marias, but in ordinary automobiles. Pending their court hearing they are housed in a separate overnight shelter.

* * *

On Friday, July 13, 1860, one of the best attended necktie parties ever presided over by a United States Marshal took place on Bedloe's Island, where the Statue of Liberty now stands.

Over 2000 ladies and gentlemen witnessed the honored guest Albert W. Hicks, who was hung in a silk pirate costume donated by P. T. Barnum.

* * *

Persons picked up on suspicion in the Dark Ages had to stand an hour barefoot in a basin of brine. They were then interrogated while a pair of billygoats licked the soles of their feet.

* * *

In the Gay Nineties the pride of the New York City police force was the bicycle squad whose function it was to overhaul civilian wheelmen who risked the limbs and lives of others by scorching along the park drives and also took into custody a large number of creatures known as mashers.

* * *

Police no longer douse packages suspected of containing bombs into a bucket of water, they use gasoline instead. Water is a conductor of electricity; gasoline is a nonconductor and dissolves grease.

* * *

The boldest crime ever committed in New York's Chinatown occurred in 1909 during a performance in the Chinese Theatre there.

It was a holiday and during the show someone threw a bunch of firecrackers in the aisle, which the audience believed was a prank. When the show was over everybody rose to leave except five members of the On Loong Tong who had been shot dead; climaxing a long tong war.

* * *

A convict escaped from a middlewest penitentiary by patiently sawing through a steel bar with strands from his unravelled woolen socks impregnated with brick dust scraped from the wall of his cell.

* * *

A prisoner broke out of an "escape proof" death cell in a Texas jail. With a spoon he dug a hole twelve inches square through eighteen inches of solid concrete to an eighteen-inch drain pipe. With nose salve he greased his body, pushing his clothes ahead of him, slipped through the pipe to freedom.

* * *

Reporters from all over the country covering the Hall-Mills murder trial in 1926, tapped out five million words of copy on the sensational case.

It took the world's largest telegraph switchboard to handle this flood of verbiage from Somerville, New Jersey.

* * *

Down Mexico way the police don't arrest evening serenaders for disturbing the peace, they cooporate by supervising the guitarists in accordance with previously issued permits. For this service they receive two and a half pesos for each session of love ballads.

* * *

In strychnine poisoning victims lips are drawn back in a hideous grin.

* * *

Sultan Abdul II of Turkey on advice of his native detectives, banned typewriters from his harem and realm when the machines were first introduced into Europe and near East in the nineties. He feared some of his wives or subjects might type him anonymous letters without leaving a clue for the handwriting experts on the palace payroll.

Six out of every ten convicts in Michigan and Pennsylvania are repeaters, in Massachusetts and Washington seven out of ten have done time before; in Louisiana and New York eight out of every ten have previous records.

* * *

Sheriff's wives of today wouldn't care much for the job their English predecessors used to have, preparing the heads of executed felons for the mounting on London Bridge. Some conscientious housewives pickled the heads to preserve the flesh. Other good wives, however, preferred parboiling out of consideration for crows and other carrion-eaters which nibbled till they picked the skull clean.

* * *

The sole survivor of a ship wrecked off the fishing village of West Hartlepool, England, during the war of the Spanish Succession, 1701-1714, was an ape. The natives had never seen one before, so they tried it, found it guilty and hanged it as a French Spy.

* * *

Under the Reign of Richard the Iron-Hearted, the law for murder was; "Whosoever slays a man on land shall be bound to the dead man and buried in the earth. Whosoever slays a man on shipboard shall be bound to the dead man and thrown into the sea."

* * *

There are approximately 4000 jails in the United States and the average prison population is thirteen.

* * *

The NKVD, secret service agency of the Soviet Union, gets its name from the initials of Narodni Kommissariat Ventrenmkh Del (People's Bureau of Internal Affairs). Lavretia Parlovich Beria is the J. Edgar Hoover of the Red G-men.

* * *

The first automobile patrol wagon in this country was of the Akron, Ohio, police force in 1900.

It was powered by a pair of six-horsepower motors operated by an electric battery. Its cruising range was twenty-five miles per hour. It carried six detectives, a driver and an officer who rode standing on the rear steps.

*   *   *

The expression "getting into hot water", goes back to the Sixteenth Century when prisoners were boiled alive in huge cauldrons.

*   *   *

Two or more bullet holes in the skull of a corpse are usually considered by most coroners and medical examiners, to be sufficient evidence that the wounds were not self inflicted. Yet a number of suicides have been known to shoot themselves in the head two or three times.

In one case on record, a man fired five bullets into his brain before he collapsed.

*   *   *

A century ago prisoners in the Massachusetts State prison at Charlestown went in for colors. A new comer was dressed in Red and Blue, repeaters Red, Yellow and Blue, third termers Red, Yellow, Blue and Black uniforms. Any convicts that broke any of the rules had to wear a yellow cap with a pair of donkey's ears attached.

*   *   *

There are about one hundred bodies on ice, at any given time, at the Brooklyn morgue.

Autopsies are performed on an average of eight cadavers daily.

*   *   *

During the French Revolution in 1789 there was a gang of Parisians, known as Chauffeurs, who gave their victims the hotfoot with red-hot pokers to force them to reveal where their valuables were hidden. The French word Chauffeur means a stoker, or someone who makes it hot for people.

*   *   *

The word "cop" comes from the Classical Latin capere meaning to lay hand on or to grab.

A hundred years ago the prison population of the United States was 7000. January 1, 1900 the figures had reached 50,000. The year 1930 saw 100,000 convicts in prison. The figure today is estimated at 200,000.

* * *

The standard hangman's knot has eight turns to the noose. Some official executioners, however, favor nine turns on the ground that even if the condemned man has as many lives as a cat the rope will still do the trick. A few superstitious souls use thirteen turns, in view of the victim's ill fortune.

* * *

The police force of New York City under former Police Commissioner Lewis J. Valentine comprised more than 19,000 men, a number equal to Chicago, Philadelphia, Detroit and Los Angeles put together.

* * *

The exacting task of firearms identification experts is rendered all the more difficult, by the fact that 75 per cent of all bullets dug out of bodies or from walls of murder rooms are fired from either a 32 or 38 caliber revolver or automatic pistol.

In the United States there are more than just a few 32 and 38 caliber around.

* * *

The French guillotine first went by the dainty name of La Louisette, after a Dr. Louis.

It was later renamed in honor of Dr. Guillotine, who recommended its use.

Neither of the doctors, however, had anything to do with inventing the lethal machine.

Its birthplace was Scotland where it was known as the Scottish Maiden at least 200 years prior to the French Revolution.

* * *

The first policemen in this country were plainclothesmen walking their beat in their regular week day business suits. When it was suggested that they be outfitted with uniforms there was a storm of public disapproval and the idea of a force in blue uniform was bitterly opposed as undemocratic, militaristic, and a badge of degradation and servitude.

*		*		*

The condemned in France do not walk the last mile; they are taken to the scene of their execution.

The gallows, which has succeeded the guillotine, consists of a portable crane mounted on a truck. The dead wagon, with the condemned, pulls up before the door of the home in which the crime was committed and in the presence of relatives and neighbors the hanging takes place.

*		*		*

The word bail comes from the Latin baiulus, meaning a fellow who took a nursemaid's place holding the baby.

*		*		*

The original United States rouges' gallery photofile was started in New York City during the administration of Theodore Roosevelt as Police Commissioner in 1897.

*		*		*

The "big ten" in state police forces are Pennsylvania, California, New York, Texas, Michigan, Illinois, Massachusetts, New Jersey, Indiana and Connecticut, in order given.

*		*		*

In Russia no uniforms are provided prisoners. Inmates are allowed to wear whatever clothes they happen to have.

*		*		*

The maximum sentence provided under Russian criminal code for a homicide committed by a jealous husband or wife is ten years.

*		*		*

There are two "ins" of the law, "in camera" and "in extremis." The first is cases in court where the public is excluded. The second refers to the point of death when a dying declaration may be taken from a principal in a murder case.

Philadelphia's Walnut Street jail, was the first real penitentiary in the world in 1793. Mrs. Mary Weed was keeper with fifty prisoners.

* * *

The earliest precedent for the use of blood-grouping tests as evidence in a criminal case was established before an Italian Court in 1916.

* * *

The type of hoisting apparatus known as a derrick was named in honor of an English hangman, Derrick, who set set up a special gallows at Tyburn.

* * *

The United States Bureau of Prisons operates six penitentiaries, six reformatories, seven correctional institutions, six prison camps, a detention headquarters and a medical center, three hospitals for narcotics addicts and the criminally insane. These accommodations are scattered in twenty-one different states. However, the government places annually approximately 4000 convicts in different state, county and city jails.

* * *

Gilles de Retz, the 36 year-old Commander-in-Chief of the French Army, 500 years ago was the original bluebeard, and not a wife slayer. At his trial he confessed to the torture and slaying of more than one hundred children. He was found guilty, strangled and roasted over a slow fire.

* * *

The term "blackmail" originated in ancient Scotland where tribute paid to lord or baron was known as "mail." If the booty was paid in farm products or small change it was known as blackmail. If the pay off was in silver it was called whitemail.

* * *

The oft quoted verse "stone walls do not a prison make" was written by Richard Lovelace, a 24 year old poet, in 1642, while in a London prison for treason.

Hired slayers in the 1870s worked on a fee basis. The notorious Whyo Gang had a sliding scale as follows;
$4.00 for a pair of blackeyes.
$10.00 for breaking nose and jaw.
$20.00 for breaking arm and leg.
$100.00 for a neat killing.
The killers of the Murder, Inc., in New York City drew regular pay checks as high as $100.00 a week.

*   *   *

The moisture which produces fingerprints is exuded from a couple of hundred sweat glands on each finger tip. The telltale perspiration is an acid liquid made up of salt, potassium, iron, sulphuric acid, phosphoric acid, lactic acid and urea.

*   *   *

The distinction of being one of the first four men to be electrocuted in Sing Sing's new electric chair in July 1891, belonged to a Jap, Shibuya Jugiro.
When he was refused permission to commit hara kiri, he begged to be hanged, but his last request was refused and he fried.

*   *   *

The original "straw men" were ne'er-do-well who hung around courtrooms. Their presence was known to shyster lawyers by a straw or two carelessly sticking up out of their shoes, being a sign that they were in readiness to testify as to anything and everything for a price.

*   *   *

The first picture transmission of a Rogues Gallery photo over a wire was that of a Parisian jewel thief whose suave likeness was flashed across the English Channel to London in March 1908.

*   *   *

The only known way for a criminal to alter his fingerprints is to contract leprosy. The ravages of this dread and disfiguring disease change the loops, whorls and arches.

When solitary confinement was introduced into the American penal system in the early 1800s, all prisoner inmates, from first offenders to the hardened lifers served their sentences in solitary.

In those times the inmates actually welcomed solitary confinement, it being a relief from the daily beating which previously had been a regular routine prison discipline.

*   *   *

There are only four states in the Union where lying in Court can carry a life sentence. So witnesses seldom perjure themselves in capital cases in Alabama, Maine, Rhode Island and South Dakota.

*   *   *

When a Japanese girl gets into trouble that may reflect dishonor on her family she is requested by her older brother to commit suicide. The girl has no choice but to comply.

*   *   *

Warden Lewis E. Lawes, this country's best known prison official, first set foot in a penitentiary forty years ago. He was assigned to a night shift, a fourteen hour hitch, seven days a week. His weekly paycheck came to exactly $12.50.

*   *   *

Lest we forget, a policeman has to chaperone in dance halls, inspect defective streets, serve summonses, help firemen, censor plays, console lost children, direct traffic, check automobiles and catch crooks as well.

*   *   *

E T A O I N S R H L D C U M F W G Y P B V K X J Q Z
These letters are arranged in the sequence showing the order in which they are most frequently used in the English language.

*   *   *

Despite the efforts of penitentiary officials to eradicate the cultivating of Marihuana, in more than one United States penitentiary, it is still cultivated by convicts in out-of-the-way places behind prison walls.

The use of ultra-violet rays has put an end to the smuggling of drugs pasted inside of envelopes or on the backs of sheets of letter paper into prison cells.

*   *   *

Favorite hiding places for stolen jewelry, by burglars, are match boxes, kitchen ranges, canary's cage, electric light fixture, back of electric switches, box of chocolates, etc.

*   *   *

Centuries ago in New England and other Eastern States the Blue Laws applied to Sunday observance and have been long forgotten.

Our blue sky laws regulate the sale of securities and are designed to protect the public.

*   *   *

City Firemen in St. Joseph, Missouri, are prohibited from going about in their undershirts.

*   *   *

In England at the trial of a young girl for the poisoning of her rich old father, medicolegal work in toxicology was born.

Sir Anthony Addington, a famous physician, startled the court when he poured a bit of the powder in question into a red hot skillet. White fumes rose and a smell of garlic filled the air. The supposed sleeping powder which the daughter had given her father was arsenic.

*   *   *

In the middle ages a jurist sentenced a female bigamist to wear two pairs of men's breeches around her neck for the rest of her natural life.

*   *   *

Nowhere in the world will one find cats, dogs and birds more petted than among affection-starved prisoners.

*   *   *

In New York and London, the world's two largest cities, authorities coping with the problem of juvenile delinquency have shared this experience, that from the day war was declared in Europe to the present time the largest proportionate increase of youngsters in trouble has been in the age group between eleven and thirteen years.

* * *

Any doctor can spot a drug addict the minute the user of drugs sets foot inside his office. The addict's eyes are a dead giveaway; using the drug causes the pupils to contract to the size of a pin point.

* * *

Criminal courts have given many broad and peculiar interpretations to kidnapping, holding that intent is not necessary and that the offense includes keeping or detaining anyone against his or her will.

In Louisiana in 1933, a man was convicted of kidnaping his wife because he had forced her to accompany him on a trip.

* * *

Many issues of postage stamps have borne pictures of monarchs and sacred personages, including Jesus. Only two were forbidden by law to be cancelled across the face, a Spanish issue in 1850 depicting Queen Isabella II and a Sicilian issue in 1859 depicting King Ferdinand II.

* * *

For nearly a generation after Abraham Lincoln's death, many attempts were made to steal the body. It had to be removed seventeen times to thwart the thieves.

During one two-year period, its location was known only to a caretaker who had hidden it in the cellar of a monument.

* * *

To determine just how reliable eye-witness descriptions really are, Robert Heindl, a celebrated German criminologist, questioned 20,000 persons. The test proved people unconsciously add as much as five inches in estimating a person's height and eight years to his age. In remembering the color of someone's hair, four out of five eyewitnesses guessed wrong.

The word ignoramus as applied to dunces, dopes and morons was originally a term in good legal usage. Juries who after due hearing failed to find cause for prosecution used to confess themselves ignoramuses by writing the word across the face of an indictment they rejected.

Translated from the Latin, means "We don't know."

*   *   *

The expression "to lynch" dates back to the time of Patrick Henry and Colonel Charles Lynch, of Pittsylvania, Va. Colonel Lynch, during the days of 1776, devoted himself to making life difficult for the British loyalists in his vicinity attempting to sabotage the Revolution.

*   *   *

The expression "bad egg" is not after Thomas Egg, one-time notorious American criminal. Credit for the expression goes all the way back to Shakespeare who used the phrase in Macbeth.

*   *   *

The expression "to be hauled over the coals" goes back to an old lie-detector test, the ordeal by fire. Judges forced the defendant to walk barefoot over a bed of glowing embers as a test of his innocence. If his feet were burned the verdict was guilty.

By a miracle anyone subjected to such a treatment escaped with his life.

*   *   *

When anyone is arrested as drunk or vagrant in Cleveland, the first thing given him is a complete physical check-up. A physician, a nurse and an X-ray operator on duty at police headquarters determine if the man is really drunk or dazed by a skull fracture.

Many culprits have died in jail who ought to have been treated in hospitals.

*   *   *

Joliet Penitentiary was the first prison in the country to have bathtubs. It was in 1884 that the Illinois State penitentiary installed sixty wooden tubs for individual weekly bathing by 1400 convicts.

Forty years after he had designed the original electric chair in 1889, Nicola Tesla, the electrical wizard, declared the alternating current made the chair "the most cruel form of torture ever invented by men."

According to Tesla, the most humane way conceivable to inflict the death penalty would be by striking the condemned felon with an artificial bolt of lightning.

* * *

The occupational diseases of lawbreakers are nervous indigestion, ulcers and other abdominal ailments.

Chronic offenders always suffer from insomnia as well, and shell out plenty of their ill-gotten gains for sleeping pills and narcotics.

* * *

The largest burglary insurance company advises its policy holders to keep a small amount of money in the cash register till overnight.

This is to prevent sorehead burglars who go berserk and indiscriminately destroy property if they find the till bare.

* * *

In the Gay Nineties the favorite loot of the Mustachioed pickpockets was the personal tooth pick every well-dressed man wore attached to his watch chain or in his vest pocket.

Some were gold, others silver or ivory encrusted with precious stones.

Some are known to be valued as high as a thousand dollars.

* * *

Not as well known as the tremendous fingerprint files of the FBI is the superefficient file of bullets involved in uncracked cases.

As the years come and go these clues remain fresh as ever waiting for the inevitable day when other missiles from the same weapons will turn up in a second shooting and the old and new cases will be cracked at one and the same time.

In New York State convicts sentenced to hard labor were formerly put to work as construction gangs on cellblocks and outer walls.

They quarried the stone, dressed it and then hauled it to the site of construction where buddies took over the actual building. The work, however, was supervised by the state.

*   *   *

Under the Royal English law whatever caused a man's death used to be automatically forfeited to the king.

Under the same token today, if a man fell out of bed and broke his neck the coroner immediately after the inquest would confiscate the bed and cart it off to Buckingham Palace.

*   *   *

The Royal Canadian Mounted Police report only one fatal shooting took place last year in the Yukon Territory, a far cry from the days of the goldrush.

Today's lawbreakers are violators of the vehicle ordinances.

*   *   *

According to the Chief of Police of the State of Chihuahua, tourists from the United States are driving their cars across the Mexican Border, having them "stolen" and then returning to collect on their theft insurance. A car that sold for $1000.00 brings in Mexico City $3000.00. The same car shipped to Spain sells for $6000.00.

*   *   *

The latest in burglar detection devices is an electric-eye gadget which snaps the burglar's picture in the dark without his knowing it. It is made possible by a built in candid camera attachment equipped with an infra-red flash bulb which gives off rays invisible to the human eyes.

*   *   *

Wardens are very careful as to handkerchiefs being sent into prisons. It is an old trick for addicts to iron into the handkerchief morphine and then try to see that it gets to a friend in jail.

So before being given to the inmates they get a sudsy rinse in lukewarm water.

*   *   *

Detectives nowadays are artists in the use of moulage for preservation of evidence. Laboratory technicians use negocoll, a sticky mixture, to make the mold and hominit, a waxy substance to set the amazing likeness in permanent form.

*   *   *

Unknown to most people is the fact that payment on a certified check may be stopped, although certification is a guarantee that the bank has and will hold the funds to meet it. When issuing a stop-payment order, however, the drawer is required to obtain a surety bond for the protection of the bank against any claim resulting from the action.

*   *   *

The first letter ever sent airmail was dispatched from Philadelphia's Walnut Street Jail in 1793. The sender was George Washington, while the keeper of the jail, Mary Weed, and the fifty prisoners of the first penitentiary in the world cheered from the yard as Monsieur Jean Pierre Blanchard released the anchoring gear of his balloon and took off.

President Washington's missive was duly delivered to the Mayor of Woodbury, N. Y.

*   *   *

The half-dozen worst sore-spots of juvenile delinquent offenders against the Federal Government are;

Northern Texas.
Western Missouri.
Southern New York.
Illinois.
Eastern Michigan.

In 114 arrests for breaking Federal laws in 1945 the offenders were not even old enough to be teen-agers; these boys and girls arrested from coast to coast had not yet reached their thirteenth birthday.

Certain leading psychologists are of the opinion that the reason a slayer sometimes returns to the scene of his crime is that he wants to get caught.

They explain that slayers may become haunted by the same kind of guilty feeling that leads a child to confess his wrong doing, so that certain types of slayers drift back to where they committed the crime and hang around until picked up as suspicious characters, afterward confessing their deed.

*   *   *

Scotland Yard Detectives on finding the body of a woman in the River Luton, Bedfordshire, England, and determining who the woman was, inquired of the husband as to his wife's whereabouts. He stated that she was alive and staying in Hampstead and to prove it he produced letters.

One of the Detectives, noticing that Hampstead was spelled without the letter P, asked the husband to write the name of the town. He spelled it Hamstead; confronted by the evidence he duly confessed to the crime.

*   *   *

The existence of crime in the United States has been blamed by experts on just about anything on the map, religious training, insufficient recreational facilities, lack of schooling, liquor, drugs, broken homes, movies, newspapers, etc.

Pros and cons on the subject of probation and parole further confuse the situation.

*   *   *

Police investigators who have mastered the technique of hypnotizing exploded the notion that a "Master criminal" could hypnotize his victim who while under his power of suggestion could produce a perfect forgery.

The officers proved that the would be forgers were unable to imitate the signatures any better than any one else.

*   *   *

Not a city from coast to coast accepts Rookie cops under five feet seven inches tall. In some cities if you have passed your twenty-sixth birthday you are considered too old to join the force, while in others if you are under twenty-eight you are too young.

*   *   *

William Tweed of New York, who as Boss of Tammany Hall controlled the city administration between 1867 and 1871, with three others looted the treasury of about $100,000,000.00.

In 1873 he was brought to trial and found not guilty by the jury. At the second trial, the District Attorney made certain of having twelve untouchable jurymen. He assigned twelve officers to watch them, and twelve watchers to watch the officers, and twelve other watchers to watch the watchers.

*   *   *

When the St. Louis team was playing the Phillies in Philadelphia on August 1, 1876, a St. Louis player, on batting a home-hit, which he thought was a four-bagger, started out to score a home run.

Exasperated by interference from the second and third basemen, he pulled a pistol, shot both of them and made his homer. When approached by the umpire he shot the umpire also.

All the victims recovered and the rowdy player was released from jail and his contract.

*   *   *

The majority of suicide attempts behind bars are phoney. The convict, playing for hospitalization or sanity test, first makes sure a guard is nearby to save his life before he strings himself up or slashes a wrist.

A desperate convict, who really means business, uses a quicker and more sure method, such as diving head first off the top gallery to the concrete floor below.

*   *   *

During the Elizabethan era, pitching an officer known in those days as "Watch," was a common sport for the young blood. Upsetting in the mud which filled the streets of London in those days confronted the Watch who could do nothing about it, for the gay blades who took part in the practice were persons of influence, or had friends of high standing.

* * *

In the middle ages, pigs, rats, cows and roosters were tried for murder.

* * *

In 1807 a rooster was tried and convicted and burned at the stake for being a witch.

* * *

In 1836 in Falaise, France, a pig trampled an infant. The pig was tried in court for murder, and convicted. Was sentenced to be dressed up like a man and so executed. The reason for the clothing was that otherwise its slaughter under the axe might have seemed the perfect normal fate for any pig.

* * *

In 1521, the town council of Antro, France, indicted the rats in the village for having destroyed the wheat crop. Henri Trounceau was appointed to defend them. He obtained several postponements of the trial, saying that his clients, the rats, had been delayed from appearing at the trial due to the great number of cats on the highway.

* * *

In Paris, France, a court tried and convicted a cow for murder. It had kicked its owner and caused his death. The death sentence was appealed. The French Parliament, sitting as a Reviewing Court, after hearing the evidence came to the same conclusion as the lower court and affirmed the sentence.

* * *

At one time tamed animals went to the Civil Courts, while any wild animal or insect had to be dealt with only by the Church Courts.

* * *

In the middle ages suits were seriously brought against all kinds of insects, including snails, flies, caterpillars, locusts, and crickets. Rats and snakes were especially prosecuted.

In the middle ages many charges of murder were leveled against pigs because they wandered through the streets and were likely to trample little children to death.

*   *   *

In the year 1474, in the city of Basel, Switzerland, an old rooster was accused of having laid an egg. Convicted, the fowl was solemnly burned at the stake.

*   *   *

By an ancient Persian law, a dog that bit without first barking was to be punished with death. Many animals were tortured on the rack because this was the legal procedure of the time, even though no possible confession could be withdrawn.

*   *   *

In ancient Rome, a farmer plowed under a boundary stone so the neighbor had a hard time proving where his land was. In the lawsuit that followed the Oxen were executed for the deed of having pulled the plow, and the farmer went scot free.

*   *   *

A goat was once exiled from Russia.

*   *   *

In Athens, when Greece was great, special courts decided the rights of dumb animals and even of inanimate objects.

*   *   *

In the middle ages a hangman publicly killed a pig without its being tried and convicted, and in punishment the executioner was banned from the community.

*   *   *

It was not only in the middle and ancient ages that animals were tried like human beings and strung up and had their heads chopped off. The strange and barbarous custom still goes on.

Lawyers continue to go through an elaborate and pretentious rigamarole to "try" dumb creatures just as they did in the dark age. Dogs are now the favorite butt of law. In McGraw, New York, four dogs were tried, convicted to death and executed for biting a six-year-old girl, little Joyce Hammond, who had to be sent to the hospital.

*　　*　　*

At Peoria, Ill., a dog was exonerated by a coroner's Jury from blame for a man's drowning, but only by a hair's breadth.

*　　*　　*

At Baldwinsville, New York, a dog without a pedigree went on trial for his life, for having sunk its teeth in a boy's back.

*　　*　　*

At Hudson Falls, New York, in 1936, a dog went on trial for biting a woman and was put on probation.

*　　*　　*

At Brockport, New York, a six-months-old pup was charged with murder, having caused a fourteen year old boy to drown. To his defense came alibi witnesses, character witnesses, with appeals for mercy.
He was put on two years probation.

*　　*　　*

It seems ridiculous that in the middle ages moles should be tried by jury; but in this country, recently two mongooses were put on trial in St. Louis. The Federal Government wanted the death penalty because they are public enemies to American birds and chickens and are not allowed to enter the country.

*　　*　　*

Among certain African tribes there is an unusual punishment for murderers. A murderer before he begins serving his prison sentence, must produce a life to replace the one he has taken. Thus, he must live with a female relative of the murdered person until a child is born.

*　　*　　*

A popular but fallacious belief is that the absence of water in the lungs of a human body found in water indicates that the person was dead before entering the water.

Actually, many victims of accidental drownings, when sinking for the first time, develop a spasm of the larynx which tightly closes their throat and causes suffocation through lack of air and not the presence of water.

* * *

The highest paid elective position ever attained by a Negro in the United States is held today by Francis C. Rivers, who, as an Associate Justice of the City Court of New York, receives an annual salary of $17,500.00.

* * *

In the past twenty years, eleven states have changed their penalty for murder. The number that impose a life sentence has decreased from eight to six, and the number that execute by hanging has decreased from eighteen to nine; while those that execute by electrocution has increased from twenty to twenty-four and those that use hydrocyanic gas have increased from one to eight.

These figures exclude Utah, which still gives the condemned his choice of being hanged or shot.

* * *

June, 1934, Congress empowered F.B.I. special agents with the right to make arrests. Previous to this time it was even illegal for them to carry firearms.

* * *

In the early nineties coal stoves placed in the corridors were supposed to provide enough heat for the convicts in their stone-walled cells. During this time forty-five per cent of all prison deaths were caused by tuberculosis.

* * *

The first United States prison to use electric lighting was the reformatory at Elmira, New York, in 1892.

* * *

In New York a spinster rooming house keeper who gets married has to turn over all proceeds she gets from roomers to her husband when she marries.

* * *

In Ohio it's against the law for women to drive taxicabs.

By an ancient Japanese tradition, a criminal led before a bar of justice, is allowed to wear a conical straw "Amegasa" over his head to save his face.

* * *

In Connecticut any female musician caught playing in an orchestra after 10:00 PM is subject to arrest.

* * *

As a woman thinketh in her heart, so is she.

* * *

At the turn of the century prison keepers figured on a ten cents a day allowance for feeding inmates.

* * *

Safe manufacturers who design an improved type of locking or security device do not patent it. This is because blueprints registered with the United States Patent Office become matters of public record.

* * *

There are three stages in the development of prostitution; first, it is labor of love; second, it is a public service to be nice to the men who are kind to her; and third, it is business.

* * *

Approximately five per cent of the prostitutes are teetotalers.

* * *

Approximately ten per cent of the prostitutes are booze hounds, and spend most of their income on liquor.

* * *

Approximately seventy-five per cent of the prostitutes are moderate drinkers when they have to buy for themselves.

* * *

Approximately ten per cent of the prostitutes are dope fiends and addicted to morphine and its derivatives by inhalation, injection or the smoking of opium.

SECRET SIGNS

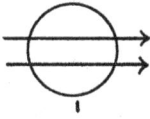
1

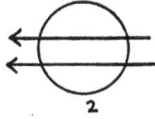
2

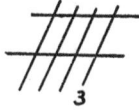
3

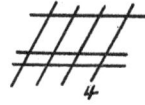
4

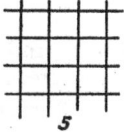
5

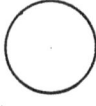
6

7

8

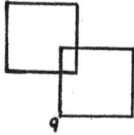
9

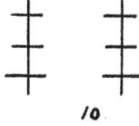
10

11

12

13

14

15

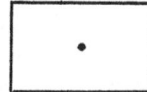
16

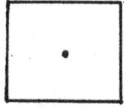
17

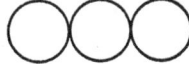
18

19

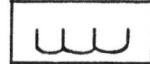
20

21

22

23

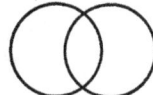
24

25

26

27

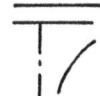
28

29

30

31

32

APPENDIX

Secret signs, the language of American hoboes and tramps, and what they mean on fences, gate-posts, trees and water tanks.

(*See illustration on preceding page*)

(1) Signifies that two men have left town together, traveling in direction indicated by arrows.

(2) A warning to get away quickly, that hoboes and tramps are eyed distrustfully.

(3) Signifies that hoboes and tramps are not welcome in the neighborhood, and will be put to work on the rockpile,

(4) A warning to hoboes and tramps that the residents are apt to turn them over to a policeman or sheriff.

(5) This sign means exactly what it represents—the bars of a jail.

(6) Signifies "keep out," "get out," or "nothing doing," the town offers poor pickings for hoboes and tramps.

(7) Signifies that the town itself is no good for hoboes and tramps, but that the Christian Missions are kindly disposed towards wanderers.

(8) Signifies food will be given here. The people are O.K.

(9) Signifies the community is a good place for hoboes and tramps to make connections with others.

(10) Signifies that all the Ministers and heads of Missions in town are inclined to help migratory visitors.

(11) A warning signal, used where a crime has been committed, for hoboes and tramps to keep away.

(12)   Signifies that the citizens of the town swing back and forth in their attitude towards hoboes and tramps—sometimes kindly, other times unfriendly.

(13)   Represents two rails and a cross tie—"a Railway Terminal or Division Point"—a good place to board trains in several directions.

(14)   Signifies that hoboes and tramps may sleep here, that they are welcome.

(15)   Signifies that police or town officers are hostile to hoboes and tramps.

(16)   Signifies that the "Calaboose," or jail, of this town, is alive with cooties and vermin.

(17)   A warning that the man is a brutal person and to expect nothing at this house.

(18)   A warning that the town is no good and hoboes and tramps should keep on moving.

(19)   Rough circles carry the glad tidings that a hobo or tramp may expect to receive money at this house.

(20)   Signifies the community is big-hearted and a good place for hoboes and tramps.

(21)   Signifies food can be had for the asking, all classes are equally taken care of and are liberal to the wandering tribe.

(22)   Signifies that there are two women in the house, that a hard-luck story may yield satisfactory results.

(23)   Signifies things are "O.K.," or very good—the town's people are kindly towards hoboes and tramps.

(24)   Signifies the town is not much good for a lone wolf and best results are secured when two hoboes or tramps travel together.

(25)   Signifies the information that a fierce dog is kept in the garden of the house.

(26)   Signifies that the people will give you car fare.

(27) Signifies that if the hobo or tramp talks religion,
      help will be readily given.

(28) Signifies that any hobo or tramp may sleep in com-
      fort in the hayloft.

(29) Signifies that a receiver of stolen goods lives in
      the house.

(30) This decoration is found only on the house of an
      officer of the law.

(31) Signifies that a woman lives alone in the house.

(32) Signifies that the occupants of the house are poor
      people.

www.ingramcontent.com/pod-product-compliance
Lightning Source LLC
Chambersburg PA
CBHW031545260326

41914CB00002B/274